The Randolph Hornets
in the Civil War

The Randolph Hornets in the Civil War

A History and Roster of Company M, 22nd North Carolina Regiment

WALLACE E. JARRELL

McFarland & Company, Inc., Publishers
Jefferson, North Carolina, and London

The present work is a reprint of the illustrated case bound edition of The Randolph Hornets in the Civil War: A History and Roster of Company M, 22nd North Carolina Regiment, *first published in 2004 by McFarland.*

LIBRARY OF CONGRESS CATALOGUING-IN-PUBLICATION DATA

Jarrell, Wallace E., 1952–
The Randolph Hornets in the Civil War : a history and roster of Company M, 22nd North Carolina Regiment / Wallace E. Jarrell.
p. cm.
Includes bibliographical references and index.

ISBN 978-0-7864-4503-5
softcover : 50# alkaline paper ∞

1. Confederate States of America. Army. North Carolina Infantry Regiment, 22nd. Company M.
2. North Carolina—History—Civil War, 1861–1865—Regimental histories.
3. United States—History—Civil War, 1861–1865—Regimental histories.
4. Confederate States of America. Army. North Carolina Infantry Regiment, 22nd. Company M—Registers.   5. United States—History—Civil War, 1861–1865—Campaigns.
6. North Carolina—History—Civil War, 1861–1865—Registers.
7. United States—History—Civil War, 1861–1865—Registers.
8. Randolph County (N.C.)—Genealogy.
9. Soldiers—North Carolina—Randolph County—Registers.   I. Title.

E573.522nd .J37 2010   973.7'456—dc22   2003026722

British Library cataloguing data are available

©2004 Wallace E. Jarrell. All rights reserved

No part of this book may be reproduced or transmitted in any form or by any means, electronic or mechanical, including photocopying or recording, or by any information storage and retrieval system, without permission in writing from the publisher.

Cover art ©2010 PicturesNow.com

Manufactured in the United States of America

*McFarland & Company, Inc., Publishers
Box 611, Jefferson, North Carolina 28640
www.mcfarlandpub.com*

This book is lovingly dedicated to my wife, Sandy,
who encouraged me to write it, helped me search records,
tromped through overgrown cemeteries,
trekked across numerous battlefields
and gave up her time with me for the research
and writing that took over two years to complete.

Contents

Preface 1
1. Onward to Victory 3
2. Turner's Romance 43
3. That Tattered Old Flag 61
4. Roster of Company M, 22nd Regiment 67
5. Old Times There Are Not Forgotten 131
6. Company M, 22nd Regiment N.C. Troops
   "Randolph Hornets" (Reactivated) 171

Appendix: Burial Sites of Company M Soldiers 175
Notes 179
Bibliography 183
Index 185

Preface

The years 1861–1865 were turbulent for our entire nation, but especially for the people of Randolph County, North Carolina. Even though the sentiment to stay in the Union was high, and remained so throughout the war, hundreds of Randolph County boys marched off to defend their native soil, many never to return. The "Randolph Hornets," Company M, 22nd Regiment N.C. Troops, left from eastern Randolph County and earned a reputation for their grit and determination in battle.

The purpose of this volume is not to dissect the political implications of the War Between the States, or even to place the people of Randolph County firmly on one side or the other. Many other books go into great depth on the politics, and the citizens of Randolph were greatly divided in their views all the way through the conflict, many changing their opinions more than once.

My purpose here is to bring together in a single volume as much documentation as possible to bring to life the men who served in Company M, 22nd Regiment. I do this primarily for their descendants, and for all the people of Randolph County, who have reason to be proud of this company of men and the service they did for their country. I want the reader to get a feel for what these men experienced, both in war itself and in the hardships they suffered while serving.

I have attempted to convey the history of the company through both official and personal accounts of the war. In addition to telling the story of Company M, this book gives insight into the actions of the entire 22nd Regiment and other units who served in the same engagements. Sergeant John T. Turner of Ramseur left us a wealth of knowledge on the events of the war through his series of articles in *The Courier* in 1914, which I have included. The story of the company battle flag helps us to look at the flag with new eyes. The newly revised roster of the company answers many questions I had about the men, and I hope it will do likewise for the reader. Numerous documents still exist to fill in the story; I have included many here. Finally, my experience as a Civil War reenactor with the

"Reactivated" Company M, 22nd Regiment, "Randolph Hornets" has helped me to gain some sense of the rigors of 19th century military life. I hope to pass this on to the reader.

I want to take this opportunity to thank the many people who have generously contributed to this book with their information and expertise, especially Mr. William D. Kivett, who helped me in sorting out information on the Kivett family and their relatives. Finally, I want to express my gratitude to my friend and former English instructor Ms. Mary Chesson, for her encouragement to write.

Deo Vindice!

1. Onward to Victory

Broken, moss-covered tombstones and cold mausoleums, ambrotype photographs, faded papers and equally fading stories handed down by some of the old folks: that's all that now remains of the lives of many a brave Randolph County son who once traveled far from home and saw sights his family had never seen or heard of, while facing hails of lead on more than one occasion.

Of course, it wasn't always this way. In an earlier time the names on the epitaphs were more than just names. They were living, breathing souls with wives, children, a family dog, friends and neighbors. They plowed their fields, worked in the mills, attended school and church, and did pretty much the same types of things you and I do today. The major difference in their lives and ours lies in the technologies of today and the rapid pace of 21st century living.

In our day we have watched with our own eyes as the enemy came into our land and took thousands of lives in one swift stroke in the tragedy of September 11, 2001. The television is constantly blaring the news of what terrorists may be up to at this very moment. It wasn't so in those days. News traveled slowly, and the rumor of war hung in the air like a heavy cloud, with lots of unanswered questions on the minds of small-farm Southern families. "Why should Northerners tell us how to run our business?" "Why would people who are supposed to be our own fellow citizens want to come down here and invade our lands?" "Why can't they just leave us alone to handle our own affairs?" "How far are they willing to go to make us even less equal to them than we already are?" "Would it really benefit us to pull out of the Union and govern ourselves?"

Northerners had often come across as cocky and belligerent to many Southerners and seemed to work every situation to their favor. They had the large mills and factories. They had the means of transportation. They obviously had the ear of the government that was supposed to be "our" government. Now it seemed the "Yankees" were about to invade Southern lands and try to abolish the little bit of self-esteem and power to self-govern that Southerners had left. They were not just the wealthy braggarts from up north anymore. They were the enemy that was coming to take away life as Southerners knew it.

In the beginning it had little to do with slavery. Slavery was a gradually dying institution that belonged to wealthy people. Randolph County had a relatively small number of people who even owned slaves. In fact, there were probably only 5 or 6 men at most in Company M who had ever owned slaves. The Baptist churches in the Sandy Creek Association resolved as far back as 1835 that it was "inconsistent with the spirit of the Gospel of Christ, for a Christian to buy and sell Negroes for the purpose of speculation or merchandise, for gain," and advised the churches of the association "to exclude members who will not abandon the practice, after the first and second admonition."[1] With a respectably large concentration of Quakers, Wesleyan Methodists and other denominations that denounced slavery, the majority of the people in this area weren't concerned with preserving the "peculiar institution." They were more concerned with being able to make their own decisions without someone else deciding for them. Most of the men who went to war from Randolph County were young, and just getting established with homes and families. Many were mere schoolboys. A few were old men. Almost all were farmers of modest means with a desire to simply work hard and live honestly. But the political atmosphere of the day was a constant reminder that a time would come when people would have to take a stand on one side or the other, and that time finally came.

The election in 1860 of Abraham Lincoln as president of the United States was an event that was anticipated and signaled to people in the Deep South that a new era was commencing. Secession had been long debated and became a reality when South Carolina seceded in December 1860. That winter, seven states seceded and formed the Confederate States of America. North Carolina was reluctant to do the same because "The Old North State" had little to gain. The state depended little on slave labor, and was beginning to see its own industrial emergence with the growth of cotton mills and other industry. Although there was much disagreement within the population on what stand should be taken, by and large the state was pro–Union. But with the surrender of Fort Sumter to South Carolina troops on 13 April 1861 and the call from Lincoln for North Carolina to send troops to put down the insurrection, the course of action was sealed. Governor John W. Ellis sent the following reply to President Lincoln:

> Your dispatch is received, and if genuine (which its extraordinary character leads me to doubt), I have to say in reply that I regard the levy of troops made by the administration for the purpose of subjugating the states of the South, as in violation of the Constitution, and as a gross usurpation of power. I can be no party to this wicked violation of the laws of the country, and to this war upon the liberties of a free people. You can get no troops from North Carolina.[2]

For most North Carolinians, the idea of remaining in the Union had now faded away, and for many, the zeal for becoming a Confederate state was greater than ever. In Randolph County the enthusiasm wasn't as great. Peace meetings had been held for some time, and would continue to be held during the war. Unionist groups known as "The Heroes of America" or "Red Strings" became active in the area. Throughout the war, many men deserted or refused to serve. Bands of organized men known as "outliers" hid in the countryside and were a constant source of trouble for local authorities. There were several skirmishes between the outliers and militia and Confederate troops; quite a few were killed on both sides. Even daily life in the communities was affected by the divided sympathies among the people. Pvt. Stephen Ward Trogdon wrote home to his brother-in-law Emsley Allred on 16 December 1861:

> you Sead that Cedar Falls was coming out in the way of fighting and you Seaid that they was A fight thare the knight before your letter was wrote I am like the duchman was I would like to know hwo in the devil fough[t][3]

But on 20 May 1861 the state held a secession convention and voted overwhelmingly to secede. Many people in Randolph County were not eager to be a part of all this, but there was no choice. A letter written on 13 May 1861 by Jonathan Worth of Asheborough, who was state treasurer and later governor, to Springs, Oak and Co., sums up the feelings of many in Randolph County:

> A large majority up to the issuing of Lincoln's proclamation were firm for the Union. Some of us would have made any sacrifice to preserve it. The small concessions made by the last Congress had strengthened us. Lincoln prostrated us. He could have devised no scheme more effectual than the one he has pursued, to overthrow the friends of the Union here.... I am left no other alternative but to fight for or against my section. I cannot hesitate.[4]

The proclamation of Lincoln and the vote to secede brought on a swell of Southern patriotism for quite a few young men, and the county quickly began to mobilize and do its part in the war effort. Before it was finished, Randolph County would give far more than its share.

The militia in North Carolina was a rather ragtag affair, and Randolph County troops were no exception. Basically, all men between the ages of eighteen and forty-five were enrolled in the militia and required to muster at least twice each year. The biannual musters were held by the local companies in their own districts. Once each year in the fall the entire regiment of nine companies met in Asheborough for a general muster, lasting several days. There were four muster fields in Randolph County, located at Trinity, Coleridge, Scott's Old Field in Tabernacle Township, and in Asheborough. The Asheborough muster field comprised about eight acres in what is presently the southeast section of Asheboro, east of Cox Street and south of Wainman Avenue. Notices were posted for the drills, such as this one from Captain John Ritter of Moore County:

Jonathan Worth (1802–1869)—Asheboro attorney, clerk and master of equity and superintendent of county schools. He was state treasurer during the war, and became the postwar governor of North Carolina from 1865 to 1868. (Photograph courtesy of Randolph Room, Asheboro Public Library.)

1. Onward to Victory

Asheborough Female Academy—Built in 1839, this and a similar Male Academy in Asheborough served as temporary military barracks during the war. (Photograph courtesy of Randolph Room, Asheboro Public Library.)

> Notice
> All persons liable to perform military duty in Dist. No. 8 are hereby
> Notified to appear in the town of Carthage on the 18th and 19th of
> October next by 10 am o'clock armed and equipped according to Law
> for the purpose of a general review this the 29th of September 1855.
> John Ritter, Capt.[5]

For the most part, it cannot be said that the men were "uniformed," although the officers did present themselves in full dress uniforms complete with plumed hats. Drums and fifes provided music. An example of how the militia soldier was to be equipped is provided in a notice in the *North Carolina Bulletin* newspaper of Asheborough in 1859:

> ATTENTION ASHEBOROUGH GUARDS!
> You are hereby commanded to appear at Asheborough, on Saturday the 4th day of July next, at 10 o'clock, A.M.—armed with Gun, Shot-Pouch, Horn, and Six Rounds of Powder.
> Also all persons wishing to join the C Company, are requested to come forward on that day.
> By order of the Captain.
> June 20, 1859   S. G. Worth, Sergeant.[6]

The militia was practically useless as it stood when the war began. Because of the long period of peacetime the country had enjoyed, the militia was trained in little except rudimentary marching, and drills were more or less attended at the whim of the men. Now some of these local militia companies would become the basis for organized units of state troops, which would eventually become reorganized into the Confederate army, as a part of the Army of Northern Virginia.

As local companies organized, the militia officers or leaders in the community attended to the recruiting. The men were encouraged to join at public gatherings, which included entertainment, food, ladies and plenty of patriotic rhetoric. A 27 March 1924 edition of *The Courier* shed some light on the organization of one such company, Company I, in Asheboro:

Elisha Clarkson Horney (1843–1863)—Mustered in as sergeant of Company L, 22nd Regiment on 18 June 1861 and rose through ranks and was appointed captain on 3 May 1863. He was wounded at Chancellorsville and again in the ankle at Gettysburg, Pa. He died 29 August 1863 following two amputations. (Photograph courtesy of L. McKay Whatley.)

> Mr. W. S. Crowson, on being interviewed about the muster field improvements being made, spoke about the general muster in 1861, "when a company was organized for the Civil War, with S. G. Worth, commander." Upon this occasion Col. Jesse D. Cox, who lived nine miles South of Asheboro on the old plank road, spoke, urging the boys to join the company if they expected to command the respect of the Randolph women. According to Mr. Crowson, the men needed little urging. The young women were present, with cakes, cider, and other edibles, which were dispensed from "cake wagons." Col. Cox was one of the county's foremost citizens. One of the features of the day's entertainment was the horse racing with headquarters at Burus Shop.[7]

Randolph County organized several such companies, nine altogether, and other local men made up a substantial portion of companies organized elsewhere. The nine full companies from Randolph were: I, L and M of the 22nd N.C. Regiment; H of the 38th Regiment; F and G of the 46th Regiment; B of the 52nd Regiment; F of the 70th Regiment and F of the 2nd Battalion. Fully half of five other companies were Randolph men. A good number of men from the Company M area served in companies other than M, some distinguishing themselves in battle. A case in point is two relatives of Alexander S. Horney of Franklinville.

Horney, one of the founders of the Cedar Falls Company and a justice of the peace, had a son and a son-in-law who served in Company L of the 22nd Regiment. Elisha Clarkson Horney was mustered in as sergeant on 18 June 1861. He rose through the ranks and was appointed captain on 3 May 1863. He was wounded at Chancellorsville, again in the ankle at Gettysburg, Pennsylvania, and died 29 August 1863 after two amputations. A. S. Horney's son-in-law, Robert Harper Gray, was married to Horney's daughter Mattie. Gray was elected captain of Company L, 22nd Regiment at its organization on 18 June 1861. He was promoted to lieutenant colonel of the 22nd Regiment on 13 June 1862, serving nine months in that position until his death near Fredericksburg, Virginia, on 6 March 1863 of typhoid fever.

A further illustration of the organization process more applicable to Company M is found in the account given by Sergeant John T. Turner in a series of articles written by him and published in the *Asheboro Courier* in 1914 entitled "Turner's Romance" (printed in its entirety elsewhere in this volume):

> In the spring of [1861], there was a free dinner set and speaking, and calls for volunteers. The clouds of war were rising fast over the Southland, and volunteers were needed. James M. Odell was making up a company of twelve months boys so I couldn't stand back any longer, as I saw the girls were liking the boys who volunteered. I gave my name to Mr. Odell for twelve months and then I had a time.[8]

Sergeant Turner's mention of James M. Odell may be an error on his part or on the part of the paper. It is generally known that John Milton Odell and his brother Laban were the organizers of the company. The Odells did have a brother named James Alexander Odell, and a cousin named James Madison Odell, one of whom may have been present at this meeting and may have served as a private in this company (see the Roster of Company M).

John Milton Odell and Laban Odell were natives of Cedar Falls in Randolph County. They had both gone on to school, attending Middleton Academy and gaining teaching certificates, and both had taught in the Cedar Falls area. John Milton Odell left teaching in 1856 to become a stockholder and salesman with the Cedar Falls Manufacturing Company. Laban was still teaching when the war began. Both were greatly admired in the community, and were influential with the people of the area. When Company M was organized on 10 June 1861, several of the men enlisting had been students and friends of the Odells. Columbus Franklin Siler, who would eventually become captain of the company and distinguish himself for his bravery, was a former student of Laban Odell.

The Odells were successful in raising a company of some 90 recruits, counting

Robert Harper Gray (1831–1863) and wife Mattie. Gray was elected captain of Company L, 22nd Regiment, 18 June 1861. He was promoted to lieutenant colonel of the 22nd Regiment on 13 June 1862 and died near Fredericksburg, Va., on 6 March 1863 of typhoid fever. (Photograph courtesy of L. McKay Whatley.)

themselves, to serve for twelve months. Then the work began. Sergeant Turner continued: "The boys had a time drilling. The company was formed and our first drill camp was at Joshua Bain's near Liberty, cooking our meals in the blacksmith shop and sleeping in the barn."[9]

Walter Clark, the father of John W. Clark of Franklinville, was then a

14-year-old student at Hillsborough Military Academy. He was called upon to come to Randolph County and help drill the troops. He later served with some of the Randolph County men, rising to the rank of lieutenant colonel in the 70th Regiment N.C. Troops, one of the youngest such officers in the Confederate Army. J. R. Cole and John Brower are known to have drilled the men in Company M.

It is not known why the company set up their first camp at Joshua Bain's near Liberty, but I can offer my thoughts. On 20 April 1861, Adjutant General J. F. Hoke issued a pronouncement which read, in part:

> The following constitute a complete outfit necessary for a Company of Volunteers, in order to be able to take the field for a campaign, vis:
> *For the Company*—Tents, Cooking Utensils, Mess Furniture, vis: Water Buckets, Knives and Forks, Tin Plates, Cups and Pans, Strong Bags for Rations, Axes and Spades (ten each,) six Hatchets.
> *For each Man*—Two pair Pants, (very loose,) two Sack Coats, two Flannel Shirts, and as few Drawers, Socks and under shirts as possible. One Felt Hat, if not supplied with Caps, two pair of Shoes. No boots except for Mounted Service, one Blanket, one Knapsack, one Haversack, one Canteen to be covered with cloth or leather, one Gutta Percha or Rubber Overcoat, if it can be procured.
> Where the generous patriotism of the community offers to supply the wants of Companies, it is recommended that the above articles be procured as far as practicable.
> The State will endeavor to supply the deficiencies when the Legislature shall have made the necessary appropriation.[10]

At first, the men had no tents to protect them from the elements. Joshua Bain was a blacksmith, associated with several others in that work. This was probably a fairly large blacksmith operation with a barn big enough to accommodate the troops until tents could be made. Secondly and equally significant was the fact that the troops would need some blacksmith work done to make some of the equipment and hardware for the months ahead. Sergeant Turner mentions the company being paraded with the regiment when they arrived in Richmond, Virginia. He said, "I thought myself that we were nice looking, for we were uniformed and our new guns and bowie knives hanging by our sides, made us look dangerous and I thought that the Yankees would run at the first sight of us."[11] Bowie knives, though sometimes issued, were generally brought from home. It may be that the blacksmith shop also manufactured these knives for Company M.

In addition, many of the men who joined Company M were from the Liberty area. The Kivett family alone furnished twelve men to the company, and a large number of the other men in the original company were Kivett relatives. This may have been a way to ease them into the military life—keep them near home while the preparations were being made to get them off to war. A couple of men were married during this encampment, so this kept them conveniently near home.

While encamped at Joshua Bain's, the company elected its officers: John

George Makepeace (1799–1872), superintendent of Cedar Falls Company and supporter of the war effort, furnished Company M with much of its equipment and supplies during its organization. (Photograph courtesy of L. McKay Whatley.)

Milton Odell, captain; Laban Odell, 1st lieutenant; Henry C. Allred, 2nd lieutenant; and James M. Pounds, 2nd lieutenant. Captain Odell appointed the non-commissioned officers and set about his work of seeing that the company was equipped and trained. The men chose to designate their company the "Randolph Hornets." According to Sergeant Turner, the company remained in camp at Joshua Bain's for about three weeks, and then moved to Middleton Academy, a school organized by the Horney and Makepeace families and located halfway between Cedar Falls and Franklinsville. It may be that by this time they had tents and needed a more spacious area to set up a camp. Also, this camp would be more central to the county and nearer the home of Captain Odell, allowing better communication with the various people he contracted with to make uniforms and equipment. During the week or so that they were here, they were also fitted with their new uniforms.

Captain John M. Odell was diligent in seeing that the men were provided for. He obtained the materials locally, much of it through George Makepeace, superintendent of the Cedar Falls Company. Makepeace was a fervent supporter of the war effort and, according to attorney and local historian L. McKay Whatley, practically outfitted the company, ordering the supplies through the Cedar Falls Company Store. Services of Cedar Falls Mill employees and other area craftsmen were obtained to make uniforms, shoes, blankets, knapsacks, cooking utensils and other necessary goods. Many of Odell's detailed records of purchases still exist today in the state archives at Raleigh. The exact design of the uniforms Company M took to war are unknown, but are thought to be on the pattern of the N.C. state regulation uniform, which consisted of a long-skirted sack coat with a

1. Onward to Victory 13

The company store of the Cedar Falls Company. Many of the supplies for Company M were purchased here. (Photograph courtesy of Cedar Falls Historical Society.)

lay-down collar and black epaulets on the shoulders. It is known that the material was jeans wool, a combination of wool and cotton. Captain Odell described it as Salem Jeans. The shirts were described in his account as being Plaid Linsey. After being wounded and taken to a hospital in Petersburg after the battle at Mechanicsville on 26 June 1862, Sergeant John Turner described their shoes: "Our shoes were made of cloth and over the toes and around the heels there was a strip of leather. The leather part was shined up. The bottoms were made of wood."[12]

By the 9th of July, the company was furnished, Captain Odell had submitted his bills to the county, and the "Randolph Hornets" were ready to go to war.

The 9th day of July 1861 was a sad day for the men. Many friends and kinfolk came to Middleton Academy to say goodbye to their brave boys. It cannot be said with certainty, but this is probably when the company flag, made by the women, was presented to the men. It was a splendid flag, a Confederate First National flag, with eleven stars on a blue satin union and measuring 55 inches by 35 inches. The red bars were made of cotton and the white bars of satin. Hand painted in red on the front of the white satin bar was the battle cry "Onward to Victory." The reverse side was hand lettered in India ink "Randolph-Hornets." The flag had a gold fringe around its edges. Surely the men were greatly inspired by the presentation of such a grand flag. The following morning, on 10 July 1861, the men marched off to High Point, many never to return home.

Franklinsville Manufacturing Company mill—This mill was purchased in 1859 by Cedar Falls Company and was operated by that firm during the war years to supply N.C. troops with clothing materials. (Photograph courtesy of L. McKay Whatley.)

In High Point the men boarded trains to Raleigh, N.C. They arrived safely in Raleigh and went into camp at Camp Crabtree. The regiment was then organized at the fairgrounds on 11 July, and was designated the 12th Regiment N.C. Volunteers. The men were sworn in and received a bounty of ten dollars. The regiment then went into camp at Camp Carolina and elected its field officers: J. Johnson Pettigrew of Tyrell County, colonel; John O. Long of Randolph County, lieutenant colonel, and Thomas S. Galloway, Jr., of Rockingham County, major. Originally composed of twelve companies, the regiment was reorganized by transferring companies C and D to other units. The remaining ten companies retained their original lettering: A, B, E, F, G, H, I, K, L, and M. Companies I, L and M were all from Randolph County, and Company E was from Guilford County. The others came from counties in the western portion of the state. The remaining field officers were elected and in place by the last of July. The regiment was now nearly 1,000 strong.

Around the first of August 1861, the regiment was ordered to Richmond, Virginia. According to Sgt. Turner, the original order was to Garysburg, N.C., and the troops traveled by cattle car to that point, but there were already enough troops stationed there. They were then ordered to Richmond and traveled by flat cars and coaches, arriving there on 7 August 1861. Upon arrival the regiment paraded through the city with crowds of onlookers watching and encamped at Rocketts

1. Onward to Victory

Cedar Falls Company mill produced textile materials for shirts and underwear for Confederate troops during the war. Capt. John M. Odell became superintendent after leaving the war. (Photograph courtesy of Randolph Room, Asheboro Public Library.)

on a hill overlooking Richmond. Many of the boys had already seen things they never imagined and wrote letters home telling of their travels and the sights of Richmond.

On 16 August 1861 the regiment was ordered to Brooke's Station near Aquia Creek. They boarded a train on the Fredericksburg & Potomac Railroad and upon arrival, went into camp at Camp Bee. On 28 August the regiment, along with others encamped there, was ordered to Stafford Court House, to be assigned to the garrison at Evansport, Virginia. Sgt. Turner gave the following account:

> They all started on their march for Evansport. Our regiment was left back for some purpose. We went into camp near the depot in a low, flat field and it began to rain. We did not see the sun for 17 days. When it was not raining it was cloudy. Our boys had a siege of the measles. The drilling and camp guards were all suspended, for it took all the boys to wait upon the sick crowd. Our regiment was called the sick regiment.
>
> We began to think that it would never stop raining. The mud was so bad that the regiment ahead had to go in camp a few days. The rain

ceased, and our Colonel sent word to the Colonel of the 13th Miss. that he would start our regiment on the march at 12 o'clock (noon), as they were about six miles ahead of us, and for them to have all their camp kettles made full of coffee for his sick boys. We made the six miles, reaching there about night. The coffee was ready for us. The next morning when we awoke another crowd was broken out with the measles. They were carried off to hospitals at different places. Some of the boys I never saw again as they were laid to rest in the soil of Va.[13]

On 13 September 1861, the regiment was organized into a brigade with the 1st Regiment Arkansas Infantry and 2nd Regiment Tennessee Infantry at first under General Theophilus Holmes. At later dates, other units were assigned to the brigade, including the 47th Virginia Infantry, 35th Georgia Infantry, and the 13th Mississippi Infantry. They variously served under General Holmes, General John G. Walker, General Isaac R. Trimble and General Samuel G. French. On 14 November 1861, the North Carolina regiments were renumbered to prevent confusion, and the 12th Regiment N.C. Volunteers became the 22nd Regiment N.C. State Troops.

At Evansport, which is now called Quantico Station, plans had been laid to set up batteries of heavy guns to blockade the Potomac River below Washington, D.C., and prevent Union ships from passing on the Potomac. The distance from shore to shore was about one and seven-eighths miles. The brigade went to work building winter quarters, and then worked at night building parapets and magazine breastworks for the gun emplacements. In the beginning, there were three batteries, mounted with 9-inch Dahlgren guns, smooth bore 32 and 42 pounders, and one heavy-rifled Blakely. Sgt. John Turner wrote of mounting these guns:

> We were ready for the big guns which were from 8 to 14 feet long. They were hung under a two-wheel cart and hauled to within a half mile of the river by oxen 8 to 12 yoke each. When the night came on 75 or 100 of the boys were hitched to the big guns by a rope and we hauled them in. We were very quiet for fear the Yankees would find out what we were doing. We kept this work up until we finished the works.[14]

Company I of the 22nd Regiment was detailed to man a 42-pounder in the Number 2 Battery. Soon the Federals discovered the batteries, and an exchange of volleys began. The blockade did its job and practically stopped navigation on the Potomac River by Federals for a while. Sgt. Turner offered this story from the batteries during that period:

> I must tell a joke on our Colonel. We boys would talk to each other when on picket across the river, and when the Colonel found it out I was on guard. He came down for a little talk with the boys. He told me to get the boys to talking and then he would take hold of them. I got them started. The first word he spoke was in a different voice. The answer from them was "Who is that?" "This is Colonel Pettigrew." "Colonel Pettigrew, you

and your men grease your heels and slip back into the Union. I will bet you $100 that you nor any one of your men haven't any hair on your breast." The Colonel turned to me, and said "Sergeant, I will quit them." He never tried them again.[15]

The winter passed cold and miserably, with volleys of artillery at various times of the day and night passing overhead from the Federal guns and enemy gunboats trying the positions. On several occasions, reports of the enemy landing on the riverbanks upstream sent the troops into battle mode, often marching miles upstream only to find that it was a false report. This angered the men and made them even more anxious for a fight. There were very few battle casualties during this time, but several men from Company I were wounded when their 42-pounder exploded. There was also quite a bit of sickness from measles. Company M suffered its first casualty on 3 October 1861. James Murdick Kivett had enlisted on the 10th of June at the organization of the company. His death on 3 October came at Camp Holmes of typhoid fever. Early in the war some of the men still referred to wherever they were as Camp Holmes, so it is probable he was at Evansport with the others when he died. At any rate he was the first to die, but certainly not the last. Several would die from disease during the winter and spring of 1861–62.

A correspondent writing from the 22nd Regiment to *The Times*—a Greensboro, N.C., newspaper—on 1 December 1861 and identified only as J. A. C. described the camps at Evansport:

> To one who had never seen anything like it, the first appearance of our camp would strike him somewhat with wonder, presenting to his view so many diminutive and variously constructed chimneys standing just out of the ground, heterogeneously about in spots, disgorging volumes of black smoke. As the story goes, the snow once fell so deep that the huntsman stepped down a cottager's chimney. It will require very shallow snows to cover up these chimneys; but should one step in them, he would hardly then discover where the fire is. I will explain. Our camp is upon the side of a hill; the men remove the dirt from the upper side of their tents, making the floor level. This gives from two to three feet of dirt wall on the upper side of the tent; in this they cut out a fire-place, and for a chimney cut and cover a trench some six to ten feet to the rear, capping it with a flour barrel, or a few stones set upright, or a little pen of daubed sticks. It is astonishing how well these chimneys draw the smoke, and how small a fire it requires to keep the tent perfectly warm. I write with as much ease and as much comfort as if sitting in your own room by a big log fire, and I doubt not a more cheerful heart than many, who, surrounded with their home comforts sympathise with the "poor" soldier. It is true now and then it is a bitter pill to stand guard in the pelting rain; and to double quick, half leg deep in mud, upon some alarm of the enemy; but a resolute heart is half the victory; besides these "bitter pills" are voluntarily taken at home as often during the winter as we are compelled to take them in camp. I do

not mean to say the camp is as pleasant as home, by any means; but necessity works out many inventions by which our apparent hardships are greatly alleviated.¹⁶

At this early juncture of the war, it was impossible for "J. A. C." to foresee the deprivations the men would suffer in the months and years ahead, when they would give anything for the "comforts" they had at Evansport. A letter written by Solomon York of Company L to his future bride, Delphina Cox, on 18 January 1862 further illustrates the life of the 22nd Regiment during the time at Evansport:

> I will tell you something about our fair. We fair tolerable well. We have plenty to eat and have tolerable good tents to stay in. The weather is verry disagreeable, it has been raining, snowing & hailing for the last week. The ground is verry muddy at present. Though we don't have much to do we have to stand Picket every fourth night which is tolerable disagreeable. We have to get wood and work every fifth day in the batteries. We have had no fight here yet though. They say that the Yankeys are going to attact us here by land and water though. Things have been verry quiet for several days with some cannonading on the River.
>
> There was heavy firing last night at a steam tug as it passed up the River. There was ninty that fired at it. It was thought that some of them took effect. It is nothing strange to hear the Cannons Roaring and hear the balls whistling over us though. Their is none of us boys been hurt yet and I hope they will all get home safe for I long to see the day that I can return home to the armes of my friends.¹⁷

Some evidence exists that not only did the blockade work well for a while at keeping boats from navigating the river, but some boats were actually commandeered. Private Stephen Ward Trogdon wrote home to his sister, Susan Trogdon Burrow, during this time: "I haven't much to write you at presant only we captured two boats the other day they was worth Severl thousan dolars but I do not know how much and they did not hurt any of us"¹⁸

In the spring of 1862, Colonel Pettigrew was offered an appointment to brigadier general in another brigade, but declined because he didn't want to be separated from his troops. A short while later he was offered the brigadier general position in his own brigade and accepted. In February of 1862 a call was given for troops to enlist for three years in return for a fifty-dollar bounty and a thirty-day furlough. Back in Randolph County, on 6 March 1862, forty men volunteered to serve in Company M in addition to a few others who had joined in the interim. Many of the men who were already serving volunteered to reenlist at this time and made plans to go home on furlough. Some who had planned to get out in June decided to wait until their 12 months was up and go home for good. This idea did not work out, because on 16 April 1862 the first Conscript Act was passed, and all men between the ages of 18 and 35 were pressed into service.

In early March 1862, the army fell back from Manassas and the Potomac and began moving troops from northern Virginia to the line of the Rappahannock below Williamsburg, to meet a Federal advance under General George B. McClellan. On 7 March the brigade was ordered to Fredericksburg. The guns were rolled into the river and the baggage was sent to Richmond. During the hasty departure, much equipment and supplies were left behind, including the beloved Company M flag. The troops were quickly moved from Evansport to Fredericksburg, this time marching the entire distance. A camp was set up at Fredericksburg, where the brigade remained until mid–April. By this time those who had gone on furlough had returned. With new conscripts and those who were impressed to remain in service, the regiment was returned to full strength. The brigade was ordered on to Yorktown, where it was to be employed in the Williamsburg and Yorktown campaign. In the course of this march, more men were left behind with measles in a hospital in Ashland, Virginia.

Back home, the folks in Randolph County had no idea what was really happening, and the rumor mill went to work. Tales that might have contained some small bit of truth turned into horror stories for uneasy wives and families. Mr. C. W. Burrow of Cedar Falls wrote to his brother-in-law, Stephen Ward Trogdon:

> Ward your cant imagine the tales that is aflote about your regiment the nuse come hear last week that 15 of cap Odell co had goined the yankees and that the reg[iment] was cut all to peices and then we heard that you were all Taken prisoners and that is the kind of nuse that is going dayley then your pa heard tuesday at coart our men [were] cut all to peices and all that did get away did so by clean running this com by a solgier that was in the engagment so it was pretty true as we thought but as for my part think the nuse must of com in the wind but gust to tell the plain truth about the mater it is gust done to flusterate the women that is left.[19]

During this transition time, on 27 April 1862, Company M elected new officers. Captain John M. Odell was defeated for reelection after his resignation due to poor health. He returned to Randolph County, and to the Cedar Falls Manufacturing Company, which continued to produce materials for shirts and drawers for the troops. His brother, Laban Odell, was elected captain in his stead. Warren B. Kivett was elected 1st lieutenant to replace Laban Odell, and Columbus F. Siler had previously been elected 2nd lieutenant on 16 March. James M. Pounds was defeated for reelection; Lewis F. McMasters was elected 2nd lieutenant in his place.

At Yorktown, Virginia, the 22nd and other forces were placed in a reserve division under the command of General W. H. Whiting. After the rest of the army reached this area from northern Virginia, the army was placed under command of Gen. Joseph E. Johnston. He felt pressure from the Federals and found it necessary to withdraw the reserve troops to Richmond, where most of the army was concentrated. The 22nd was positioned with their division on the Brooks Turnpike. While at Richmond, on 18 May 1862, Private Stanley Kivett wrote home and described their conditions. He had just learned a few days earlier of the death of his brother, Daniel M. Kivett. Daniel was one of those left behind at Ashland in mid–April. The text of Stanley Kivett's letter to his parents, brother and sisters is quoted here in part, and will be found elsewhere in this volume in full:

> I have know good news to rite to you. We have hard times hear. We have bin marchin for a month or more through rain and mud sometimes knee deep and sometimes all knight. We have aheap of sickness hear. I have never had the chance to rite to you since I heard that D. M. Kivett was dead. I never heard that he was dead till a few days ago.... I don't know what ailed him.... We haven't been in any fight yet but I expect we will have the hardest battle hear that ever was red of. We are in tooo miles of Richmond. We came hear last knight. I think we will stay hear till the fight comes on.[20]

The fight came soon enough. On 31 May 1862, General Johnston found that the Federals had crossed the Chickahominy River near Seven Pines and decided to attack. The 22nd reached the Nine Mile Road at 4 o'clock in the afternoon and the battle had already begun. The troops faced thick brush and logs in the woods and found the enemy in a low bank or ditch. With the thick foliage, the troops could not see each other to stay together well. Sergeant Turner gave this report:

> We stayed here in camp until May 30. We then drew rations for two days. We lay down to rest. About 9 o'clock the bugle sounded to fall in line. All baggage was left in camp except what we had on and one blanket each. We marched about two miles and formed in battle line on the extreme left. The line of battle was about one mile long when the morning came.
>
> Not much was done until evening. From the roaring of the muskets near the Fair Oaks farm and beyond the Williamsburg road the battle was severe. In the evening at our end of the line the Yankee troops tried to pass our left wing. It was charge after charge by both sides. We gained with every charge. The last charge made by us was made through a swamp knee deep in mud and water.
>
> The enemy fell back to their breastworks. Night came and the battle was over. So ended the 31st day of May, 1862. On Sunday, June 1, the battle began early in the morning and lasted all day long. It was a severe engagement and along the line and we gained ground at every charge. At last we beat them back to the last line of their breastworks. The 22nd Regiment made the last charge.
>
> We charged their strong breastworks. It was a costly effort. They greeted us with fearful volleys and we turned in plain view of them to retreat. Col. Pettigrew, Lt. Col. John O. Long were wounded and seven of our company, including First Lieutenant W. B. Kivett [and] L. F. McMasters. Emsley Allred and Alvin Pugh were killed. All were left in the lines of the enemy. We marched back to where we had camped on May 30. Our

regiment being out of a colonel, Colonel Connor was temporarily assigned over our regiment. Gen. Johnston was wounded and so Gen. Robert E. Lee took charge at this time of the army of Northern Virginia.[21]

Company M had suffered its first battle casualty in the deaths of Emsley Allred and Alpheus "Alvin" Pugh. Sergeant Turner supposed that Pugh had been killed on the battlefield, but he was actually wounded and captured, then died the following day in a Federal hospital in Fort Monroe, Virginia.

With Robert E. Lee taking command of the Army of Northern Virginia, many other changes followed. There was an attempt to brigade together regiments from the same states, and as a result, General Pettigrew's brigade was broken up. The 22nd Regiment was now brigaded with the 2nd Battalion Arkansas Infantry, the 16th Regiment N.C. Troops, the 34th Regiment N.C. Troops and the 38th Regiment N.C. Troops under the command of General William D. Pender as part of General A. P. Hill's division.

On the afternoon of the 25th of June 1862 General Pender's brigade was marched from its camp near Friend's House on the Chickahominy River to a place near the Meadow Bridge crossing where it joined General A. P. Hill's division for a planned attack on the Federal right flank at Mechanicsville. Hill and General Thomas J. Jackson were to force a crossing of the Meadow Bridge, and then Generals D. H. Hill and James Longstreet were to follow and join an attack on the flank. The attack on the flank never took place and the fight was more of a frontal assault, which was repulsed. Sergeant Turner gives this account:

> On the 25th day of June we drew five days' rations and marched for the Chicahominy river. We went about eight miles in the night and took up. Next day at 3 o'clock we crossed at Meadows' Bridge where the C. and O. R. R. crossed the river. When we got to the river we were halted. Every man had to have a good cap on his gun for we were marched down the stream.
>
> We saw the Yankees retreating so we formed in line. We reached the little village called Mechanicsville. They opened fire on us with their shells. We were ordered to lie down as flat as we could for it was getting hot for us. We lay down as flat as a board but it didn't help us any. We got up and went to fighting again. It got too bad for us so we lay down the second time. Their troops fell back beyond a stream called Beaverdam Creek and got behind their breastworks. We went after them again. And the third time we had to lay down.
>
> We lost many of our boys in the fight. We were ordered now to go for them. We got within eight feet of them and we found out that they were the Fourth Michigan Regiment. We fired upon them and they hotly returned the shots. I received four of the shots. I received a wound in the right arm through the elbow. I came very near bleeding to death. I was carried off the battlefield.[22]

Over night, the Federals moved back into a defensive position with the entire Federal V Corps at Gaines' Mill. Early on the morning of 27 June 1862, A. P.

Hill's division was in the advance forces that moved on Gaines' Mill and made first contact with the enemy, with Longstreet on the right and with Jackson and D. H. Hill on the left. A series of frontal assaults, supported by R. S. Andrews' battery, was made and succeeded in driving the enemy slowly before them for about 250 yards. At one point the 16th and 22nd N.C. regiments gained the crest of open ground and moved into the enemy's camp, but found themselves being flanked and fell back. The 37th N.C. came in for support and another push was made, but it did not hold and the troops once again fell back, due to fresh Federal troops continually being brought in. A. P. Hill's troops were driven back from the wood. However, Hill stated: "My men fought nobly and maintained their ground with great stubbornness."[23] During the afternoon, General Robert E. Lee had brought in John B. Hood's Texas Brigade, who broke the Federal center and caused their retreat during the night. Thus ended the battle at Gaines' Mill.

The next day, the Confederate army stayed encamped on the battlefield while the enemy positions were ascertained. On 29 June 1862, Lee ordered Longstreet and A. P. Hill to recross the Chickahominy River at New Bridge while Jackson crossed at Grapevine Bridge, hoping to flank the enemy. Pushing into enemy territory, the brigade reached the junction of Long Bridge and Darbytown roads and came into contact with the enemy near Frayser's Farm. Joseph B. Kershaw's and Charles W. Field's brigades were in front of Pender's brigade, but strong forces of Federals passed between them and to the right of Pender. Lee's troops succeeded in driving the Federals back and putting them in disarray, but Confederate ammunition was running low, preventing them from capturing many Federal troops that otherwise could have been taken. Jackson was never able to get in position for the planned flank attack either. Some enemy batteries were taken, however, and as darkness came on, the Confederates held their ground.

The Federals escaped up Quaker Road to a very strong position at Malvern Hill, supported by gunboats nearby. Here the Confederate forces made unsuccessful attacks on 1 July 1862. Longstreet's and A. P. Hill's troops were held in reserve until late in the battle, when Pender's troops were ordered forward. Because of the lateness of the day, the density of the woods and the darkness, the 22nd Regiment did not see much action here. On 8 July 1862, Lee withdrew the army to Richmond and ended the campaign. The 22nd Regiment had lost 28 men killed and 133 wounded during the Seven Days battles. Company M had lost Andrew J. Fields, Daniel Wilkerson, John R. Sumner, Calvin Allred, Samuel Trogdon and Braxton York. Still, many of the men were determined that the South would win the war, and Federal troops saw the determination of the Southern army. Pvt. Stephen W. Trogdon wrote home to his brother-in-law, C. W. Burrow, on 20 July 1862: "I thinke our men aimes to drive them out of virginia if they can but I think it will be hard to do but if they try hard A nuff they will do it the yankies Sayes that the North Carolinaines will charge hell with A Barlow knife for A canteen and haversack."[24]

Now back in Richmond, Lee took the opportunity to reorganize his army, which included putting A. P. Hill's division under General Jackson's command.

Also, the 2nd Battalion Arkansas Infantry and 22nd Battalion Virginia Infantry were transferred out of Pender's brigade. Pender's brigade now consisted of the 16th, 22nd, 34th and 38th Regiments N.C. Troops. Jackson was ordered on 13 July 1862 to move his troops to Gordonsville to challenge the advance of the Federal army under General John Pope, and on 27 July A. P. Hill's troops joined them. Jackson moved to take the offensive against Pope on 7 August and the armies met on the 9th at Cedar Mountain, also known as Cedar Run, near Culpeper, Virginia.

At about 3:00 P.M. a detachment of Pope's troops attacked the Confederate forces and a sharp battle ensued. Eventually, Jackson's men drove the Federals back, but then the main body of Pope's army came into view and Jackson withdrew. The Federals thought they were winning with their smaller force and attempted to flank Jackson on the left, but Hill's troops were moved to the left flank to stop them. The 22nd N.C. was moved to the far left, where at dusk they put a detachment of cavalry on the run by coming up on their rear and cutting them off. Hill's division then moved well to the front before the battle ended at around 9:00 P.M., and Pope's army had been defeated in their attempt to take the railroad junction at Cedar Mountain. Jackson's men remained in camp on the battlefield until the night of 11 August and then moved back to the area of Gordonsville.

After Pope's defeat at Cedar Mountain, the Federals began sending more troops to reinforce him, and Jackson began to make the necessary moves to cut off Pope's right and his communications at Manassas Junction. On the way there several small skirmishes were fought along the Rappahannock River. In one such skirmish, Samuel M. Burgess of Company M was hit by artillery fire and decapitated. Jackson's troops reached Manassas Junction on 26 August, and then on the 27th moved north to Groveton. On 28 August Jackson's right engaged a column of Federals at Groveton, then put his men in a strong defensive position along an unfinished railroad branch of the Manassas Gap Railroad and Pope turned to engage him. On the 29th the Federals launched a general attack on Jackson's left. Pender's brigade was held in reserve on Jackson's left at the beginning, but eventually was brought forward to retake a section of the railroad cut that had been captured by Federals. This they did in the face of grapeshot and drove the enemy back beyond their batteries. The enemy began flanking Pender's men and he withdrew back to the cut. Jackson then put Pender's men back in reserve to rest while guarding his left flank.

On morning of the 30th, the Federals renewed their assault on the railroad cut, but apparently didn't realize that Longstreet had arrived with 28,000 more troops. Longstreet advanced on the Federals' left, crushing them as they went. Jackson's army then moved forward as well and the entire Federal line gave way. As the Federals retreated, they tried once more to hold some ground at Henry House Hill, but around 8:00 P.M. Jackson's troops, including the 22nd N.C., hit them hard and Pope ordered a retreat to Centerville. This ended the battle of 2nd Manassas with a great Confederate victory. Of the six men killed from the 22nd Regiment, three were from Company M: William Fields, William A. Hayes and John D. Spinks.

As the Federal army retired towards Washington, Lee ordered Jackson to pursue and try to turn them in a more advantageous direction. The advance troops of Jackson's force contacted the enemy rear guard at Ox Hill, also called Chantilly, on 1 September 1862. A battle ensued, with only a portion of Jackson's troops being engaged and the rest in reserve. The 22nd Regiment was present but not engaged to any great extent. The Federals held their ground until dark, and then retreated. At this point, Lee decided it was time to for his army to enter Maryland and he turned the army north.

Jackson's army marched through Leesburg, crossing the Potomac River on the 5th of September, and continued toward Hagerstown. On the 9th the order was given by Lee for him to take Harper's Ferry from the west while other units occupied the Maryland Heights across the Potomac and Loudon Heights southeast of Harper's Ferry. Jackson marched to Williamsburg, Maryland, and crossed the Potomac on 11 September 1862, reaching Martinsburg the next day. Enemy troops there retired and on the 13th A. P. Hill's men met the enemy at Bolivar Heights, west of Harper's Ferry. Pender's brigade advanced from the point where the river and railroad met, and at one point were within about 60 yards of the enemy breastworks on the western point of Bolivar Heights. Following a Confederate bombardment of the town, the Federals surrendered it. Lee then ordered a concentration of troops at Sharpsburg. Jackson left A. P. Hill's men in Harper's Ferry to receive the surrender, and departed to join Lee.

Hill's troops left Harper's Ferry at 7:30 A.M. on 17 September 1862 and were marching towards Sharpsburg while the battle there was already in progress. In the afternoon, Hill's men began arriving just in time to blunt a strong attack on Lee's right, helping the Confederate lines to hold. Pender's brigade, which included the 22nd Regiment, was not actively engaged except for long-range musket and sharpshooter fire. However, Sergeant John Turner seems to indicate that Company M took part in at least some of the action, so it may be that the 22nd Regiment was with Jackson's troops rather than with Hill's men who were left at Harper's Ferry. At least one man from Company M, John C. Lane, died that day. This gives further evidence that Company M may have participated. Turner wrote:

> We went to fighting about 9 o'clock in the morning. Our army had not all crossed the Potomac River. The boys who had crossed over began fighting soon [too]. We held them back steady until about 1 o'clock when they got the better of us. We kept giving back every charge. Late in the evening A. P. Hill crossed the remainder of his troops and came up at double-quick movements and helped us out. The battle lasted until late in the evening. It was hard on both sides, as the Yankees numbered about seven to our one.[25]

The next day the army rested on the battlefield and that night retired across the Potomac. On 20 September 1862, Hill's division moved on the crossing near Shepherdstown to take part in driving Federal forces back across the river. There the troops suffered heavy artillery fire, and two men from Company M were killed:

Alfred N. Arnold and John R. Williams. Seven others were wounded and three taken prisoner. Brigadier General William D. Pender, brigade commander, reported the events in this way:

> At Shepherdstown, September 20, my brigade formed the left of our division. Advancing to within about 500 yards, we were opened upon by the artillery from the opposite side of the river, which lasted all day, at a most terrible rate. We came upon the infantry which had crossed. I had gone to the left to oppose this force, which was far superior to my own. Finding an effort made to flank me, I placed two regiments under cover from artillery, facing the river, and threw the other on my left flank, so as to check this new disposition of the enemy. Holding this position a short while, General Archer came up with three brigades to the support of the advanced line, and, upon seeing the flanking movement of the enemy, moved quickly to the left, when we advanced, driving them headlong into the river. After driving them from the plain, I sent the Twenty-second North Carolina, under the gallant Major Cole, to the river bank to take them as they crossed, and this it did nobly. Others of my brigade had gone to the river, but, finding them too much exposed, I called them back under a hill just overhanging the river. I called out those I had first left in that exposed position, leaving Major Cole with 20 men, who remained all day, the enemy being in heavy force in the canal on the opposite side. We were exposed all day to a tremendous fire of artillery, and also to the fire of their sharpshooters.
>
> In conclusion, I would beg leave to bring to the notice of the major general the distinguished gallantry and efficiency of First Lieut. R. H. Brewer, volunteer aide on my staff, whom I recommend for promotion. I would also beg leave to mention the names of a few whose actions entitle them to notice. In the Twenty-second the list will be rather long, as it is upon it and its commander that I usually call when any special and dangerous services are to be performed. Maj. C. C. Cole, commanding Twenty-second, always acts with coolness, courage, and skill. Captain Odell, acting field officer, has invariably behaved in a highly commendable manner.[26]

The division subsequently helped destroy a section of the Baltimore & Ohio Railroad, and then went into camp near Bunker Hill, Virginia, and remained in the Shenandoah Valley through most of October. Pvt. Stephen Ward Trogdon wrote home in October 1862:

> Dear Brother I haven't any thing of importance to write you at present only we march to this plase the other day and exspected to fight the yankies but they took the hint and Crossed the river and I was not Sarey of it for I have fought the yank as much as I want two we have ben tareing up the Rale road for the last two day I exspect we will go back to wards [toward] Stauton [Staunton, Virginia] when we get the Rale road tore up as much as they want it and we have burnt up Martinsburg I think the

yankies is A fraid of us A little we may have A fight here yet before we leave this plase.[27]

On 17 October the 13th Regiment N.C. Troops was added to Pender's brigade, making it a five-regiment brigade. It now included the 13th, 16th, 22nd, 34th and 38th N.C. Regiments, and it remained this way for the rest of the war.

On 26 October the Federals began crossing the Potomac east of the Blue Ridge, and Lee began moving his troops to confront them. He first ordered Longstreet's corps to Culpeper Court House and Jackson to Winchester, but realized the Federals were concentrating near Fredericksburg, Virginia. He then moved Longstreet to that place and Jackson's corps to near Orange Court House, where it remained until 26 November, when Jackson was ordered to join Longstreet at Fredericksburg. Pvt. Stephen Ward Trogdon wrote home on 7 December 1862:

> [T]he weather is very cold in this part of the country at present and no tents yet and only one Blanket A pice our Boxes has not got here yet we are A looking for them to day Dear Brother we had A very hard march coming from the valley to this place we March from Winchester to this plase in twelve days A distance of about two hundred miles and they was Snow on the Blue Ridge when we Crossed it and they was none on the other side nor on this Side but plenty on the top of it and they is A plenty here at this place now.[28]

On the 12th and 13th of December, the Federals began crossing the Rappahannock River at Fredericksburg, and Pender's brigade, which included the 22nd Regiment, was eventually stationed to the right of Longstreet near Marye's Heights next to Deep Run Creek. On 13 December 1862 the Federals launched an attack on A. P. Hill's line, and Pender's brigade came under heavy artillery fire. One Federal brigade advanced up Deep Run Creek but was driven back by the 16th N.C. Regiment and two regiments from another brigade in Longstreet's corps. The enemy finally retreated from in front of A. P. Hill, and during the night Hill's division was relieved. The Federals remained on the bank of the river at Fredericksburg until the night of 15 December, when they began re-crossing to the north bank. Company M performed well during the battle. Captain Laban Odell gained the recognition of senior officers for his daring and courageous action, which eventually led to his promotion. The 22nd Regiment lost one man killed and 44 wounded.

The regiment then went into winter quarters at a place eight miles below Fredericksburg on the Rappahannock River, known as Quinney's Station. They called it Camp Gregg. During the winter the regiment performed picket duty on the river there.

The winter passed quietly, as far as the Southern troops were concerned. The Union army now had a new commander, Major General Joseph Hooker, who set about reorganizing his army and its hospital and supply services so that the Union forces would be more mobile and more able to rapidly change with the troop situations. He also worked on the morale of Union troops, who were generally feeling that the Confederates could match them at every move. Confederate forces were being resupplied as best they could and endured the harsh Virginia winter. In January and March, Company M received ten new recruits, seven of them having been enlisted in Moore County on March 13. These men started their career in muddy, vermin infested camps, and without the innocence that the new recruits in the early days of war enjoyed. On 16 March 1863, Captain Laban Odell received his much deserved promotion to major of the 22nd N.C. Regiment, and 1st Lieutenant Warren B. Kivett was promoted to captain of Company M.

In the early spring of 1863, the weather was still quite cold and wet. The Confederates took the time to do some work in the background, making preparations for the 1863 campaign, which would eventually lead them onto Union soil in Pennsylvania. At least some detachments, including Company M, left Camp Gregg for a time. Sergeant John Turner reported: "In the spring of 1863 we broke up camp and took our march to the mountains of Virginia. We went to Culpepper and Jordansville, near Winchester. We also went into the Valley of Virginia near New Market on the Shenandoah river. We tore up the Baltimore and Ohio Railroad and then fell back near Chancellorsville."[29]

During this period of time, Warren B. Kivett was shot in the left leg and resigned as captain on 14 April. Sergeant Columbus Franklin Siler was promoted to 1st Lieutenant on 16 April, and evidently the company went without a captain until Siler was promoted to that rank on 2 May 1863 at Chancellorsville. Captain Siler was wounded numerous times, and though hospitalized for a period of time, remained in command throughout the remainder of the war, surrendering with his men at Appomattox.

The troops were being rallied for the invasion of Union troops under Hooker. On 29 April 1863, the Army of the Potomac began crossing the Rappahannock in the area of the Wilderness upstream from Fredericksburg. General John Sedgwick's Federal forces also remained facing the Confederates at Fredericksburg. General Lee deduced that Federals at Fredericksburg were a ploy, and decided to move most of his troops to confront Hooker, who had set up a defensive position around Chancellorsville.

About three miles from there, the Confederates began engaging enemy troops on 1 May 1863, but pushed on to Chancellorsville, where they found the main army entrenched. Early on the morning of 2 May 1863 Lee sent Jackson's corps, including Company M, on a hard march four miles to the west around the Union's right to flank them. Company M, being part of Pender's brigade, was placed in the third line along the Orange Turnpike. At about 5:15 P.M. the attack began. The Federals were totally surprised and were driven in disarray towards Chancellorsville. The first and second lines merged and pushed forward until meeting such strong resistance that they halted for the night. The third line came under heavy artillery fire, but pushed on, and became the first line during the night. At about 9:30 P.M., General Thomas J. "Stonewall" Jackson was accidently wounded by his own men while returning from a scouting patrol and riding across the front of his lines in the darkness.

At about 6:00 A.M. on 3 May 1863, the Confederate assault resumed under the command of General J. E. B. Stuart. After advancing about 150 yards, Pender's brigade found the enemy behind a breastworks of logs and brush in an area that was densely covered with undergrowth. Charge followed charge, and ground was gained, then lost. The Confederates pushed the Federals far beyond the breastworks, but then were forced to retire back to the breastworks. The 13th N.C. was able to push farther than the rest of the brigade, but eventually had to fall back as well because of a shortage of ammunition and support. Finally, other troops came up in support and a general advance of the entire Confederate line was made, forcing the Federals out of Chancellorsville. On May 3-4 the Confederates entrenched there, while Lee sent a portion of his troops to confront General Sedgwick, who had pushed through Fredericksburg while the battle was taking place at Chancellorsville. The third day's fighting was described by Sergeant John Turner:

> General Stuart took charge of Jackson's part of the army and managed it well. It was and hand-to-hand battle on both sides. The battle ground part was fought where there was a great deal of small brush which in the evening caught fire from the explosion of the Yankee magazine. The smoke was so thick we could not see anything in our front except the flash from their guns. So we got the better of the Yankees and ran them across the Rappahannock river. It was a heavy loss on both sides. Next day we had to bury their dead as well as our own. I was one of the boys to help. The fire had burned all of their clothing off, except what was between their bodies and the ground. It was an awful sight to see boys killed and then burned. I suspect several who were wounded so badly that they could not help themselves were burned to death.[30]

H. Spain Carroll of Company M was killed at Chancellorsville. Many others were wounded. Major Laban Odell and Lt. Colonel C. C. Cole of Guilford County were both killed within a few feet of each other on 3 May 1863. Captain Frank Siler was wounded in the right arm and thigh. The regiment had lost 219 men and 26 out of 33 officers were killed or wounded.

Around the 6th of May Lee moved his army back to Fredericksburg, and the regiment went back into camp at Camp Gregg. During this time a reorganization took place, and the Army of Northern Virginia was divided into three corps under generals James Longstreet, Richard S. Ewell and A. P. Hill. Pender was promoted to command a division of A. P. Hill's corps, and Colonel Alfred M. Scales was promoted to brigadier general and placed in command of Pender's former brigade. Thus the 22nd Regiment was now a part of Scales' brigade, Pender's division of Hill's corps.

On 4 June 1863, the army began its movement toward the Shenandoah Valley to begin the Gettysburg campaign. Ewell and Longstreet led the way, followed later by Hill, who had been ordered to watch Federal forces opposite Fredericksburg. As Hill's corps moved northward, the 22nd Regiment was engaged for a short time at Brandy Station, near Culpeper, on 9 June until General J. E. B. Stuart's cavalry took over the fight. Moving northward, Ewell's corps crossed the Potomac and entered Maryland on 16 June. Hill's and Longstreet's men followed on 24 June. By 27 June 1863, Hill's corps was encamped near Chambersburg, Pennsylvania. On 29 June the order came for Hill to go to Cashtown with Longstreet following the next day. Ewell's corps had gone eastward to Carlisle, and was ordered to rejoin the rest of the army at Cashtown or Gettysburg, depending on circumstances.

General Henry Heth of Hill's corps arrived at Cashtown on 29 June and the following morning sent General James J. Pettigrew's brigade to Gettysburg for shoes and other supplies. Finding the enemy occupying the town, Pettigrew returned to Cashtown. General Hill arrived at Cashtown late in the evening and made the decision to attack the enemy the next morning with Heth's and Pender's divisions.

On 1 July 1863, battle lines were formed with Heth's divison in the lead and Pender's behind. Scales' brigade was next to last on the far left, with the left of the brigade on the Chambersburg Pike. After marching forward for about a quarter mile, the far left brigade was moved to the right of the division, leaving Scales' brigade on the far left. The troops waited for about thirty minutes and moved forward. General Ewell's Corps arrived from Carlisle and struck the enemy on their right flank as Heth's troops came under fire. The enemy was driven from defensive lines three times. Heth's troops soon were out of ammunition and halted twice. Pender's division then began moving ahead of Heth's, and Scales ordered his brigade to pass over Heth's men. Scales reported that the brigade crossed McPherson Ridge and descended just opposite the theological seminary, where they encountered "a most terrific fire of grape and shell on our flank."[31] About midway between the ridge and the seminary, General Scales was wounded by a piece of shell, and Colonel William Lee J. Lowrance of the 34th N.C. assumed his command. About ten minutes after Scales was taken off the field, the enemy lines broke and the brigade and the rest of the division pursued the Federals into Gettysburg. General Scales reported 9 officers killed, 45 wounded and 1 missing. In the ranks 39 were killed, 336 wounded and 115 missing, although during the night some of the wounded and missing returned.

During the night of 1 July the brigade was moved to the extreme right of the army, and the following morning on 2 July was moved even farther to the right, on line with the artillery. Sgt. John Turner described the day of 2 July as follows:

> We lay there all day, under the fire of those shells. Lee was waiting for the Yankees to come to us, and they were waiting for us to go to them. The infantry had little to do except they would try to find the end of our line of battle, and we would drive them back. Large numbers of our boys were killed by bursting shells. In front of our brigade lay General Sycles and his New York troops.[32]

At about 1 P.M. the brigade was relieved by General Richard H. Anderson's division and was ordered to rejoin Pender's division in the center of the line.

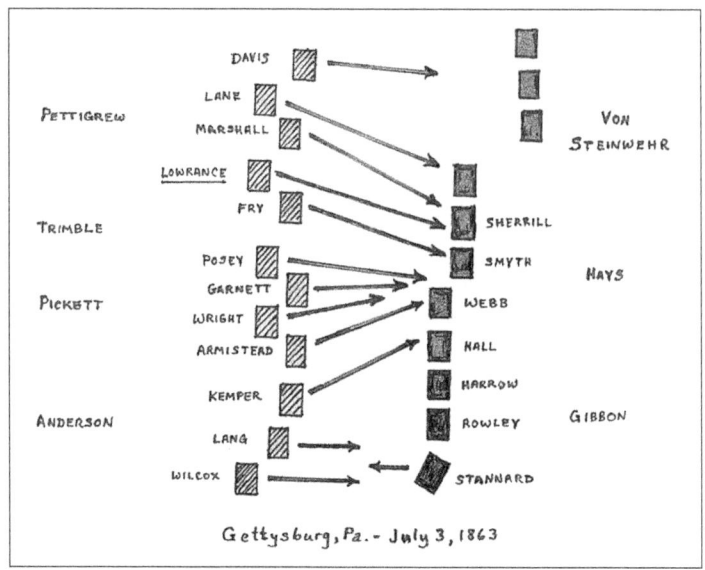

Map of the troop positions during the Pickett-Pettigrew-Trimble charge at Gettysburg, Pa., on 3 July 1863, popularly known as "Pickett's Charge." Company M was part of the Lowrance brigade.

During the day General Pender was mortally wounded and was temporarily replaced by General James H. Lane until General Isaac R. Trimble could get there.

On the morning of 3 July 1863 Lane's and Scales' (now Lowrance's) brigades received orders to move to the right to take part in an attack on the Federal center. General Trimble arrived to take command of the two brigades. The attack would be carried out by General George E. Pickett's division of Longstreet's corps on the right, supported by Cadmus M. Wilcox's brigade on the right rear, and by Heth's division (commanded by General Pettigrew) of Hill's Corps on the left, supported by the two brigades of Pender's division under General Trimble. The two Pender brigades (which included Company M), would follow about 100 yards behind Pettigrew.

At about 1 P.M. the Confederates began a two-hour cannonade. The attack columns then moved in front of the artillery and formed battle lines. Col. Lowrance reported the attack as follows:

> Then we were ordered forward over a wide, hot, and already crimson plain.
> We advanced upon the enemy's line, which was in full view, at a distance of 1 mile. Now their whole line of artillery was playing upon us, which was on an eminence in our front, strongly fortified and supported by infantry. While we were thus advancing, many fell, but I saw but few in that most hazardous hour who even tried to shirk duty. All went forward with a cool and steady step, but ere we had advanced over two-thirds of the way, troops from the front came tearing through our ranks, which caused many of our men to break, but with the remaining few we went forward until the right of the brigade touched the enemy's line of breastworks, as we marched in rather an oblique line. Now the pieces in our front were all silenced. Here many were shot down, being then exposed to a heavy fire of grape and musketry upon our right flank. Now all apparently had forsaken us. The two brigades (now reduced to mere squads, not

This 22nd N.C. Infantry Regiment battle flag was captured at Gettysburg on 3 July 1863 by Private Michael McDonough of the 42nd New York Volunteers. (©North Carolina Museum of History. Used by permission.)

numbering in all 800 guns) were the only line to be seen upon that vast field, and no support in view. The natural inquiry was, "What shall we do?" and none to answer. The men answered for themselves, and, without orders, the brigade retreated, leaving many on the field unable to get off, and some, I fear, unwilling to undertake the hazardous retreat. The brigade was then rallied on the same line where it was first formed.[33]

Colonel Graham Daves reported that during the charge, "Archer and Scales' brigades occupied and held for a time the Federal works"[34] and then retreated to the Confederate lines. Lowrance and Scales' brigade apparently reached the wall at or about the location of the 126th New York Regiment. During the fight, the 42nd New York "Tammany" Regiment moved over to assist the 126th N.Y. Private Michael McDonough of the 42nd N.Y. captured the 22nd N.C. Regiment flag, probably during this time. Sergeant John Turner had previously reported that he was with the 22nd Regiment flag and had seen two men killed and another wounded in the leg while carrying the flag on the previous day at Gettysburg. Sgt. Turner had this recollection of the charge from the perspective of Company M:

> The Yankees stopped firing their cannon to let them cool off, and Lee, thinking he had silenced them, charged with his whole army across the open space for a thousand yards. The Yankees did not fire a shot, and we, looking as if on dress parade, got within fifty yards of them, when they threw lead in our faces from both musket and cannon. It was a terrible time around there with those who were not killed or wounded. Several of our boys did not get a scratch. We retreated and night coming on, we left many of our boys sleeping their last sleep near Gettysburg.[35]

Lee expected a counterattack on his troops and held his army in place to repulse the enemy, but the counterattack never occurred. On the night of 4 July the army began its retreat to Virginia. The battle had been costly. The total loss to Scales' brigade was 102 killed and 322 wounded. During the three-day battle Company M lost one man killed (Private Wesley Siler) and 14 wounded or captured. Nathan David Barker died at Chester, Pa., of his wounds on 4 August.

The army retreated to Hagerstown, Maryland, arriving on 7 July and remaining until the 11th. The army set up defensive positions there because the Potomac River was too swollen to cross. Ewell's corps forded the waters above Williamsport, while Lee planned to cross with Longstreet's and Hill's corps at Falling Waters. Some of the men tore lumber from surrounding buildings and built a pontoon bridge at Falling Waters, while others, including Company M, held the defensive positions. Scales' brigade (under Col. Lowrance), of which Company M was a part, acted as part of the rear guard for the army and arrived at the bridge on the 14th at 10 A.M., resting before crossing. Just as the brigade began to cross, cavalry under Judson Kilpatrick and John Buford attacked, and were it not for Pettigrew's brigade defending them, Lowrance's troops would have been decimated. Lowrance was separated from his men during their crossing and had to ford the river about three-fourths of a mile upstream. After Pettigrew's men crossed, the bridge was cut, and some of the men who were unwilling or too exhausted to cross were killed or captured. Lowrance later reported that during this action about 200 men were lost. Company M lost John W. Kivett captured and John Jackson killed. General Pettigrew was mortally wounded during the defensive and died a few days later.

The army marched on to Bunker Hill, Virginia, where it remained encamped for a few days. Then they moved on to the Rapidan River, crossing at a place called German's Ford, where according to Sgt. Turner, a small skirmish took place. By 4 August 1863, the Army of Northern Virginia was occupying the Rapidan River line. According to Adjutant Graham Daves, General Cadmus M. Wilcox had replaced General Trimble, who was captured on 3 July.[36] In addition, during the time on the Rapidan, General Scales returned from being wounded. This now made Company M part of Hill's corps, Wilcox's divison and Scales' brigade.

During the late summer the Federal army under George G. Meade had entered Virginia and taken a position on the Rappahannock River line. On 10 October 1863, Lee ordered his troops to strike the Federals' flank, causing the Federals to retire northward to Centreville. As the rear guard of Meade's troops passed through Bristoe Station, Gen. A. P. Hill attacked with Heth's division in the lead, but did not wait for all his troops to come up. Hill's division suffered heavy losses during the attack. Scales' brigade was not engaged at Bristoe Station because it had been detailed to guard the corps train at Buckland. In early November some of Lee's troops fought a short engagement at Rappahannock Bridge, then the army retired to the Rapidan River again. On 26 November, Meade again moved into Confederate territory, hoping to cross the Rapidan below Lee. As Lee saw the plan unfold, he shifted his forces to confront Meade and made strong entrenchments at Mine Run before Meade could attack. Meade, seeing he could not find a weak defense to attack, began to entrench his troops as well. Lee then sent an attack force, composed of Wilcox's and Richard H. Anderson's divisons, to attack what was thought to be an exposed Federal flank on 2 December 1863. As the divisions moved, however, they found that the Federals had already retired. Wilcox and Anderson pursued, but the Federals succeeded in re-crossing the Rapidan. Lee's army then went into winter quarters. The 22nd Regiment camped with Scales' brigade near Orange Court House, Virginia.

The armies took advantage of a long winter quarters to recover from the devastation of 1863 and made no attempts to reposition themselves until early May. It was on the early morning of 4 May 1864 when the Federal army, now under the command of General Ulysses S. Grant, began crossing the Rapidan and moving into the area called the Wilderness. The Wilderness was part of the area called Chancellorsville, a battle site exactly one year before. Just to the south and west of Chancellorsville, much of the six by twelve mile area was covered with dense, second-growth trees and heavy underbrush. Sergeant John Turner described the place as "a thicket of small green briers and bush of all kinds."[37]

When Lee learned of the enemy movements he ordered his troops to move on the area with Ewell's corps on the left along the Orange Turnpike and Hill's corps in the center on the Orange Plank Road. Longstreet's corps would arrive from Gordonsville and move to the right of Hill. On the morning of 5 May 1864, the Confederate forces were advancing when Hill's corps encountered Federal cavalry near Parker's Store. With Heth's division in the lead, Hill drove the Federals back and occupied the crossroads. At the same time, Ewell's men were facing a corps of Federals on the Orange Turnpike. Hill ordered Heth's and Wilcox's divisions to turn and join with Ewell's corps on his right. Scales' brigade of Wilcox's division was posted on Chewning Plateau.

At around 4 o'clock in the afternoon the Federals made a strong assault on Heth. Heth was forced to bring up his reserves, and Wilcox received orders to support him. The Scales and Samuel McGowan brigades were ordered forward, along with the Lane and E. L. Thomas brigades, leaving a gap between Ewell's corps and Hill's. With Heth and these reinforcements holding off seven enemy brigades, the enemy brought more troops into action. At one point McGowan's and Scales' brigades passed over Heth's men and drove the Federals back until they themselves finally had to retire.

The Federals then attempted to turn the Confederate right flank as darkness fell. It was during this fight that Captain C. Frank Siler of Company M was first commended for his heroic actions. Three color bearers of the 22nd Regiment had been shot down when Captain Siler himself took the flag and shouted, "Follow me, my brave men." Years later, Col. W. P. Wood recalled that Captain Siler took the colors and, "waving it aloft, led his men in a gallant charge which took the ground the enemy were holding and prevented their flank charge. Soon afterwards General Scales embraced the Captain and said: 'God bless you! I saw your conduct with that flag! You have saved the army, and you shall be promoted.'"[38]

During the night Hill's corps regrouped with Scales' brigade on the right of the Plank Road and McGowan on the left. Other brigades were posted on either side and to the rear of them. At about 5 o'clock on the morning of 6 May 1864, Federal columns under command of Gen. Winfield Hancock struck Hill's line on the front and left flank. There were some thirteen Federal brigades against eight Confederate brigades, and the Confederate line was unable to hold. First Scales' line broke, then the others followed. Had it not been for the arrival of Longstreet the entire right wing of Lee's army would have collapsed. With Longstreet leading and the Wilcox and Heth divisions reformed behind his left, the Confederates succeeded in ending the Federal assault and driving them back. Night finally came to end the battle. There were nearly 18,000 Union casualties and about 10,800 Confederate casualties. Many wounded men became entangled in the dense undergrowth, which caught fire, and the cries of men being burned to death filled the air. Memories of the scene would haunt soldiers for many years to come. Company M had no men killed here, but many were wounded, and Talton Kivett was captured and died the next year in Elmira Prison, New York.

Finding that Grant was moving his army towards Spotsylvania Court House, Lee sent his forces to try to get there before Grant. Lee won the race, arriving early on the morning of 8 May 1864. The Confederates quickly began constructing a strong defensive works as other troops continued to arrive and preliminary fighting began. Lee's troops formed their line in a sort of V shape, with Longstreet's corps on the left, Ewell's corps in the center and Hill's corps (under temporary command of General Jubal Early) on the right. Wilcox's division was on the left of Hill's (Early's) corps, connecting with Ewell's. In the early morning hours of 12 May 1864 the Federal army opened an attack on the Confederate center, and overpowered the tip of the V-shaped position. Lane's brigade counterattacked on the enemy's left, while Thomas' and Scales' brigades hit their right and center. This caused the Federals to retire and take a new defensive position behind the former Confederate works at the tip of the V. Close fighting resumed, and lasted some 23 hours. It was reported by some Federal troops that around midday on 13 May a large oak tree some twenty inches in diameter was clipped in two by musket balls.

The Confederates finally fell back and established a new position across the base of the former V-shaped line. On 19 May, Ewell took his men around and behind the enemy in an attempt to find their right flank but ran into newly arriving Union troops near the Fredericksburg Road. The fighting there was known as the Harris Farm engagement, and accomplished little on either side.

Grant made several unsuccessful attempts on the Confederate line and finally decided to move eastward. On 21 May 1864 Thomas' and Scales' brigades (which included the 22nd Regiment) were ordered forward to explore the enemy positions. Following a short but intense skirmish, the Confederates advanced, finding that the Federals had abandoned their works. Lindsey Williams of Company M is reported to have died that day, although it is not known if his death was the result of this skirmish. General Lee then decided to move his army east to the North Anna River just north of Hanover Junction. Here he hoped to set up a defensive line against the Union advance. General Hill had returned to his command on the 21st of May and the next day moved his troops into the Confederate line on the left flank. Grant's men moved to positions opposite the Confederate line and along the North Anna River.

Meanwhile, the Federal V Corps under General G. K. Warren began crossing the river northeast of the line at Jericho Mills. General Hill ordered Wilcox's division forward to stop the V Corps' advance. Wilcox put three brigades on line, with Scales' brigade following the brigade on the left flank. As the division advanced and met the enemy, the left brigade gave way, and Scales' brigade moved up to the front. The advance halted as the fight ensued, and at nightfall, the Confederate brigades retired to their defensive position with the rest of the army. During the Jericho Mills portion of the North Anna campaign, Wilcox's division sustained 642 casualties. Two men from Company M, Henry Breedlove and James Cannon, were captured and imprisoned at Point Lookout, Maryland. Neither of them survived their imprisonment.

Lee's lines again formed an inverted V shape, with the tip of the V on the North Anna River. Grant crossed the river on 24 May 1864 and tried both flanks of the Confederate line, but was not able to push in the center as he had at Spotsylvania Court House. The Confederates had succeeded in building some of the most formidable works Grant had ever encountered. He found that his army was divided, and seeing the danger of remaining that way, they re-crossed the river during the night of 26-27 May.

As Grant moved eastward, Lee decided to move southward in protection of Richmond. The army marched about 24 miles and set up a line between Beaver Dam Creek and Pole Green Church. Ewell's corps was in the center of the line with Hill on the left and Longstreet on the right. On 30 May, Lee ordered Ewell's corps forward at Bethesda Church to attack the Federal left and attempt to turn it. The attempt failed, but provided valuable information about the intentions of the Federals. Grant seemed to be moving his troops to the Confederate right. Lee saw the situation unfolding and moved his men in the direction that would lead to the next meeting of the two armies at a crossroads called Cold Harbor.

On 30 May 1864 Maj. General Philip Sheridan's Union infantry and cavalry had succeeded in forcing the Confederate Cavalry out of the Old Cold Harbor Crossroads. By 31 May the main armies began staking their positions, with the Federals defending the crossroads and facing the Confederates of Anderson's corps and the Shenandoah Valley brigades of Maj. General John C. Breckinridge, who had joined Anderson in mid–May. The Confederates had their backs to the Chickahominy River.

Lee, seeing the movements of the Federals in recent weeks, had been calling for extra troops, and finally the division of Maj. General Robert F. Hoke reached the field. Hoke's troops fanned out to the right of Anderson towards Turkey Hill. On 1 June, Sheridan pulled back from Old Cold Harbor, but was ordered back at all costs. Upon returning his men poured deadly repeating carbine fire into the Confederates, while two more Federal corps moved in to take Sheridan's place. The Federals made a general advance and nearly reached the Confederate breastworks but were stopped by heavy fire, except for the two center corps, which made a small break in the Confederate line. Anderson's troops soon sealed the break by bringing up three brigades of reserve troops. Grant had captured around 750 Confederates and lost 2,800 men in the process.

On 2 June, General Hill, who had been occupying a position on the far northern end of the line, was ordered to leave Heth's division there and take Wilcox's and William Mahone's divisions south to join Breckinridge on the far right of the line. Wilcox arrived on the right of the line at about 3:00 P.M. and the two brigades joined Breckinridge in the attack and occupation of Turkey Hill. From that point, the Confederates fanned out farther, making a six-mile line extending to within half a mile of the Chickahominy on its right.

At 4:30 A.M. on 3 June 1864, the Federal army made a general assault on the whole Confederate line, with the exception of Wilcox's division, which was too far to the right for them to reach. The attack finally ended about 11:00 A.M. with the Federals having been bloodily repulsed. Some artillery and infantry firing continued until about 1 P.M., but the battle was over. Grant had lost heavily in a scene reminiscent of Pickett's Charge. There were about 13,000 Union casualties and nearly 5,000 Confederate. Half of the Federal casualties occurred in that final assault. The armies held their positions for several days, and Grant finally requested a truce on 7 June to retrieve his wounded men, but by then most of them had died.

Many prisoners had been taken on both sides. Sergeant John Turner had this story to tell about one of them:

> After the battle was over we had a few prisoners our boys had taken. They were brought to our colors for us to hold until a guard was selected to take them to Richmond. One of the men looked at me and said, "Sergeant, I

want to talk with you." "Owing to what you want to talk about, whether I will answer you," I replied. "I want to ask if General Lee has any men in his army from any state besides North Carolina," he said. "Why do you ask that question?" I enquired. "Well," said he, "I've been in 23 battles and have not met a man except from that state, and I thought his whole army was from there."[39]

Grant finally began moving southward in the direction of the James River on 12 June and Lee followed the next day. Contact was made on 13 June at Riddell's Shop, when the 22nd Regiment had a brief skirmish with the Federals. Grant then crossed the James River and moved on Petersburg. Scales' brigade crossed the James River about eight miles below Richmond at Drewry's Bluff, then went to the Halfway Station on the Petersburg & Weldon Railroad. From there, they went about 4 miles south and according to Sergeant Turner had another skirmish. Afterwards, the Confederates went southward, arriving at Petersburg about 18 June, passing through Petersburg, and crossing the Appomattox River. After traveling about three-fourths of a mile downstream they formed breastworks, with Scales' brigade occupying the works south of Sycamore Street. Here they remained until mid–August.

Sergeant Turner had been examined by doctors in March and recommended for discharge due to his wounds. He received his discharge orders and left the company on 3 August 1864. He was later placed in another light duty unit, serving on the Weldon Railroad until the end of the war.

General Grant gave orders to extend his line to the west, and on 18 August the Federals occupied Globe Tavern on the Petersburg & Weldon Railroad. A contingent of Confederate forces, including all of Hill's corps with the exception of Scales' brigade, made an assault on the Federals at Globe Tavern on 21 August, but was unsuccessful in forcing them out. Meanwhile, Federals were also occupying Reams' Station on the railroad south of Globe Tavern. General Hill ordered Scales' and six other brigades, along with two divisions of cavalry, into action at Reams' Station. They arrived on the morning of 25 August 1864, and at 2:00 P.M. Scales' and Lane's brigades launched an assault. After failing at two attempts to take the Federal works, the rest of the brigades there joined in. Together they succeeded in driving the Federals out. Adjutant Graham Daves wrote:

> The Sixteenth, Twenty-second and Thirty-fourth North Carolina regiments, and Benning's Georgia Brigade, were ordered to charge. On reaching the edge of the woods, Benning's men, seeing a strong line of works, well manned, in their front were halted. The Twenty-second Regiment charged up to the works, but, having lost their support on their right, were withdrawn. They were not repulsed. Private Ellison, of Company L, snatched an United States flag from the earth works in this charge, and brought it away with him. Shortly after this Lane's, MacRae's and another brigade of Heth's Division, with the Twenty-second Regiment covering their left flank, charged the position and carried the works in

splendid style. Hampton's cavalry shared in the attack and rendered most efficient service.[40]

J. E. Dollinger of Company M was killed at Reams' Station. That evening, Hill's corps returned to their position at Petersburg and Wilcox's division saw no more action until 29 September. Grant was extending his line westward from Globe Tavern and on that date, Confederate forces met with Grant's troops under Maj. General Benjamin Butler at Fort Harrison. Butler had crossed the James River, aiming at the northern defenses of Richmond. He had some success against Confederate defenses at Fort Harrison and New Market Heights, but the Confederates soon rallied and contained the Federal advance. Lee then counterattacked in an action known as Jones' Farm. The attempt at halting the Federal activities failed, and Scales' brigade was nearly captured when Wilcox's division was struck on the left flank and forced to withdraw. The Federals entrenched and Wilcox's division then fell back to its Petersburg defenses.

Hill's corps received orders on 8 December to deploy to Belfield to meet an advance of Federals on the Petersburg & Weldon Railroad. A few miles from Belfield, Hill received intelligence that the enemy had already retired, and tried to cut off their retreat. He caught up with Federal cavalry at Jarratt's Station, where a short skirmish ensued. Finding that the main Federal forces were three hours ahead of them, Hill ended the pursuit and had his men camp for the night. The next morning, they started back to Hatcher's Run, reaching that place on 13 December 1864.

During the winter of 1864-65 at Petersburg, Captain Siler of Company M was again recognized for his heroism. The 22nd N.C. was on duty on the lines south of Petersburg, in support of Battery 45. General A. P. Hill sent the following order to General Scales:

> I am at sea as to the location of the enemy; and unless I can learn it to-night, our army may be ruined. Send your sharpshooters and a part of General Lane's to-night about twelve o'clock as quietly as possible to the enemy's rifle pits and take as many prisoners as they can, and ask them as soon as captured as to the location of their army. They will tell the truth, just aroused from sleep.[41]

Captain Young, who commanded the sharpshooters, was temporarily absent. General Scales then chose Captain Siler from among his one hundred and sixty officers to take charge of them. Captain Siler, a few days before, had been to the enemy rifle pits under the ruse of exchanging newspapers with the Federals, which was often done during the war. While in that area, he had carefully observed a worn path along the edge of the woods that might be used in reaching enemy positions more easily. He was ordered to General Lane's regiment to get his sharpshooters and was given General Scales' own horse to ride.

The 22nd Regiment had constructed a small dam on the nearby stream to creat a pond in front of Battery 45 as an obstacle to enemy troops. The dam was the shortest route between the regiments, so Captain Siler rode across the top of the dam. However, it was dark and as Captain Siler soon discovered, the horse was "moon-eyed." The horse lost footing and fell, carrying the captain for a fifteen- to seventeen-foot fall into the mud and water. Uninjured, Captain Siler seized his horse and continued to General Lane's brigade, where he met Major Thomas J. Wooten and obtained his sharpshooters.

Joining the two groups of men together, he led them along the same path he had chosen earlier, and reached the rifle pits. All of the enemy troops were asleep, with the exception of a sentry. As the men stormed the pits with Captain Siler in the lead, the sentry tried to use his bayonet, but Siler snatched it from his own breast, turning it aside, and secured the sentry before he could fire his weapon or give any alarm. The Confederates were able to sweep the rifle pits, taking about 60 prisoners with them as they returned to the Confederate lines. The Federals, discovering the surprise, poured heavy fire on them as they left, but did no damage because of the darkness. The captured prisoners furnished all the information General Hill needed on the location of the Federal lines, and he ordered General Scales to promote the officer in command of the raid—Captain C. F. Siler. There is no record that he was ever promoted, though he was twice recommended for it.

In early February 1865, General Grant made the decision to extend his line on his left to Boydton Plank Road at Hatcher's Run. He thought this would be a good opportunity to head off some supply trains from reaching the Confederates. He sent Brevet Brigadier General David Gregg's cavalry division to the Boydton Plank Road, followed by the Federal V corps and elements of the II Corps. Gen. Hill's corps was engaged on 5 February in the defense of Hatcher's Run, but achieved little for their efforts. The Confederate lines were then extended farther to the right to meet the extension of Federal lines. This moved Wilcox's division to the right and away from the main action. By the time the battle was ended on 7 February, the Confederate forces had stopped the Federal advance, but had lost precious ground in the process.

In late March 1865, Gen. Grant began a new series of attacks on the Petersburg defenses. General Philip Sheridan's cavalry was sent on 29 March to the area of Dinwiddie Court House, followed by the Federal V Corps, to turn Lee's right flank at the Petersburg defenses. The Federals succeeded in driving the Confederates back to their entrenchments on White Oak Road. The next day, Lee shifted reinforcements to meet the attempt at turning his flank by placing Maj. Gen. Fitzhugh Lee's cavalry divisions at Five Forks and moving Gen. Pickett's division to the extreme right. On 31 March, Sheridan's cavalry and the V Corps moved against the Confederate entrenchments on White Oak Road, but were dealt a hard counterattack by Confederates under Maj. Gen. Bushrod Johnson. The Federals suffered 1,870 casualties to the Confederates' 800 casualties, but the Federal line soon stabilized and set the stage for the fight of 1 April 1865 at Five Forks.

Lee ordered Pickett and Fitzhugh Lee along with Rosser's cavalry to hold the Five Forks crossroads at all hazards, because this protected his last major supply line, the South Side Railroad. On 1 April, Sheridan's cavalry pinned the

Confederate lines in place while the Federal V Corps attacked Lee's left flank. The attack was disastrous to the Confederates. Many prisoners were taken. This time the Federal casualties were only 830, while the Confederate loss was nearly 3,000. The next morning Lee informed President Jefferson Davis that Petersburg and Richmond had to be evacuated. Meanwhile, the Federals were launching a general attack on the entire Confederate line at Petersburg.

Wilcox's and Heth's divisions were at this point attempting to defend the South Side Railroad near a place called Sutherland's Station. On 2 April 1865, Federal troops under the command of Maj. Gen. Nelson A. Miles attacked the position held by the Confederate brigades of John R. Cooke, Scales, William MacRae and McGowan. Scales' brigade was driven back to its second line of defense, and meanwhile, three Federal brigades overran the left flank of the position. The Confederate defenders were forced to leave their positions and the Federals took control of the South Side Railroad. During the day the Confederates suffered another blow with the death of General A. P. Hill, who was killed while trying to reach his troops in the confusion of the battles around Petersburg. Though the Confederates lost the battle at Sutherland's Station, the men of Randolph County displayed exactly what they were made of.

Colonel T. S. Galloway reported that during the battle, Captain Siler of Company M was ordered to take Companies I, L and M of the 22nd Regiment and hold a small piece of woods to his right. With about 70 men, Captain Siler charged through the woods and captured the Federal picket line. An ammunition wagon had broken down nearby, and Siler had several boxes of ammunition brought to his lines and distributed. When General Miles' division came in sight, the Union commander, seeing the advantage of the woods, deployed a regiment of about 300 men to take the woods back. The Federals launched three attacks on Siler's men. Col. Galloway later wrote:

> The third attack was made with full regiment and colors advancing to within about one hundred and forty yards; but they fell back with loss, the gallant stand of our line making it seem that a heavy force was there. All the time I could see Siler, with hat in one hand and sword in the other, rushing up and down his line encouraging his men, which so thrilled General Cooke that he cried out: "Who is that gallant officer in command?" In this way that much-desired ground was held until the arrival of other forces.[42]

The men from Randolph County continued to hold their ground until they were finally ordered to retire, due to the failure of the Confederate lines to hold back the general assault by Miles' forces.

That night, General Lee evacuated the defenses of Petersburg, pulling his army out of the trenches and marching them in the direction of Amelia Court House. Reaching that place on the 4th and 5th of April, Lee regrouped his army and continued the retreat. At Sayler's Creek on 6 April 1865, Sheridan's cavalry and portions of the Federal II and VI corps cut off nearly one-fourth of the retreating army. Confederate generals Ewell, Seth Barton, James Simms, Joseph Kershaw, Custis Lee, Dudley Dubose, Eppa Hunton and Montgomery Corse surrendered their men, signaling the end of the Confederate army.

On 7 April, Scales' brigade (under temporary command of Colonel Joseph Hyman of the 13th N.C., due to the sickness of Gen. Scales) participated in perhaps the last victory of the Army of Northern Virginia, at a place called Farmville (otherwise known as Cumberland Church). The Federal II Corps came upon the retreating Confederate column here and prepared an attack. The Confederates entrenched on high ground near the church. The Federals attacked twice but were repulsed, and during the action, Scales' brigade drove off a body of Federal cavalry preparing to attack the right of the Confederate column.

The retreat continued until the armies were facing each other at Appomattox Court House. On the morning of 9 April 1865, Wilcox's division was moving to support an attack by General John B. Gordon on the Federals just west of Appomattox Court House. The word came to cease-fire. That afternoon, the surrender was completed, and the parole conditions agreed upon. The Army of Northern Virginia ceased to exist, and on 12 April a formal turning over of arms and flags was held. Only 22,000 Confederates remained for the ceremonies.

Only 97 men from the 22nd Regiment were paroled at Appomattox Court House, and only eight men from Company M. They were Captain Columbus Frank Siler, William Allridge, Jacob B. Foust, Lorenzo Dow Stout, Andrew Jackson Turner, David Wright, Jabez Lindsay York and William Joseph York. These men took part in the heartbreaking ceremony of laying down their arms and flags. On 12 April 1865, Union Brigadier General Joshua Chamberlain formed his troops along either side of the Richmond Stage Road leading out of town towards the Confederate camps. The Confederates left their camps and formed ranks, almost as if they were on parade, and marched into town, with Major General John B. Gordon in the lead. As the Confederates entered town, a bugler was ordered to "sound a marching salute. The Federals snapped to 'carry arms.' [General] Gordon, astride his horse, caught the spirit of the event, rose erect in his stirrups, wheeled his horse magnificently, and brought the point of his sword to his boot toe, at the same time ordering his men to the same position at arms, 'honor answering honor.'"[43] General Chamberlain later wrote that there was "not a sound of trumpet more, nor roll of drum; not a cheer, nor whisper of vain-glorying, nor motion of man standing again at the order, but an awed stillness rather, and breath-holding, as if it were the passing of the dead!"[44]

Arms stacked and paroles given, the men started on their long journey home. The war wasn't over, because there were still other commands out in the field for as long as two months afterwards, but for these men, it was time to go home and start over. For the next several weeks, the same poignant scene was repeated many times. Families at home were about their daily duties when, up the road, they saw a singular figure dressed in rags of gray, making his way to the home he loved. Many of the folks at home were not even sure when or if anyone was coming home. Some watched in vain.

There were a few of the other men already at home, recovering from wounds or sickness, and preparing to come back to the army. Some men apparently left the army at Appomattox before receiving their parole. Others, in the closing days of the war, may have slipped away and started home before the end came. For whatever reasons, there were about 21 members of Company M who received their paroles in Greensboro, North Carolina, between the 2nd and 22nd of May 1865. Another 31 men were being held prisoner at the time of the surrender or just before. The last of these prisoners, James Furgerson of Rockingham County, was released at Point Lookout, Maryland, on 26 June 1865. Several other men have no military record after October 1864, though we know that some survived and either came home or moved west. Another 14 men of Company M were captured or deserted and joined the U.S. Army for the remainder of the war.

Some of the surviving men were maimed for life, having lost a leg or arm, or the use of them. A couple of them were blinded. Whatever their lot, these men were of a stronger mettle than most, and came home to pick up the pieces, determined to work hard and live honestly, just as they had done before they went off to war.

The first casualty of the war for Company M had been James Murdick Kivett, who died at Camp Holmes on 3 October 1861. The last was Newman Breedlove, who died at Point Lookout Prison on 6 June 1865. Though the records are not complete, the last known surviving member of Company M was Daniel P. Pulley, who died on 17 June 1931, and was buried at Oak Ridge Baptist Church cemetery in Vance County, N.C. The final old soldier to die lived nearly 70 years longer than the first.

2. Turner's Romance

The following history came from a series of articles written by Sergeant John T. Turner of Ramseur, who enlisted as a private and was promoted to corporal and sergeant in Company M, 22nd Regiment. He later served in Company B, 1st Battalion light duty men, where he was orderly sergeant. These articles were published in the *Asheboro Courier* as a continuing series that ran from 29 January 1914 to 2 July 1914. Mr. Turner also wrote several obituaries for some of his comrades, which are found elsewhere in this volume. These articles are unique in that they tell the history of Company M from the perspective of one of the participants. I have attempted to reproduce the articles as written, with a few noted exceptions to clarify or correct misprints.—Wallace E. Jarrell

Romance No. 1
Life of John T. Turner Written by Himself

Note—John T. Turner who writes the deaths of all the old soldiers that he was acquainted with before the war and after, is beginning with this issue a sketch of his life and this sketch will appear in The Courier *in installments for the next several weeks. The sketch will deal mainly with incidents connected with the war and will be written in his own familiar style, not having the opportunity for a school education. It would be well for his friends and those interested to save the papers containing his sketches as they will be interesting in the after years.*

This is the first month of the year 1914 and as I take up my pencil to write a sketch of my life and my experiences in the Civil War, when all my life was before me, I realize that I am one of the old men having lived my allotted time and the world has little to claim my attention.

I hope that the readers will bear in mind that this sketch will be written, much of it from a boy's standpoint and will leave out the history that has already been recorded, and as I am writing from memory, I hope to interest the young folks telling of the old-time ways of old folks—the young children who ate bread baked on the shovel.

I, John T. Turner, was born on Sandy Creek, Randolph County in 1842, and was raised on the farm much of the time. I was hired out by the day or the month, so I had a good chance to find out how other folks lived, who was a good cook and who was not. I came to the conclusion before I was a man that one of the worst faults with many a man was quarreling with his wife.

Today being the first month of the year, my mind goes back to 1854, when the Christmas that had just passed. I thought it a long time before another would come, but somehow they roll around.

Looking back 65 years we had no railroads, nor automobiles, nor even a buggy to carry the girls to church.

Well, I guess you wonder what we did for amusement in those days. Hogs were killed before Christmas, and the old folks would go to see each other, and the women would bring pipes and a big twist of our home made tobacco, and talk of everything that had happened, or was to happen in time to come.

These were the days of slavery, and it was customary for all farmers to clear a new ground every winter and have "chopping frolics" in the spring, so all the girls were invited to come in to quilt and after supper the house was turned over to the young folks and the fun commenced and always winding up each play with a kiss.

Turner's Romance No. 2

As my mind runs back to my school days, we had from two to three months term in winter. Our teachers got from eighteen to twenty dollars per month and held school from morning until night. We had but one book to study, Webster's Blue Back Speller. When we got so we could spell and read in that, our studies were Emmerson's Arithmetic first, second and third parts. We had slates that cost ten to fifteen cents each and would last our life time if not broken. Now days it is tablets that cost the parents from one dollar to five per session.

It was customary to turn the teacher out before Christmas. All knew the time, also the old folks, but kept it a secret from our teacher. The old men, especially the committeemen, were there to see the fun. Most of the times passed and not much fun. Mr. W. M. Reece taught one session for us and when the time came for our treat we had the door shut and four of our largest boys were placed at the back of the house to get in the rear of him and then the treat was demanded. His answer was "I will not give you the treat." Then the boys took hold of him but he got loose and ran. We all ran after him and he threw off his coat so away we went after him. He got about a half mile from the school house and sat down and we tied him on his back to a plank and got some hand spikes and carried him to the house. Still he refused to treat so we carried him down to the run below the spring and dipped his head in and asked him if he would treat and he still refused, so every time we dipped him in a little deeper and finally we held his head under the water until the blubbers began to raise and he said "I will treat you all." It was real enjoyment to the old folks.

In these days we had sales, musters, elections and other gatherings. It was customary to have something to eat and drink, so the dishpies, sugar cakes, cider and whiskey were all prepared and hauled out in wagons. The clerk sat in the wagon and you could see the old men coming in with their fiddles. They would take a few drinks of the stuff and the music would commence, some of the folks patting and the others dancing. Some of the younger boys would take our girls and treat them with cake. I have stood back and looked on and wished I was an old man with them. It looked to me as if it was heaven on earth for them. We boys in those days would not drink whiskey for fear the girls would smell it and turn us down. For the girls would not go with a boy who had been drinking in those days, the young men did not drink the stuff but now it is changed.

My next number will dwell upon the commencing of the Civil War.

Turner's Romance No. 3

The school buildings in my boyhood days were built of logs and filled up between the logs with mud. Our parents would meet every fall before time for school to start and fill all the open places, ready for the school to start. The seats were made of slabs and punchings split out of logs with legs put in them. Some were higher than others, to suit the big and the little folks. I have seen the little tots fall off backward, as the seats had no backs to them. After dinner all the big boys had to carry one load of wood and if you wanted a drink of water you had to go to the spring after it, and drink out of a gourd. But it is not that way now. Times have improved.

The girls wore shoes [with] the heels from one to two taps high. Now they must be from two to three inches. I notice now that when the girls walk they are mostly on their toes, and I look for them to grow pitched forward. The little tots that pass by every day carry a satchel full of books that I look to see them all bow legged when 15 years of age. But there I am not criticising for I don't blame people for keeping up with the style and fashions, for if I was a young man, I would be in the "ring" with them.

My teachers are all dead except two—Benjamin Moffitt of Asheboro and Miss Lov An Pugh [Lou Ann Pugh?] of Franklinville.

My school days ended and I began farming. It did not look like farming but fighting grass. In the spring of 1859 I asked my father to let me go and learn some trade. He told me he could not spare my time, as all apprentices, to learn any trade, had to serve three years. Their wages were only ten cents per day, so I did not say any more to him. In the spring of 1860 I told him if he would let me go, I would give him, after I had learned a trade, all I could make for twelve months. He then gave me permission to go.

There was a good carpenter in our neighborhood by the name of Dorris York. I started to work for him and every thing moved on nicely. Every few weeks there was speaking at different places. I would go to hear what was said and it was always on "war." They urged the boys to go to war, telling them that they could wipe up all the blood spilt with their handkerchief. They also said that Yankees could not shoot a gun. But when I went to war I found all this different.

On Saturday evenings we would meet our neighbor boys and they would meet me with "Well, John, what is the news?" "Nothing," I replied. "What with you?" "War, I think I will go," one replied.

In the spring of [1861], there was a free dinner set and speaking, and calls for volunteers. The clouds of war were rising fast over the Southland, and volunteers were needed. James M. Odell was making up a company of twelve months boys so I couldn't stand back any longer, as I saw the girls were liking the boys who volunteered. I gave my name to Mr. Odell for twelve months and then I had a time. The boys had a time drilling. The company was formed and our first drill camp was at Joshua Bain's near Liberty, cooking our meals in the blacksmith shop and sleeping in the barn.

Turner's Romance No. 4

We elected our officers: J. M. Odell, captain; Laban Odell, first lieutenant; J. M. Pounds, second lieutenant; L. F. McMasters, third lieutenant; Henry Allred, fourth lieutenant. The non-commissioned officers were appointed by the captains. We remained at this camp about three weeks, then we moved to Middleton Academy, half way between Franklinville and Cedar Falls. It was a good thing that we did not know what was before us.

After the company had been uniformed, a day was set for us to go to Raleigh. It was a sad time for us, as many of our friends and kindred had come to bid us good bye. We marched to High Point next day. We reached Raleigh safely, and went into camp Crabtree, a military [camp] of instruction. In a few days we were sworn in and paid a bounty of $10, which was the first ten dollars of Confederate money that I ever seen. From that day we were Confederate soldiers.

One of the first things that we had to learn was that our liberty to do as we pleased had ceased and [that] we could not do anything outside of camp without a pass. We began to learn what was required of a soldier and very soon found that we had no use for repeaters and bowie knives of which we had many.

We were soon formed in regiments with the following companies: I, L and M from Randolph, A from Caldwell county, B from McDowell, E from Guilford county, G from Caswell, F from Alleghany and two other companies from the Western counties.

Our regiment was the 12th volunteers and went by that number until the first Conscript Act passed. Our first Colonel was J. J. Pettigrew, of Johnson county. We remained in camp until September and was then ordered to Garrysburg. Upon arrival there we were told that there were enough soldiers stationed there and our Colonel to report his regiment at headquarters at Richmond, Va. We had been riding in cattle cars so now we were put on flat cars, some having coaches to ride in.

Upon arrival at Richmond we fell into line and stacked our arms. Our Colonel gave us command to "rest at ease." He rode off for orders, and [then] gave the command: "Twelfth Regiment, fall in line! Take arms! Forward, march! Keep step with fife and drum!"

We marched toward the capital and struck Main Street and filed down the part called Rockett. The sidewalks on each side were lined with old and young men and women and girls. The Colonel put us through the manual of arms in march. Some of the onlookers said, "Where are you all from?" Another said "Look at the flag" for it said, "Twelfth North Carolina Regiment." Another said, "They are fine looking young men. Wonder if they left any more back home." I thought myself that we were nice looking, for we were uniformed and our new guns and bowie knives hanging by our sides, made us look dangerous and I thought that the Yankees would run at the first sight of us. We went into camp near the city, on the James river upon a high hill on a level higher than the city. We raised our tents and the guards were strung around us so that no man could pass out without a pass signed by his captain.

We had a fair view of the river with the city facing us. When night came on and the lights at Richmond were lit, some of the boys said that the world was upside down, that the stars at home were above us, out here they were below us. In a few days there was a heavy mail set to our homes telling our friends what we had seen, for many of us had not been so far from home before.

Our regiment was next ordered to Evansport on the Potomac river. We broke camp and took the Fredericksburg and Potomac railroad and went to Brooks station, the last stop before you get to the river, and went into camp.

Turner's Romance No. 5

As I am writing as one of the Twelfth Regiment boys, I will soon pass to the Twenty-second Regiment, then later on to the First Battalion and finish my war tramps under Johnson in North Carolina.

I am now at Brook's Station. In November 1861, we were formed in a Brigade with the following regiments: Twelfth N.C., Thirteenth Miss., Thirty-fifth Ga., Forty-seventh Va., and a Battalion from Ark., with General Holmes commander. They all started on their march for Evansport. Our regiment was left back for some purpose. We went into camp near the depot in a low, flat field and it began to rain. We did not see the sun for 17 days. When it was not raining it was cloudy. Our boys had a siege of the measles. The drilling and camp guards were all suspended, for it took all the boys to wait upon the sick crowd. Our regiment was called the sick regiment.

We began to think that it would never stop raining. The mud was so bad that the regiment ahead had to go in camp a few days. The rain ceased, and our Colonel sent word to the Colonel of the 13th Miss. that he would start our regiment on the march at 12 o'clock (noon), as they were about six miles ahead of us, and for them to have all their camp kettles made full of coffee for his sick boys. We made the six miles, reaching there about night. The coffee was ready for us. The next morning when we awoke another crowd was broken out with the measles. They were carried off to hospitals at different places. Some of the boys I never saw again as they were laid to rest in the soil of Va.

By this time our regiment was getting small. On the second day we started on our march for Evansport. We reached Stafford Court House by night. We camped there. It was called Camp Washington. It was in sight of the Potomac river. There we had another beautiful night. Another heavy mail left for North Carolina, telling our people what we had gone through with and what we had seen on our way. I thought I had volunteered to fight the Yankees but we were put to work. We were sent to blockade the river to keep the Yankees from going up to Washington. When I first saw the river I could not see how we could build a dam across it, but I soon saw how we could do it. The place was surveyed and plans were laid out. This was December; we moved our camp down near the river and built our winter quarters. Every night a certain number were detailed out of each company to work all night. We built parapitts [parapets] and magazine breastworks and parapitts. We were ready for the big guns which were from 8 to 14 feet long. They were hung under a two-wheel cart and hauled to within a half mile of the river by oxen 8 to 12 yoke each. When the night came on 75 or 100 of the boys were hitched to the big guns by a rope and we hauled them in. We were very quiet for fear the Yankees would find out what we were doing. We kept this work up until we finished the works. This was spring and the day was fixed for firing upon the boats which were passing up and down the river, which was one and seven-eighth miles from shore to shore.

Turner's Romance No. 6

When that day rolled around it was foggy on the river. We opened fire on the Yankees with our big guns. I never heard such noise. The whole earth shook, everything was aquiver around us. Across the river they had found out what we had done so the Yankees raised some guns over on their side. It was fun to see our boys and the Yankees shoot at each other across the river. They started a railroad on their side out of reach of our guns and run around us and connected to the river above us. So all of our work profited the South nothing.

In February they called for men to volunteer for three years, or during the war. They would pay the boys $50 bounty and 30 days furlough. A great many of the boys volunteered. I did not volunteer as my time was out in June.

On April the 16th the first conscript act was passed, that all men between 18 and 35 years of age were to be pressed into service. So that included me.

I must tell a joke on our Colonel. We boys would talk to each other when on picket across the river, and when the Colonel found it out I was on guard. He came down for a little talk with the boys. He told me to get the boys to talking and then he would take hold of them. I got them started. The first word he spoke was in a different voice. The answer from them was "Who is that?" "This is Colonel Pettigrew." "Colonel Pettigrew, you and your men grease your heels and slip back into the Union. I will bet you $100 that you nor any one of your men haven't any hair on your breast." The Colonel turned to me, and said "Sergeant, I will quit them." He never tried them again.

By this time our boys that had reenlisted were making arrangements to start home with their $50 and 30 days furlough. The Yankees were dividing their army into two parts. Jackson and Breckinridge was to watch north of Richmond and Johnston to look after the southeast part of Richmond. We were with Johnston. March was here and our big guns were rolled in the river and lay there. Our necessary baggage was sent to Richmond. Our brigade all left for Yorktown and marched down there 125 miles. The 12th Regiment was left back for some purpose. In a few days we started our march for the point. We got to Fredericksburg and took up camp.

It was now April and the boys who had been on furlough had returned. Others had joined us. We now had a full regiment. We now became the 22nd Regiment. North Carolina had 10 regiments of three-year volunteers and 12 regiments of 12-months boys. They were all put together and ours was raised to the 22nd Regiment. We were reorganized and new officers were elected. In Company M, our company, we elected Laban Odell captain, W. B. Kivett first lieutenant, C. F. Siler second lieutenant, L. T[F]. McMasters third lieutenant, Milton Lawrence fourth lieutenant. All were new men except McMasters. Before our time was up these old commissioned officers had a right to resign and come home, which they did, except for McMasters. Everything was straightened out.

We started on our march for Yorktown. We got as far as Ashland and went into camp. The new boys that had joined had the measles. In a few days we started on our march again. We left the boys who had the measles at the hospital. We reached Richmond and stopped for the night. Next day our regiment took the boats for Harris' landing, near Yorktown. We marched about eight miles and went into camp. We were sent down to the Warwicks swamps to relieve our boys who had been there for some time. We were not allowed any fire, and it was April, 1862, then I have told my readers I would tell when I got to the war. I have gotten to the firing line after twelve months of traveling. Next number will tell what the war really is.

Turner's Romance No. 8

[The numbers of the articles here skip from six to eight due to a missing issue of the *Asheboro Courier* of which no copies have been located. This creates a gap in Sgt. Turner's story of about one month. However, the articles presented here remain in sequence and in correct order.]

We stayed here in camp until May 30. We then drew rations for two days. We lay down to rest. About 9 o'clock the bugle sounded to fall in line. All baggage was left in camp except what we had on and one blanket each. We marched about two miles and formed in battle line on the extreme left. The line of battle was about one mile long when the morning came.

Not much was done until evening. From the roaring of the muskets near the Fair Oaks farm and beyond the Williamsburg road the battle was severe. In the evening at our end of the line the Yankee troops tried to pass our left wing. It was charge after charge by both sides. We gained with every charge. The last charge made by us was made through a swamp knee deep in mud and water.

The enemy fell back to their breastworks. Night came and the battle was over. So ended the 31st day of May, 1862. On Sunday, June 1, the battle began early in the morning and lasted all day long. It was a severe engagement and along the line and we gained ground at every charge. At last we beat them back to the last line of their breastworks. The 22nd Regiment made the last charge.

We charged their strong breastworks. It was a costly effort. They greeted us with fearful volleys and we turned in plain view of them to retreat. Col. Pettigrew, Lt. Col. John O. Long were wounded and seven of our company, including First Lieutenant W. B. Kivett, L. F. McMasters. Emsley Allred and Alvin Pugh were killed. All were left in the lines of the enemy. We marched back to where we had camped on May 30. Our regiment being out of a colonel, Colonel Connor was temporarily assigned over our regiment. Gen. Johnston was wounded and so Gen. Robert E. Lee took charge at this time of the army of Northern Virginia. And this is my account of the battle of Seven Pines. [Here Mr. Turner relates some harrowing experiences of the boys in the trenches.]

In my next account, I shall tell about the seven days' battle in which I, among the thousands of others, suffered a bad wound.

Turner's Romance No. 9

While we were in this camp our baggage, which had been sent from Evansport in March, was brought to camp and our regiment dressed up for the last time during the war. On the 25th day of June we drew five days' rations and marched for the Chicahominy river. We went about eight miles in the night and took up. Next day at 3 o'clock we crossed at Meadows' Bridge where the C. and O. R. R.

crossed the river. When we got to the river we were halted. Every man had to have a good cap on his gun for we were marched down the stream.

We saw the Yankees retreating so we formed in line. We reached the little village called Mechanicsville. They opened fire on us with their shells. We were ordered to lie down as flat as we could for it was getting hot for us. We lay down as flat as a board but it didn't help us any. We got up and went to fighting again. It got too bad for us so we lay down the second time. Their troops fell back beyond a stream called Beaverdam Creek and got behind their breastworks. We went after them again. And the third time we had to lay down.

We lost many of our boys in the fight. We were ordered now to go for them. We got within eight feet of them and we found out that they were the Fourth Michigan Regiment. We fired upon them and they hotly returned the shots. I received four of the shots. I received a wound in the right arm through the elbow. I came very near bleeding to death. I was carried off the battlefield.

I can't say what took place between the two armies until the last of August, when I returned to the regiment. Now I will tell my readers where I was and how I was treated as a wounded soldier.

As soon as I was wounded I was carried to the place where we crossed the river. We were thrown on flat cars, about two hundred of us, just like loading wood. We were carried to Richmond. When we arrived in the city we were carried in carts to a large livery stable which had been cleaned for us. We were placed on planks to sleep. We were fed on rough food for two days, then we were carried to Winder Hospital where we stayed two weeks. The worst of the wounded were given a hospital gown while our clothing was sent to the wash-house. Orders came that the wounded were to be transferred from Richmond elsewhere. Some went to Gorden's Mill, Winchester. I with about two hundred others were sent to Petersburg. When the time came for us to depart, our clothes were at the washhouse, so we had to go with only our gowns on. No shoes nor hat.

We started to the depot. On our way we met a nice looking lady selling pies. I asked her what she would sell me two pies for. She said fifty cents each. I told her I had no money and asked her to give me two as I was hungry. She looked at me and when she saw I was wounded she gave them to me. I thanked her and went on my way to the depot. We were placed in box cars and were inspected by a doctor to find out who was able to stand the trip. When he got to me he asked me why I was eating. I told him because I was hungry. He said, "You will die after this." I told him that I expected to die. He kicked my hand and out went my pie. I looked at him and told him that it was a good thing for him that I did not have Betty (my gun) with me.

The train started for Petersburg at last. When we arrived there we were met by a large crowd, as the people knew that we were coming. I got away from the crowd and sat down to rest. A Negro woman came up and looked at me, then peeped in my face. She stepped back and said, "Boss, are you a woman or a man?" I answered that I was neither, as I was a wounded soldier. "Boss, where are you from?"

"I am from North Carolina," I [said]. "Dat is my good old state, too, Boss soldier. I wants to kiss you." So I reached out with my face and she kissed me all over my face with one stroke. She wanted to know where I wanted to go. I told her to the nearest North Carolina hospital. "Boss, I will go with you."

She helped me up and put her arms around me and supported me down the street. When we got tired we sat down and rested. We met ladies and gentlemen, but they all looked downcast and paid no attention to us. At last I felt that my strength was gone. I told "Aunty" that I would have to give up. We sat down on the pavement and she told me to lay my head in her lap. Some time passed. People passing each way but all looked ashamed to stop. Two fine looking men stepped up and looked at us.

They said, "I see you are a wounded soldier. Where are you from?" I told him from North Carolina. "That is my state." I turned around and saw that it was Governor Vance.

"Governor Vance, I voted for you." At that, the Governor said, "Thank you. I see that you are very weak. I will see you later. Aunty, see that this soldier is taken to our hospital immediately." I believe he thought that I was not long for this world. Aunty reached the hospital with me, and when she left she said, "Boss soldier, don't forget me. I have to go after some one else." And I haven't forgotten her and never will.

Turner's Romance No. 10

I remained in the hospital 18 days. In a few days our clothing which was left in Richmond came to us all right. Our shoes were made of cloth and over the toes and around the heels there was a strip of leather. The leather part was shined up. The bottoms were made of wood. The bullet holes through our coats and pants and torn places were neatly mended; it reminded us of home.

I was sent home for 30 days on furlough. After I arrived home some of the boys that went off to the army when I did came to see me. I will not say how they got home, I will leave it to the reader to say. My 30 days seemed a long time to me as I wanted to go back to my command. I had received my $10 bounty and taken the oath to support the laws of the Confederate States. The day my 30 days were out I started back; my wound had healed but little. Had I not gone back I would have been called a bushwhacker, which is not an enviable reputation to carry through life. I took the train at Greensboro, went by Raleigh, Wilson, Petersburg and Richmond. I went to headquarters in Richmond to learn where my command was. Here I was given a way-bill which carried me straight to my regiment, going over the C. and O. Railroad towards Gordonville; at some station, I do not remember the name, before I got to Gordonville, I reached my regiment near Manassas. I found a change in our brigade. All states took their own troops and put them in their own brigade, so ours was the 13th, 16th, 22nd, 34th, and 38th regiments. Our commander was General Pender throughout the war.

I was told by the boys that they finished up the Seven Days' fight and went through the Cedar Run near Culpepper court house while I was in the hospital and on furlough. I found several of my company missing, some killed, some wounded, and some taken prisoners. I received my wound in two days after I got back. We went in battle at Manassas. For two days I could not handle a gun. Some of the other boys and I who were shot carried the ammunition up to the line of battle so that the rest could keep firing.

In the morning of the first day the battle was severe and hard on both sides. The next morning we had to change our lines some, our position then was preferable to that of the Yankees. It was the same that the Yankees had back in '61, the first battle at that place where McDowell and Scott tried to run over Bouregard and he bent them. Later they were defeated by Lee and Jackson. The killed and wounded on both sides were heavy. Late in the evening our boys got them on the retreat and the battle was over for the second day with a victory for the South.

The next day as I was crippled and could not handle a gun the captain sent me to remain with the colors of the regiment and I was excused from carrying a gun, so I remained with them until August, 1864. The second battle of Manassas was over. We started north across the mountains of Virginia, across the Shenandoah river at Raccoon Ford and then towards Leesburg and Martinsburg. We crossed the Potomac river near Leesburg. We were in A. P. Hill's corps. We then started on our march towards Hagerstown, Md., on our way we halted to rest near a dwelling house. While there I saw two women come out with a tub, one on each side, carrying it toward us. As we lay on each side of the road they set it down and stepped back a short distance, threw up their hands and said, "Apple butter, free treat." So the boys took their tin cups and went for it; I got mine about half full and wished later that I had got it full. This was the first time I ever heard of apple butter. We marched on to Hagerstown. When we got near the little town we found it in possession of the Yankee infantry and cavalry, and there after a short fight with them, they retreated to Sharpsburg [and] we took up for the night. The next morning the whole Yankee army [was] in Maryland on the 16th day of September, 1862. In the next number, I will tell how the battle ended.

Turner's Romance No. 11

We went to fighting about 9 o'clock in the morning. Our army had not all crossed the Potomac river. The boys who had crossed over began fighting soon [too]. We held them back steady until about 1 o'clock when they got the better of us. We kept giving back every charge. Late in the evening A. P. Hill crossed the remainder of his troops and came up at double-quick movements and helped us out. The battle lasted until late in the evening. It was hard on both sides, as the Yankees numbered about seven to our one.

We were not willing to cross back over the river back into Virginia, more so than when we went over. In my company two were killed, seven wounded and three taken prisoners. We crossed back at Williamsport in the night and took up for a few days and then took up our march down by the Wilderness and Chancellorsville on to Fredericksburg. This was in November. We lay there until the 12th or 13th of December, when we had a hard battle for two days. We beat the Yankees back across the Rappahannock with a slaughter on each side. This battle was called the First Battle of Fredericksburg.

When the battle was over we had to bury the dead on both sides. I was detailed to help and I can't tell the number that were killed. It was a large number on both sides.

We moved down near [Quinney's?] Station and went into winter quarters for the winter of 1862. The camp was called Camp Gregg. We passed the winter here. In the spring of 1863 we broke up camp and took our march to the mountains of Virginia. We went to Culpepper and Jordansville, near Winchester. We also went into the Valley of Virginia near New Market on the Shenandoah river. We tore up the Baltimore and Ohio Railroad and then fell back near Chancellorsville. Here we had a heavy battle on the 1st, 2nd and 3rd days of May, 1863. The first day in the evening the battle commenced. On the second day our brigade was put under Jackson and we were in his famous flank march around the Yankee army. We struck them in the rear, while Lee struck them in front. The battle was hard.

Night came on and the fight was over for the second day. That night Jackson was wounded by his own men and died eight days later. General Stuart took charge of Jackson's part of the army and managed it well. It was an hand-to-hand battle on both sides. The battle ground part was fought where there was a great deal of small brush which in the evening caught fire from the explosion of the Yankee magazine. The smoke was so thick we could not see anything in our front except the flash from their guns. So we got the better of the Yankees and ran them across the Rappahannock river. It was a heavy loss on both sides. Next day we had to bury their dead as well as our own. I was one of the boys to help. The fire had burned all of their clothing off, except what was between their bodies and the ground. It was an awful sight to see boys killed and then burned. I suspect several who were wounded so badly that they could not help themselves were burned to death.

The battle ended. The dead were buried at Chancellorsville. In the meantime I was wounded but not enough for a furlough. We marched back in the mountains of Virginia and ran into their cavalry near Brandy Station. We held them in check until our cavalry came up and halted. We fell back near the Potomac river up above Martinsburg. We are now on our way to Gettysburg. Will say something about that battle in my next number.

Turner's Romance No. 12

We made our arrangement to cross the Potomac river again. Lee's army crossed about June 26 or 27, and camped for a day or two at Carlyle, Pa., and then marched toward Harrisburg. Before reaching there, however, we turned south and went about twelve miles on the first day of July.

We found the village of Gettysburg, in possession of the Yankee infantry and cavalry. We drove them back beyond the town and then fell back and camped for the night. All through the night we could hear them at work, hauling their cannon up on Cemetery Ridge, and when morning came we were looking into the mouths of about 225 of their cannon. We moved a short distance to the left and formed a line of battle in a piece of woodland. Lee's artillery, coming up was placed in readiness and the two armies were in line of battle about one thousand yards apart. There was a small ravine between them and all the land was cleared.

We lay there all day, under the fire of those shells. Lee was waiting for the Yankees to come to us, and they were waiting for us to go to them. The infantry had little to do except they would try to find the end of our line of battle, and we would drive them back. Large numbers of our boys were killed by bursting shells. In front of our brigade lay General Sycles and his New York troops. So when night came, Lee's lines were changed some, our part being moved to the right something like a mile, near what was called the peach orchard. When morning came there were the same New York troops in front, and we again ate a small cold breakfast and then went to fighting. Both lines were firing as fast as they could load, with charge after charge, and about 225 cannon on each side, all firing as fast as they could be loaded; it was a shocking time around Gettysburg, one long to be remembered by all old soldiers who took part on either side. I was with the flag of our regiment, and saw two men, who carried it, killed and another shot in the knee who lost his leg and was captured.

About 12 o'clock, the Yankees stopped firing their cannon to let them cool off, and Lee, thinking he had silenced them, charged with his whole army across the open space for a thousand yards. The Yankees did not fire a shot, and we, looking as if on dress parade, got within fifty yards of them, when they threw lead in our faces from both musket and cannon. It was a terrible time around there with those who were not killed or wounded. Several of our boys did not get a scratch. We retreated and night coming on, we left many of our boys sleeping their last sleep near Gettysburg. The battle was over, and in the night we took up our march back to Virginia.

Lee's entire army did not cross the Potomac at the same place, but some crossed at Williamsport and others at Falling Water. I was among those who crossed at Falling Water. When we got there, the river was swollen and we had to lie over a few days.

During this time, the Yankee cavalry was after us, and one morning they charged in among us, firing and wounding General Pettigrew, who died eight days later. We crossed the bridge and marched to Bunker Hill, Virginia, where we stayed for some time. The next battle was at German's Ford, where we crossed the Rapidan River. This was just a small engagement, and we remained in that part of Virginia until we went into winter quarters near Orange Courthouse for the winter of 1863. Here General Pender was promoted, and General Scales was our brigade commander for the remainder of the war.

Turner's Romance No. 13

This is the opening of the campaign of 1864. We broke up camp and made our way into the Wilderness near Chancellorsville, where we had fought in May, 1863. The Wilderness was the right name for the place. The large growth was all cut and gone, and it was a thicket of small green briers and bush of all kinds. We could not get along without falling and tangling our feet. We fought there all day early in May, 1864. Both sides did all they could, and it was hard on both Yankees and Confederates. There were lots of our boys and theirs killed and wounded. When the battle was over, we marched northward. It seemed to me we were looking for those Yankees to get to fight them again. It was skirmish and fight them every day. We fell back and ran up with them near Spottsylvania Courthouse, where we had another heavy battle. I think this was May 11, 1864. Then we marched towards Petersburg, going about the same way Jackson went before the Seven Days' battle below Richmond.

We reached Cold Harbor, on the Chickahominy River, and here we met them again for another fight. There were the most men killed here in the shortest time that I saw in any battle during the war.

After the battle was over we had a few prisoners our boys had taken. They were brought to our colors for us to hold until a guard was selected to take them to Richmond. One of the men looked at me and said, "Sergeant, I want to talk with you." "Owing to what you want to talk about, whether I will answer you," I replied. "I want to ask if General Lee has any men in his army from any state besides North Carolina," he said. "Why do you ask that question?" I enquired. "Well," said he, "I've been in 23 battles and have not met a man except from that state, and I thought his whole army was from there."

After this, we started on our way to Petersburg, crossing the James river eight miles below Richmond at Drewe's [Drewry's] Bluff. We then went to the Halfway Station between Richmond and Petersburg, a part of the army going by railroad and the others marching. We went about four miles south, on the Weldon Railroad, where we had another hard battle. Here we lost several of our boys. After the battle, we marched back through Petersburg, crossed the Appomattox river and went down it about three-quarters of a mile and formed breastworks. We lay in them for several days. We could not show a head above them, or a ball would come at us.

In March I was examined by our doctor and recommended for a discharge. The order came to my captain August 2, 1864, and on the 3rd I left the army of Lee and Jackson, in which I had served since 1861. I came home, and on the 18th day of the same month was conscripted on light duty and was attached to Company B, first Battalion of light duty men. Our commander was Major Hahar of

Wake county. I was orderly sergeant of the company and was present at Greensboro when Johnston surrendered to Sherman, April 26, 1865.

In my next I shall tell of my travels in this State through the last year of the war.

Turner's Romance No. 14

Our battalion was formed at Raleigh and went to Goldsboro, from there to Kinston, there to New Bern and from there to Wilmington. We were then sent down the Cape Fear river between Sugar Loaf and Fort Fisher to do picket duty. We remained there through the winter of 1864. We had no winter quarters and had to lie behind the breastworks. I suffered more with cold there than I did with Lee and Jackson in Virginia during three winters. All of the army that could be spared was sent to the battle at Bellfield, Va. In December my battalion took the cars for Weldon. It rained and snowed all the way as we rode on flat cars. When I called the roll of my company at Weldon there were 82 to answer to their names. Two of them were frozen to death on the way.

We moved on to Bellfield and relieved some troops that were fighting. We charged the enemy four times but fell back as Lee's troops came down from Petersburg to help us. The Yankees saw them coming and gave way. I got 12 bullet holes in my hat. The battle over, we replaced the railroad irons which had been removed, and marched back to Weldon where we stayed for a few days. Next day when I called my roll there were thirteen who answered to their names. We went back to our old stand in the trenches below Wilmington and saw the bombardment and fall of Fort Fisher. It reminded me of the second and third days of the battle at Gettysburg. I saw but little difference between the armies of Virginia and North Carolina. A few days after the downfall of Fort Fisher our battalion was sent to Wilmington to do guard duty.

Turner's Romance No. 15

Our commissioned officers in each company were: A captain, two lieutenants, who, in my company had been returned home on a pass and did not come back, so I was left in command of the company during the remainder of the war. Our major had a call for 18 men to do guard duty on the train from Wilmington to Weldon made in three relieves of six each. I went with these. The remainder of my company remained with the battalion in charge of the second corporal.

The Relieve that was off duty on the train was at the public road entering the city. My post when not on the railroad was at the ferry across northeast river. The citizens of the town could not pass without a pass from the provost marshal's quarters, so no one could pass into the city without giving a strict account of himself. Johnston's army commenced leaving in the morning and by night all were on the way to Goldsboro. The next morning we were informed that Sherman's cavalry was in sight, so my guard and I started for Goldsboro. We caught up with some more of our boys who were trying to get to Johnston's army. We got in eight or ten miles of Goldsboro and Sherman's cavalry came in sight. Then it was run for life to keep out of their way. We reached Neuse river, where Johnston had left a strong guard. Here we formed a line of battle and commenced firing on each other. Johnston heard the firing and sent a brigade to help us, so the tide turned and we drove them back a mile or two. We fell back to Goldsboro and our guards took up the old run from Weldon to Raleigh, so I missed the battle at Smithfield, though my battalion was at the last battle in North Carolina. When Johnston got to Raleigh my guard run from there to Salisbury. I asked Major Whiten for a pass to visit home and he gave me one for eight days. Next day was my time to make the trip to Salisbury. Before time to start he wrote me a note telling me to make my run and he would lengthen my time. When we reached Durham the next day there was a part of Johnston's army heading for Greensboro. When we got near Raleigh we got on the train.

Turner's Romance No. 16

When we got near Raleigh, we got on the train and rode to the company's shops, now Burlington. I left my guard there and then went to Greensboro, where I met my battalion. I saw one man there who belonged to my company. His name was Phelen, who had charge of our company when I was absent on duty. He lived near Salisbury, Rowan county. I found him near the depot and said to him, "Where is our company?" His answer was "In hell I hope." "Don't have such talk," I said to him, "This war is over and let us go to the provost marshal's office and take the oath and get our payroll and then we will be free men once more." He looked at me and said, "Sergeant, I will follow them to hell before I will take the bushes." "You don't know what I mean, Mr. Phelen, go with me." We got through all right. On our way back he came to his senses and said, "What a fool I was, I can see it now." I saw that he was a good soldier and would die before he would bushwhack.

As I am now about through my war tramp I will write one more number and dwell on the old soldiers that are living. I have left out several of the small battles I was in and as I said in the beginning, I have told my story as I saw the things happen. Some of the old soldiers saw the war in a different way and I would like for some other old Confederate soldier to take it up as I have done. I want to see how they saw the war. It was hard times on all Southern people, especially the women and the girls who were large enough to work. When I was at home on furlough I saw them in the field carrying the scythe and cradle. Some of them could do as good or better than some men I have seen in the field with me. But my time is past. The older I get the more I can see how they had to do back in those days. The folks at home turned their hands a thousand different ways to support the Southern cause, and their little children too, while their husbands and sons have a war ahead of us in which I expect to gain the victory: an answer to the last roll call.

John T. Turner."[1]

> [Evidently, Sgt. Turner intended to write one more article devoted to telling about the soldiers who were still living at that time, but no other article has been located at this writing.]

3. That Tattered Old Flag

> Bright Banner of freedom with pride I unfold thee:
> Fair flag of my country with love I adore thee,
> Gleaming above us in freshness and youth;
> Emblem of liberty, symbol of truth;
> For the flag of my country in triumph shall wave,
> O'er the Southerner's home and the Southerner's grave!
> —Borrowed from an original
> Confederate letter mailed
> from Evansport, Va. in 1861[1]

In early July of 1861 as the Randolph County soldiers prepared to leave their homes and loved ones, they finally comprehended that war had really arrived and now it was time to go. They might never see home or loved ones again. Loved ones knew that the men needed something to spur them on and give them courage to do what they had to do. What they needed was a flag.

The Confederate States of America on 4 May 1861, only a little over a month before Company M was organized, adopted a national flag. The flag spread quickly over the South, but was not necessarily uniform in appearance. The design was intended to be as follows:

> The flag of the Confederate States of America shall consist of a red field with a white space extending horizontally through the center, and equal in width to one-third the width of the flag. The red space above and below to be the same width as the white. The union blue extending down through the white space and stopping at the lower red space. In the center of the union a circle of white stars corresponding in number with the States in the Confederacy.[2]

Many variations existed, and the Randolph Hornets' flag was no exception. The flag that they carried off to war followed the basic pattern of the official flag, having two red bars and one white in the center. It measured fifty-five by thirty-five inches. The two red bars appear to be made of a cotton material, while the white bar is satin, backed by cotton. The white bar on the front side is hand painted in red lettering with the battle cry "Onward To Victory." The white bar on the reverse side is hand lettered in India ink, "Randolph-Hornets." The union was made of blue satin with cotton backing, and matched the official description, except that it was narrow in comparison to most flags of this type. It had nine satin stars, not in a circle but in more of an egg-shaped pattern, with two more stars, one above the other in the center, for a total of eleven stars. This odd-shaped pattern may have come about because of the rapidly changing number of states that seceded during the time the flag was made, and the need to modify it before presenting it to the men. The eleventh state was added to the Confederacy on 2 July 1861, just seven days before the men said goodbye to their families. The Hornets' flag may have had gold stars, rather than white, which was not unusual on early flags. This is not a certainty, because the flag has faded to the point that the union and stars are now the same off-white color. Finally, the flag was finished with a gold fringe around three sides, probably three to four inches in length.

The 9th day of July 1861 was set as the day for the men to say their goodbyes to family and friends before marching early the next morning to High Point to board trains for Raleigh. This is when we can presume that the women presented the flag to the men. Many local volunteer companies across the South were honored with an elaborate flag presentation ceremony, and we can only imagine that the Hornets were also given such a send-off. No matter how the presentation was accomplished, we can be sure that the men were swelled with pride to hold such a grand banner before them. This flag led their way out of Randolph County on 10 July 1861 and wasn't seen here again for over 100 years.

Company M carried the flag with them to High Point, then to Raleigh and on to Richmond, Virginia, where they no doubt held the flag high as they paraded through the streets. It was carried in the sun and rain as they traveled northward to Evansport, Virginia, on the Potomac River. Here they camped and worked on the batteries to blockade the river, and it was here that the flag saw its only battle action, the cannonading of enemy artillery from across the river, and that of enemy gunboats attempting to breach the blockade. Here the flag also suffered the elements of a harsh winter.

Several years ago, Barbara Newsom Grigg finally solved the mystery of when and how the flag was captured by the enemy. She discovered an old newspaper, the *Weekly Times*, printed in Philadelphia, Pennsylvania, and dated 20 December 1879. An article in the paper written by Oliver C. Cooper of the First Massachusetts Infantry, Hooker's Division, told about the blockading of the river and the capture of the flag:

3. *That Tattered Old Flag* 63

The "Randolph Hornets" battle flag that was captured at Evansport, Virginia, is now on display in the Asheboro Public Library. (Photograph courtesy of Randolph Room, Asheboro Public Library.)

About the 1st November 1861, Hooker's Brigade comprising the First and Eleventh Massachusetts, the Second New Hampshire and the Twenty-ninth Pennsylvania ... was ordered down the Potomac to help look after the rebel force which had "gathered at the river" and established formidable batteries with the view of cutting off Federal water communication with Washington....

On Tuesday, March 9, [1862], the unusual movements about the rebel batteries attracted the attention of our people. During the forenoon one of the gunboats—the "Anacosta," I think—cautiously approached the upper battery, dropping shells into the works as she moved down. Getting within close range and finding no signs of occupation, a detachment of men landed from the gunboats, who scrambled up the steep embankment, and soon the multitudes of our soldiers who, from the opposite river banks had been anxiously watching these proceedings, saw the Stars and Stripes wave

Randolph Hornets battle flag, reverse side. (Photograph courtesy of Randolph Room, Asheboro Public Library.)

out to the breeze above the hostile guns, and then such a cheer went up as had never before rolled over the waters of the Potomac. At the same time a loud explosion occurred at the Shipping Point battery, clouds of smoke and earth ascending high in the air. It was now evident that the enemy was evacuating and that the blockade of the Potomac was at an end. All was excitement on our side. The long-roll was beat in every camp and the men eagerly responded to the order to 'Fall in!' Three barges loaded with men from the Massachusetts First started for the Virginia shore and landed at the Shipping Point batteries simultaneously with portions of the crews of the gunboats, which had steamed down to the scene, throwing their shells as they proceeded, and soon the starry flag of the Union also floated here. Two or three of the guns of the battery were found bursted. All of the pieces had been heavily wadded, then crammed to the muzzle with sand and fires built under the carriages with the expectation that they would burn and the heat cause the gun to discharge and burst. But this failed except in a few instances. The guns were mostly rifled 7 and 9 inch Dahlgrens, with one magnificent 120 pounder Blakeley gun, which had been brought from England but a few months before. This, with its fellows, was subsequently taken to the Washington Navy Yard, where they were all put in good condition and did much excellent service for the Union thereafter.

Our troops penetrated to the rebel camps and saw abundant indication of very hasty departure. Plenty of fresh beef was found in the quarter, and but recently killed. A sutler's store containing a large stock of goods, was discovered and the contents appropriated. On a desk in the store was found a letter, partially finished, directed to parties in Richmond. It seemed as if the late occupants had been seized with a sudden panic and had precipitately fled, glad even to get away with life. In the deserted camps were found an abundance of cooking utensils, with other indications that the 'Johnnies' had not by any means been in a starving condition. On the following day five hundred men crossed the river, and while some of them cautiously excavated the exploded magazines in quest of shot and shell, other companies went on a reconnaissance. The camps were again visited and many relics obtained, almost every man going away loaded. Among the captures was a fine litter of bloodhound pups, which were presented by the Captain to Colonel Austin of Hooker's staff. Many regimental papers, reports, etc., as well as private letters, addressed to officers and soldiers, were picked up in the camps. The writer of this has a letter addressed to 'Lieutenant W. T. Irvine, Brooks Station, VA.' from his wife, on the back of which is a memorandum of officers and men, doubtless selected for guard or other detail. Two handsome banners were obtained in one of the camps—one of silk, having belonged to an Arkansas company and the other, of satin, bearing on one side the inscription, 'The Randolph Hornet's,' and on the other, 'Onward to Victory.' A building was found containing fifteen or twenty ready-made pine coffins, and the numerous graveyards, filled with fresh graves, which were met with, showed that sickness and death had been busy in the Confederate camps during the winter. In fact this was also shown by the company and regimental reports found....[3]

The soldier who wrote this article was, of course, writing from a Union point of view, and was not aware that the Confederates had been ordered on 7 March 1862 to abandon the batteries and quickly move to below Williamsburg to meet a Federal advance under General George B. McClellan. The move necessitated disabling of the guns and leaving any extraneous equipment and supplies behind because the men would be marched the full distance. At any rate, the beloved Company M flag was left behind and was now in enemy hands.

It was nearly a century before the flag was heard from again. The late Dr. Joseph R. Suggs, a Randolph County genealogist and historian, wrote an article in the May 1969 issue of *The State* magazine that relates how the flag surfaced and was returned to Randolph County. In it, he also described the flag and gave a capsule history of Company M. Dr. Suggs indicated in the article that Dr. and Mrs. Marion B. Roberts of Hillsborough, N.C., learned of the flag in 1961 and began a long and determined effort to bring it home to North Carolina. The article also quoted Dr. Roberts from the minutes of the Randolph County Historical Society as saying:

> While visiting with some Civil War buffs in Doyleston, Pennsylvania, I heard a member of the group from New Jersey mention that someone in Connecticut had a flag made for the Randolph Hornets, but he had no idea who it might be. I was determined to get this flag; therefore I got in touch with a friend in Nashville, Tennessee. He knew a buff in Pennsylvania who knew a gentleman in New Jersey who knew where the flag was. I still do not know who had the flag, nor how it got to Connecticut. I have an idea it was captured. As you can see, I obtained this flag from and through my friend in Nashville.[4]

Research revealed that "although there were other Randolph Counties in the Confederacy, North Carolina's Randolph was the only one with a 'Hornet' Company."[5] Dr. Roberts said that he had debated for over a year whether to keep the flag or bring it back to Randolph County. He finally decided to donate it to the Randolph County Historical Society with the provision that its care be perpetuated and that it would be displayed in a suitable case. The flag was mounted in a special case made just for this purpose, and a ceremony was held in the fall of 1968 presenting it back to Randolph County.

The flag is still on display in the Asheboro Public Library. Efforts are underway to determine how to better preserve and protect this unique and important piece of history for future generations. Though it may be faded and tattered, it still hangs proudly and if you listen closely, you might still hear the rattle of musketry and feel the pride those Randolph County men of 140 years ago felt as they marched off to defend their native soil.

4. Roster of Company M, 22nd Regiment

This roster is based on a compilation of several different rosters and lists, including *Roster of North Carolina Troops in the War Between the States* (otherwise known as *Moore's Roster*),[1] *North Carolina Confederate Soldiers 1861–1865* (otherwise known as *Broadfoot's Roster*),[2] *North Carolina Troops 1861–1865: A Roster*,[3] North Carolina Confederate Pension applications,[4] and the listing compiled by Gary D. Reeder, Daniel J. Whatley, and Cheryl L. Martin, which was published in *The Heritage of Randolph County North Carolina, Volume 1*.[5] I have attempted to, as much as possible, identify each soldier and illustrate him with a description of his military service from the *North Carolina Troops 1861–1865* series,[6] along with biographical information that I have gathered from various sources, which are listed in the bibliography at the end of this volume. Some names, because of scanty information have defied identification, while others are only tentatively identified, leaving room for further research by others. In some cases, the only information available was found through Internet sources, and could not be verified. Certainly, errors are likely to be found, and I do not intend this roster as a definitive genealogical source, only as a starting point for your own research. Unless otherwise specified, all geographic locations are in North Carolina.

Captains

KIVETT, WARREN B.

Warren B. Kivett was born in May 1835 in Randolph County to John Aldridge and Mary Welborn Kivett, and was a resident of Randolph County when he married Elvira "Alva" Kivett there on 2 February 1860. They farmed in the Sandy Creek area.

On 10 June 1861 Warren and his younger brother, Troy, enlisted in Company M at its organization and were mustered in as privates. According to family sources their older brother, Zeno Kivett, also enlisted in the Confederate army and never returned home. On 27 April 1862 at the reorganization of the regiment, Warren Kivett was elected 1st lieutenant. He was wounded at the battle of Seven Pines, Virginia, on 31 May 1862, but continued to serve as 1st lieutenant until 16 March 1863, when he was promoted to captain, filling the position vacated by Laban Odell, who was promoted to major. He served as captain only about a month, until 14 April 1863, when he resigned due to a gunshot to the left leg.

Returning home to Randolph County and residing in the Liberty area, he and Alva raised a family of four children. Alva died in 1878, leaving him with at least two of the children still at home. According to Randolph County marriage records, he was married a second time on 31 May 1883 to Angeline Kivett. At some point he became a carpenter, and was still working at that trade by the time of the 1900 Census. According to his estate records, Warren B. Kivett died sometime between 10 June and 12 November 1901 in Liberty, Randolph County. His burial location has not been identified at this writing, but a likely location is the McMasters Cemetery, as some of his relatives are buried there.

ODELL, JOHN MILTON

John Milton Odell was born 20 January 1831 near Cedar Falls in Randolph County to James and Anna Trogdon Odell. He was educated at Middleton Academy, and at the age of 20 he was listed in the census as a schoolteacher. He is known to have engaged in this vocation for at least three years. On 9 March 1854 he was married to Carrie Rebecca Kirkman in Randolph County. Two sons and a daughter were born to this union. In April of 1856 he became interested as a stockholder in the Cedar Falls Manufacturing Company, and until the spring of 1861 he was engaged as a salesman in the store of that company. With the start of the war, he and his brother Laban organized Company M on 10 June 1861, and the men elected him captain. He began his duties of organizing, equipping and training his men, and served as captain while the company was in Virginia at Evansport on the Potomac River and during part of the Peninsular Campaign. In April 1862 the regiments were reorganized and new officers elected. He had served with a fine record and was suited for a conspicuous military career, but since his enlistment period had expired and he was in feeble health, he resigned. His brother, Laban, was elected as captain on 27 April 1862.

John returned to Randolph County, where he served as the business agent for the Cedar Falls mill from about 1862 to 1869. He then moved to Greensboro where he was also engaged in the mercantile business. In 1877 he bought the McDonald Mill and moved to Concord. He was instrumental in organizing the Odell Manufacturing Company, the Cannon Manufacturing Company, and the Kerr Bag Manufacturing Company in Concord, among others. He became one of the most successful textile industrialists in the state, being engaged in that business for more than 40 years. Another brother, James Alexander Odell, founded the Odell Hardware Company in Greensboro.

Capt. Odell's first wife, Rebecca, died on 13 June 1889, and on 4 August 1891 he married a second time, to Addie Allison White of Concord. John Milton Odell died at his home in Concord on 21 July 1910, and was buried there in the family mausoleum at Oakwood Cemetery.

John Milton Odell (1831–1910), organizer and first captain of Company M. Following the war, he became one of North Carolina's major textile industrialists. (Photograph courtesy of L. McKay Whatley.)

ODELL, LABAN

Laban Odell was born 8 November 1836 in Randolph County, to James and Anna Trogdon Odell. He taught school in the Cedar Falls area, and was married about 1857 to Mary Craven. They were the parents of one son, John Laban Odell. At the outset of the war Laban and his brother, John Milton Odell, organized a company of men from their community on 10 June 1861. The men elected Laban 1st lieutenant of Company M. He served in that capacity until the regiments were reorganized and new officers elected on 27 April 1862. At that time his men elected him to serve as captain in the place of his brother John, who had resigned and returned to Randolph County. During his term as captain, Company M took part in the Virginia battles at Fair Oaks (Seven Pines), Mechanicsville, Ellison's Mill, Gaines' Mill, Frayser's Farm, Cedar Mountain, Harper's Ferry, Shepherdstown and Fredericksburg. His daring and courageous action at Marye's Heights,

Virginia, earned the attention of senior officers and soon brought a deserved promotion.

After wintering at Fredericksburg, some reorganization took place, and Laban Odell was promoted to major of the 22nd Regiment on 16 March 1863. He served in this capacity until 3 May 1863, when he was killed at Chancellorsville, Virginia. He was brought back to Gray's Chapel Methodist Church cemetery for burial and a monument was later erected in his memory.

His final hours were recorded by Captain Columbus Frank Siler in a newspaper article dated 10 August 1899.

A HERO'S PRESCIENCE OF DEATH
By Frank Siler

Osgood, N.C., August 5, 1899

Major Laban Odell was a brilliant man of a ten talented family, born in Randolph County, N.C., on a small farm near my home. I loved him fondly. He was one of my teachers. I volunteered in his brother, J.M. Odell's company at the beginning of the war. Ere long Laban became Major of the 22nd N.C. Regiment, and I the Captain of his Company.

At Chancellorsville, on the night of the 2nd of May 1863, my dear Major came to me (all then lying in line of battle) and lay down beside me and took me in his arms and said, "Dear Frank, I have been under the fire of the enemy 21 times and in 13 regular engagements, and I have not been touched by a ball, but tomorrow morning when we go forward I shall be killed. Please take this gold watch and these photos to my dear wife." I refused to take them and tried to convince him that it was only a notion of his, but he said he knew he would be killed and put the watch and pictures in my vest pocket, and said "Take them to Mary." I then entreated him not to go into battle at all. He said he "must do his duty," and then drew me closer to his bosom, kissed me and said "Goodbye Frank. Tell Mary to raise our dear Johnnie right and meet me in Heaven."

This was just as day was breaking on the morning of the 3rd of May 1863. About sunrise we went forward. Soon I was wounded, and coming off the field, I saw that most gallant young hero lying in a dying condition, just as he said (he never spoke to me any more above a whisper). He said, "I told you so; do as I requested," and these were his last words. I was wounded in my right arm and right thigh, but with my left limbs, I aided best I could in partially concealing his body and marking the spot so that his noble brothers secured it, and now in the old cemetery at Gray's Chapel near where he was reared, by the side of his grand old parents and loved ones, lie his remains, over which towers a costly monument, the only one in the county known to me over a Confederate Soldier.

God bless all who are near and dear to this hero of heroes, and grant that they may all meet again where there is no more war.

Since then I have always signed my name,

C. "Frank" Siler

P.S. I also had in my care the remains of my dear Lieutenant Colonel L. L.

Laban Odell (1836–1863) helped organize Company M and served as 1st lieutenant and later as captain. He was appointed major of the 22nd Regiment and was killed at Chancellorsville. (Photograph courtesy of James L. Odell and Peggy Wilburn.)

Cole of Greensboro, who fell dead in a few steps of my Major. General Lee had in his Army no one who surpassed these two noble Godly glorious officers in all the qualities that go to make up the Christian soldier, and very few equals, I think.[7]

SILER, COLUMBUS FRANKLIN

Columbus Franklin Siler, known as Frank, was born December 1840 in Chatham County to Andrew J. and Ruth Barker Siler. His father was shown in the 1850 Chatham County Census as a tanner by occupation. By 1860 the family was living in Randolph County, in the Franklinville area.

On 10 June 1861 he enlisted in Company M, 22nd Regiment and was mustered in as 4th sergeant. He was subsequently promoted to 2nd lieutenant on 16 March 1862, during the reorganization that took place after wintering at Evansport. He was wounded in the battle of Frayser's Farm, Va., on 30 June 1862, and returned to duty in October of that year. After the resignation of Warren Kivett as captain, he was promoted to 1st lieutenant on 16 April 1863, and a few days later he was promoted to captain on or about 2 May 1863. The following day, he was wounded again at the battle of Chancellorsville and hospitalized in Richmond, both in Virginia. At an unspecified date he returned to duty, served as captain until the end of the war, and was paroled with the remainder of his men at Appomattox Court House, Va., on 9 April 1865.

Captain Siler was revered by his men and his commanders alike as a "hero of heroes." He received a total of six wounds to both thighs, upper right arm, left shoulder and flesh wounds to the right chest area and neck. Several articles have been written about him in various publications, including this undated clipping from the *Asheboro Courier* written by L. M. Caudle:

> We had the pleasure of having with us Capt. C. F. Siler, the great hero of the South, and bravest of all; justly called so by many distinguished men, and should be by all for he is a noble and great man. Great in many ways; great as a captain in the war; great as a Christian gentleman; educator and armor bearer for his country; always kind and gentle, and trying to help his fellow-travelers to be happy and good. He deserves to be remembered by the State of North Carolina for his many acts of heroism in the great struggle of 61-'5. He was twice taken prisoner and made hair-breadth escapes, twice promised promotion by General Scales for most daring deeds, once snatched a Yankee bayonet from his own breast before he could fire, and captured sixty Yankees in front of Petersburg. He bears six wounds received while in the service. Many prominent men have said that the South should give him free passes on all the railroads for life, and also a salary, and yet they have not seen nor heard the half that can be justly said of him. Awake ye that sleep and arouse to a sense of duty and let us applaud this noble man while yet with us, and not only that, but give him a position that he justly deserves. The above facts I have gathered from Mr. J. M. Hayes, one of his men, that was an eyewitness to many brave and daring deeds performed by Capt. Siler.

References:

Gov. C. B. Aycock, Raleigh, N. C. Gen. J. S. Carr, Durham, N. C. Hon. W. P. Wood, Asheboro, N. C. Col. T. S. Galloway, Sommerville, Tenn. Maj. Davis, New Bern, N. C. Capt. J. M. Odell, Concord, N. C. Rev.

W. H. Moore, D. D., Raleigh, N. C. Hon. R. N. Page, Biscoe, N. C. Dr. Will Staley and Mr. Dave Wright, Liberty, N. C.

One of Capt. Siler's brave incidents occurred at the Wilderness, Va., when, one after another, three of the regiment's color bearers were shot down. Capt. Siler picked up the colors himself and charged to the front shouting, "Follow me, my brave men." This charge took the ground the enemy was holding and prevented their flank charge. General Scales later embraced him and said, "God bless you! I saw your conduct with that flag! You have saved the army, and you shall be promoted." At Petersburg, Va., Capt. Siler rode Gen. Scales' horse into enemy lines, found out the enemy positions for Gen. Hill, and with his men, captured sixty prisoners in the process. Gen. Hill ordered Scales to promote Capt. Siler. At Sutherland Station, Va., Col. T. S. Galloway tells of Capt. Siler and 70 men holding off an entire regiment of Union troops, and all the while the captain was rushing up and down the line, hat in one hand and sword in the other, encouraging his troops. Gen. Cook later asked, "Who was that gallant officer in command?" Captain Siler was also known to be one of the only officers in the army who personally led his men in their prayers.

Columbus Franklin Siler (1840–1909) served as captain of Company M from 2 May 1863 until the surrender at Appomatox. He taught school after the war and served as major in the United Confederate Veterans state organization. (Photograph from Confederate Veteran magazine, February 1907.)

After the war, Captain Siler became a schoolteacher, primarily in Montgomery County. In 1881 some friends deeded him a lot, and presumably a small dwelling, in Troy, where he taught for several years. He taught for a short time in Wadeville as well. In the early 1900s he moved to Star and taught there for a few years, joining the Star #437 Masonic Lodge while there. In 1905 he was teaching at Candor. At some point he was at Mt. Olivet in Erect for a short time and was living in Erect just before his death. He was an active member of the United Confederate Veterans, Randolph Camp No. 1646, and held the rank of major in the state organization in 1901.

The circumstances of his death are not known, but he died at the Confederate Soldier's home in Raleigh on Wednesday, 28 July 1909, and was buried in the Oakwood Confederate Cemetery in Raleigh.

Lieutenants

ALLRED, HENRY C. (2nd Lieutenant)

Henry C. Allred was born in 1838, probably to Reuben and Sarah Spoon Allred. He resided in Randolph County and enlisted in Company M on 10 June 1861. He was elected 2nd lieutenant by his men. He served in that capacity until being defeated for reelection on 27 April 1862. There is no further military record. He may have served in Company E 63rd Regiment afterwards.

LAWRENCE, AUSTIN WILLARD

Austin Willard Lawrence was born about 1842–46 in Randolph County to Austin and Mary Lawrence. The family had just moved to North Carolina from Virginia at the time he was born. His father was superintendent of the Cedar Falls mill for a time. An older brother, John Milton Lawrence, was born in Virginia and served in this same company as 2nd lieutenant.

Austin resided in Randolph County as a farmer when he enlisted at age 16 on 6 March 1862, mustered in as a private and was assigned to Company M. He was wounded in the side at the second battle of Manassas, Va., 29 Aug. 1862. He was later captured at or near Gettysburg, Pa., 1–5 July 1863 and confined at Fort Delaware, Del. He remained there until being transferred to Point Lookout, Md., 15–18 Oct. 1863. He was paroled at Point Lookout and transferred to Cox's Landing, James River, Va., where he was received 14–15 Feb. 1865 for exchange. *Moore's Roster* indicates that at some point he was promoted from the ranks to 2nd lieutenant. I have no records to corroborate this, and no further military record is known. He returned to Randolph County after the war, where he was married 13 Jan. 1867 to Priscilla Trogdon. He is not found in Randolph County's 1870 Census, and apparently was not in North Carolina. He may have gone west.

LAWRENCE, JOHN MILTON (2nd Lieutenant)

John Milton Lawrence was born ca. 1840–41 in Virginia to Austin and Mary Lawrence. The family was in Randolph County by 1845, and lived in the Cedar Falls area. His father, Austin Lawrence, was superintendent of the Cedar Falls mill for a time. John enlisted in Company M at its organization on 10 June 1861 at 20 years of age, and was mustered in as 1st sergeant. A younger brother, Austin Willard Lawrence, enlisted in the same company the following year.

John Milton Lawrence was wounded at the battle of Seven Pines, Va., on 31 May 1862, and returned to duty after 31 October 1862. He was promoted to 2nd lieutenant on 10 April 1863. He was wounded a second time at Chancellorsville, Va., 1–3 May 1863, and was wounded a third time and captured at Gettysburg,

Pa., 3 or 4 July 1863. He was then hospitalized at Chester, Pa., until being transferred to Johnson's Island, Ohio, on 3 September 1863. He was held here until being transferred to Point Lookout, Md., on 21 March 1865. He was released after taking the Oath of Allegiance on 12 June 1865.

He returned to Randolph County, and was married 16 September 1865 to A. E. Williams. In a letter written in 1866 he stated that he was getting ready to move to Texas or Mexico.

MCMASTERS, LEWIS FRANKLIN (1st Lieutenant)

Lewis Franklin McMasters was born in 1833, probably to William J. B. and Huldah Welborn McMasters. He was married 14 January 1855 to Cynthia L. Siler, sister of Capt. Columbus Frank Siler of this company.

Lewis enlisted in Company M at its organization on 10 June 1861 at age 28 and was mustered in as 2nd sergeant. He was elected 2nd lieutenant on 27 April 1862. He was wounded in the left arm and captured at Seven Pines, Va., 31 May 1862. He was then confined at various Federal hospitals until being imprisoned at Fort Delaware, Del., on or about 15 July 1862. He was subsequently paroled and transferred to Aiken's Landing, James River, Va., where he was exchanged on 5 August 1862. He returned to duty on an unspecified date, and was promoted to 1st lieutenant on 16 March 1863. He resigned on 19 March 1863 because of disability from wounds.

Cynthia McMasters apparently died sometime after the birth of their second child in 1859, because upon returning home to Randolph County, Lewis remarried on 7 August 1864 to Mary Susan Lednum. This marriage produced one child before Lewis F. McMasters died in 1866. According to the stone placed there, he is buried in the McMasters Cemetery on Soapstone Road.

POUNDS, JAMES M. (2nd Lieutenant)

James M. Pounds was born 19 November 1840 in Chatham County to Archibald T. and Mourning Lowe Pounds. Moving to Randolph County, the family resided in Cedar Falls. James enlisted in Company M at its organization at age 20. His men elected him 2nd lieutenant on that same date. He served in this capacity during the encampment and blockading at Evansport into the Yorktown Siege, but was defeated for reelection on 27 April 1862. Further details about his service are unknown. William A. Pounds of this same company was his brother.

He was married on 4 September 1866 to Malinda Leonard. He was a highly respected citizen in his town and was a member of Cedar Falls Baptist Church for 60 years. He drew a Confederate pension, and was a member of Randolph Camp No. 1646 United Confederate Veterans. He died 25 March 1929 and was buried at Cedar Falls Baptist cemetery.

ROBBINS, JAMES M. (1st Lieutenant)

I believe this may be the James Robbins who was born 23 November 1829 in Randolph County, to Rev. Nathan and Mary Frazier Robbins. He was married to Rosanna Coltrane in Guilford County, 3 December 1855, and resided in Randolph County as a farmer when he enlisted here in Company M on 6 March 1862.

His age could have been misstated as 21 instead of 31. He was mustered in as a private and was elected 2nd lieutenant on or about 16 April 1863. He was wounded at Chancellorsville, Virginia, 1–3 May 1863. He was promoted to 1st lieutenant on 5 May 1863. He was then wounded in the arm at or near Wilderness, Virginia, in May 1864. He was wounded a third time at Reams' Station, Virginia, 25 August 1864. He was returned to duty 27 September 1864, and was present or accounted for through October 1864. James Robbins died 21 July 1867 and was buried at Ebenezer Methodist Church in Randolph County.

Non-Commissioned Officers and Privates

ADKERSON, STEPHEN

Stephen Adkerson was born about 1820–22, and was apparently a resident of Rockingham County. He was married to Martha J. _____. He enlisted at Camp Holmes on 29 March 1864 for the war, and was assigned to Company M. He died less than two months later in a hospital in Gordonsville, Va., of "diarrhoea chronic," on 13 May 1864.

ALLEN, SIMON ELWOOD

Simon Elwood Allen was born 24 Feb. 1844 in Randolph County to Samuel and Edith Henson Allen. He enlisted in Company M at age 18 on 6 March 1862 as a substitute. He was captured at the second battle of Manassas, Va., 29–30 Aug. 1862, and was paroled 29 Sept. 1862. He returned to duty on an unspecified date and was later captured a second time at or near Cold Harbor, Va., on 9 June 1864. He was then confined at Point Lookout, Md., until released on 20 June 1864 after joining the U.S. Army. He was assigned to Company K, 1st Regiment U.S. Volunteer Infantry on 27 June 1864, and served until being discharged on 20 November 1865 due to the effects of sunstroke. He was married in Hendricks County, Ind., on 27 Nov. 1866 to Ursula A. Masten. They returned to Randolph County to live by 7 September 1868, when their first child was born. Simon farmed and at one time was Postmaster of the Empire Post Office, which was about one mile north of Holly Spring Friends Meeting. He was in attendance at the Confederate reunion held in Asheboro on 1 September 1906, as a member of Company M. Simon E. Allen died 11 March 1924 and is buried next to his wife at Pleasant Ridge Christian cemetery, near Ramseur.

ALLRED, BENJAMIN F.

Benjamin F. Allred was born about 1842–43 probably to William and Mary Routh Allred. He resided in Randolph County where he enlisted in Company M

Private Simon Elwood "Doc" Allen (1844–1924) is pictured with his siblings. He enlisted in Company M on 6 March 1862 as a substitute. Back row, left to right: Simon Elwood "Doc" Allen, Mary Martitia "Titia" (Allen) Davis, Braxton Nathaniel "Bud" Allen. Front row, left to right: Uncle Matt Henson, Joseph James "Joe" Allen, Henry Milton "Henry" Allen. (Photograph from *The Allen Family—Descendants of John and Amy Cox Allen with Allied Lines*, by Lester M. Allen. Courtesy of the Allen family.)

at age 18 on 10 June 1861. He served about a year in this company, and then was reported as being absent sick from 1 August 1862 through October 1864. He was married 1 Februrary 1865 in Randolph County to Caroline Rose.

ALLRED, CALVIN C.

Calvin C. Allred has not been positively identified at this time. According to his service records he was born about 1839–40 in Randolph County. If the birth date is correct he could have been the son of Lemuel and Sarah Allred, or if he was born about 1831–35 he may have been a son of "Tennessee" John and Polly York Allred. He resided in Randolph County and enlisted in Company M at age 21 on 10 June 1861. He had served only a year when he was killed at Frayser's Farm, Va., on 30 June 1862.

ALLRED, EMSLEY

Emsley Allred was born about 1832 in Cedar Falls, Randolph County, to Jeremiah and Fanny Johnson Allred. He was married to Anna Trogdon in Randolph County on 30 March 1853. He is listed in the 1860 Census of Randolph County as a cooper. He gave his occupation as a farmer when he enlisted at age 30 on 6 March 1862. He was killed less than three months later during a charge on an enemy position at Seven Pines, Va., on 31 May or 1 June 1862, and was left behind enemy lines. His widow applied for a Confederate pension while living in the Proximity neighborhood of Greensboro in Guilford County on 20 Dec. 1911, and gave her name as Anna Trogdon Leonard.

ALLRED, JAMES A.

James A. Allred was born in 1845 in Randolph County to Samuel Hogan and Abigail Trogdon Allred. He resided there as a farmer when he enlisted at age 17 on 6 March 1862 as a substitute. He was wounded in the head at Fredericksburg, Va., 13 Dec. 1862. He was wounded again at Chancellorsville, Va., 1–3 May 1863. He was captured at Cold Harbor, Va., 1 June 1864, and was confined at Point Lookout, Md., until being released on or about 17 June 1864 after joining the U.S. Army. He was assigned to Company I, 1st Regiment U.S. Volunteer Infantry.

ALLRED, SAMUEL HOGAN

Samuel Hogan Allred was born about 1823–24, probably to "Tennessee" John and Mary "Polly" York Allred. He was married 9 January 1845 in Randolph County to Abigail Trogdon. He enlisted at Camp Holmes on 28 Dec. 1863 for the war and was assigned to Company M. He was captured at or near Jericho Mills, Va., on or about 23 May 1864. He was confined at Point Lookout, Md., until paroled on 17 Jan. 1865 and transferred for exchange. Company records do not indicate whether he returned to duty, but he may have done so, because he was paroled again at Greensboro on 10 May 1865. He and his wife Abigail are shown living in Franklinsville, Randolph County, in the 1880 Census, with four children and Abigail's mother in the household.

ALLRED, WILLIAM F.

This William F. Allred has not been positively identified, but he enlisted in Randolph County on 10 Aug. 1861 and was assigned to Company M. He served with that company until being wounded in the neck at or near Mechanicsville, Va., on 26 June 1862. He returned to duty on an unspecified date, and was captured at or near Sharpsburg, Md., on or about 17 Sept. 1862. He was paroled on 20 Sept. 1862. Company records do not indicate whether he returned to duty, but he may have done so, because he was hospitalized at Richmond, Va., 27 May 1864, which would have been just after the battles at Spottsylvania Court House and North Anna. He was furloughed for thirty days on 13 June 1864.

ALLRIDGE, WILLIAM

William Allridge was born 18 Jan. 1845, possibly to William and Satha Allridge. He enlisted at Camp Holmes on 12 April 1864 for the war and was assigned to Company M. He served with this company until the surrender, and was paroled at Appomattox Court House, Va., on 9 April 1865. He returned to Randolph County and resided there until being admitted to the Soldier's Home in Raleigh on 17 Jan. 1905. He remained an inmate there until his death of "consumption" on 4 Dec. 1910. He died with no immediate family, and was buried in Raleigh at Oakwood Confederate Cemetery.

ARNOLD, ALFRED NORMAN

Alfred Norman Arnold was born about 1833–35, possibly to Elizabeth Arnold. They resided in Randolph County when he enlisted at age 28 on 10 June 1861 at the organization of Company M. He served with this company until he was killed at Shepherdstown, Va., on 20 Sept. 1862.

ARNOLD, THOMAS

Thomas Arnold was born about 1837, probably to Elizabeth Arnold, and was most likely a brother of Alfred Norman Arnold of this company. Randolph County marriage records show a Thomas Arnold married to Martitia Hutton 7 Aug. 1855. He was livng in Randolph County when he enlisted in Company M at age 25 on 10 June 1861. He was wounded in the thigh at the second battle of Manassas, Va., on 29 Aug. 1862. He was present or accounted for through October 1864. A document written on 20 March 1865 in Franklinsville states that he had been at home on furlough prior to that date and had been acting as a guide and spy for a Major Harris. He is believed to have moved to Indiana sometime after 1870. He is found in Brown Township, Morgan County, in the 1880 Indiana Census with Martitia and eight children, the last three born in Indiana.

BAKER, JOHN HENRY

John Henry Baker was born in Cumberland County about 1834–35, and was married there to Elizabeth Harvel on 31 Oct. 1850. By the time the war began, he and Elizabeth lived in Randolph County, where he enlisted at age 26 in Company M at its organization on 10 June 1861. He died in a hospital in Richmond, Va., on or about 26 May 1862 of typhoid fever.

BARKER, NATHAN DAVID

Nathan David Barker was born about 1833 in Randolph County. He resided in Randolph County when he enlisted in Company M at age 27 on 10 June 1861. He served until being wounded in the big toe and captured at or near Gettysburg, Pa., on or about 1–3 July 1863. His big toe was amputated, and he was hospitalized at Chester, Pa., where he died on 1 Aug. 1863 of "angeroleucitis." He was buried at Philadelphia National Cemetery in Pennsylvania.

BIRNE, WILLIAM C.

William C. Birne has not been identified, although he may be William Byrns, born about 1831 in Randolph County to Enoch and Catherine Beckerdite Byrns. William C. Birne enlisted at Camp Holmes on 1 May 1864 for the war and was assigned to Company M 22nd Regiment. He was present or accounted for through October 1864.

BREEDLOVE, ABRAHAM

Abraham Breedlove was born about 1841, probably in Guilford County to Wesley and Quenette Hesley Chappell Breedlove. He was a resident of Randolph County when he enlisted in Company M on 9 Jan. 1864 for the war. He was listed as a deserter on 15 April 1864. Returning to duty, he was wounded ("one finger off") at or near Wilderness, Va., in May 1864. He was reported under arrest 7 Oct. 1864 and returned to duty on an unspecified date. He deserted to the enemy on or about 31 Dec. 1864, and was confined at Washington, D.C., until released on or about 4 Jan. 1865 after taking the Oath of Allegiance.

BREEDLOVE, HENRY

Henry Breedlove was born about 1841 to Levi Sr. and Sarah Wheeler Breedlove. He and his family resided in Randolph County at the time of the 1850 Census. He was married 31 Jan. 1862 to Julia Ann Wrenn in Guilford County. He and his older brother, Joseph Madison Breedlove, enlisted together in Company M at Camp Holmes on 6 Feb. 1864 for the war.

Henry remained with this company until he was captured at or near Jericho Mills, Va., 23 May 1864. He was then confined at Point Lookout, Md., where he died on or about 6 June 1865 of "diarrhoea."

BREEDLOVE, JOSEPH MADISON

Joseph Madison (Joe) Breedlove was born 20 Jan. 1840 in Guilford County to Levi Sr. and Sarah Wheeler Breedlove. He was married in Randolph County on 1 Oct. 1865 to Mary Jane McMasters Wood. He and his younger brother, Henry Breedlove, enlisted together in Company M at Camp Holmes on 6 Feb. 1864 for the war. He was reported absent due to sickness on 1 July 1864 and returned to duty sometime after 31 Oct. 1864. He was paroled at Greensboro on 16 May 1865. He lived in the Liberty area and drew a Confederate pension. On 24 Nov. 1915 he was walking on a railroad track north of Liberty and was struck by a train. It was said he could not hear well. He was buried next to his wife, who had preceded him in death in January of that same year. They are buried at Shiloh United Methodist cemetery, near Julian.

BREEDLOVE, NEWMAN C.

Newman C. Breedlove was born about 1838 to John and Sarah Breedlove. The place and date of Newman's enlistment were not reported, and it is unknown when and where he was captured. It is known that he was confined at Point Lookout, Md., where he died 6 June 1865 of an unreported cause. He is buried at Point Lookout Cemetery, Scotland, Md.

BREWER, HENRY

Henry Brewer was born in 1825 and resided in Moore County when he enlisted at Camp Holmes on 22 Jan.1863 for the war. He deserted on an unspecified date and was reported under arrest on 7 Oct. 1864. He was returned to duty sometime before 3 April 1865, when he was captured at Petersburg, Va. He was then confined at Hart's Island, New York Harbor, until he was released on 19 June 1865, after taking the Oath of Allegiance. He returned home to Moore County to live with his wife, Talitha A. Brewer. He died in 1902 and is buried at Bensalem cemetery.

BROWN, JAMES B.

James B. Brown was born about 1834. He was a resident of Moore County, in the Long Street Post Office area, when he enlisted in Randolph County at age 27 on 10 Aug. 1861 and was assigned to Company M. He served until being reported absent without leave in July and September 1862. He was later listed as a deserter.

BROWN, PETER P.

Peter P. Brown was born 15 April 1847 to Adam and Mary Brown. He enlisted in Company M at Camp Holmes on 15 May 1864 for the war. He was wounded in an unspecified engagement on or about 10 June 1864, probably during the Petersburg Siege in Virginia. He returned to duty sometime during September or October 1864 and served with this company until being captured near Petersburg, Va., 2 April 1865. He was confined at Point Lookout, Md., until being released on 24 June 1865 after taking the Oath of Allegiance. He returned home to Randolph County and was married to Rosannah H. Coble. They resided in the Julian Community where they were prominent farmers. After an illness of about ten days, Peter P. Brown died 23 Jan. 1929 and was buried at Shiloh Methodist cemetery.

BROWN, RILEY J.

Riley J. Brown enlisted in Moore County along with several others on 13 March 1863 for the war, and was assigned to Company M. He was captured at or near Gettysburg, Pa., 3–5 July 1863, and was confined at Fort Delaware, Del., until he was paroled and transferred to City Point, Va. He was received there on 1 Aug. 1863 for exchange. He was reported absent without leave on 1 May 1864, but returned to duty on 1 Sept. 1864, and was present or accounted for through October 1864.

BROWN, S. P.

S. P. Brown is listed in *Moore's Roster* as having enlisted in this company on 15 May 1864. This is believed to be the same person as Peter P. Brown of this company, who did enlist on that date.

BRYANT, W. P.

W. P. Bryant left behind far too little information for identification. The place and date of his enlistment were not reported, but he was assigned to Company M, 22nd Regiment. Company records dated July 1862 report that he died at Richmond, Va., but the date and cause of death are not given.

BURGESS, FRANKLIN F.

Franklin F. Burgess was born 1824–28 in Randolph County and was married 13 Jan. 1846 to Matilda Elizabeth "Betsy" York. He lived in Randolph County as a farmer when he enlisted at age 37 in Company M on 10 June 1861. Company records indicate he was discharged on 13 June 1862 by reason of being over age. He came home and reenlisted in Randolph County at age 40 on 30 Jan. 1864 in Company G, 46th Regiment. He was wounded in the hip at Cold Harbor, Va., 2 June 1864. He returned to duty by 31 Aug. 1864 and was present or accounted for through December 1864. He was paroled at Greensboro on or about 10 May 1865 and returned to Randolph County. He resided in the Ramseur area, drawing a Confederate pension for some period of time. His wife drew a widow's pension in 1902, but was reported in 1903 as having died. Franklin Burgess' date of death and place of burial are not known at this time.

BURGESS, JOHN P.

John P. Burgess was born about 1841 in Randolph County and was living there when he enlisted in Company M at age 19 on 10 June 1861. He was wounded at Frayser's Farm, Va., on 30 June 1862. He was wounded a second time at an unspecified battle, probably Harper's Ferry or Shepherdstown Ford in Virginia, in September 1862. The company records do not show whether he returned to duty, but he was hospitalized at Richmond, Va., 11 July 1863 with a gunshot wound to the left thigh, and was furloughed for forty days on 19 July 1863.

BURGESS, SAMUEL M.

Samuel M. "Sam" Burgess was born about 1826 in Randolph County and was married there on 4 Oct. 1848 to Catherine L. "Katie" Craven, born 18 May 1828. They had the following known children: Edward Clinton "Clint" Burgess, James Austin "Jim" Burgess, Robert Stevenson "Bob" Burgess, Mary Elizabeth "Lizzie" Burgess, and Lovie Ellen Burgess. They resided in the Rehobeth Church area as farmers when he enlisted in Randolph County at age 36 on 6 March 1862, and was assigned to Company M. He was killed at the Rappahannock River near Fredericksburg, Va., on or about 24 August 1862 in one of a series of small skirmishes fought there just prior to the battle of 2nd Manassas. These skirmishes, named Waterloo Bridge, Lee Springs, Freeman's Ford and Sulphur Springs, resulted in about 250 casualties. Family members relate the story that when his death came, he was sitting beside a tree and was hit by enemy artillery fire that decapitated him. This story is confirmed by his wife's Confederate Widow's Pension application, filed on 23 May 1885. Catherine remained in the community where they had lived and survived until 12 May 1920. She is buried in the cemetery at Rehobeth United Methodist Church between Ramseur and Siler City where she was a member for more than fifty years.

BURGIS, W.

This name is presumed to be W. Burgess, but cannot be identified. The place and date of his enlistment were not reported; however, he was assigned to Company M, 22nd Regiment. Company records dated September 1862 indicate he was killed at the second battle of Manassas, Va., on or about 28–30 Aug. 1862.

CAMPBELL, JAMES E.

James E. Campbell was born 16 Dec. 1839 in Randolph County to Isaac and Nancy Williams Campbell. He lived in Randolph County and worked as a blacksmith prior to enlisting at age 22 on 6 March 1862. He was mustered in as a private and promoted to corporal before 28 May 1862. He was wounded and captured sometime during the battle of Gettysburg, Pa., 1–5 July 1863 and hospitalized at Chester, Pa., until he was transferred to Point Lookout, Md., arriving 4 Oct. 1863. He was paroled at Point Lookout and transferred to City Point, Va., on 6 March 1864, for exchange. He was returned to duty on an unspecified date and promoted to sergeant by 1 Sept. 1864. He retired to the Invalid Corps on 17 Nov. 1864 by reason of disability, and was paroled at Greensboro on 17 May 1865.

James was married on 19 Oct. 1865 in Randolph County to Martha E. Pugh. He died 3 June 1907 and is buried at Cedar Falls Baptist cemetery, along with two infant children.

CANNON, JACKSON

Jackson Cannon was born about 1820. He resided in Rockingham County and was married to Sarah F. ____. He enlisted at Camp Holmes on 10 May 1864 for the war, and was assigned to Company M. He was captured at Hatcher's Run, Va., 21 March 1865 and was confined at Point Lookout, Md., until he was released on 24 June 1865 after taking the Oath of Allegiance. He and his wife Sally are found living in Oregonville, Rockingham County in the 1880 Census, with a son, Johnnie.

CANNON, JAMES

James Cannon resided in Rockingham County and enlisted at Camp Holmes on 29 Nov. 1863 for the war. He was wounded in the thigh at or near Wilderness, Va., in May 1864. He was captured at or near Jericho Mills, Va., on or about 24 May 1864. He was then confined at Point Lookout, Md., where he died on 28 June 1864. The cause of his death was not reported. He was buried at Point Lookout Cemetery, Scotland, Md.

CARROLL, H. SPAIN

H. Spain Carroll was born about 1841 in Chatham County to Edward W. and Nancy Carroll. He and his mother resided in Randolph County as farmers when he enlisted at age 19 on 6 March 1862 and was assigned to Company M. He served in Company M until he was killed at Chancellorsville, Va., 1–4 May 1863.

CARTER, W. B.

W. B. Carter is listed in *Broadfoot's* as having been a member of Company M. I have found no evidence of a man by this name in any company records. It is probable that this is a misreading of another name, such as W(esley) E. Caudle, for example.

CAUDLE, WESLEY E.

Wesley Caudle was born about 1824 in Orange County. He married Sarah M. Lane in Guilford County on 25 May 1853, and resided in Randolph County working as a carpenter. He was a mechanic when he enlisted in Company M in Randolph County on 10 June 1861, at age 36. He was discharged 20 June 1862 by reason of being over age.

CAVINESS, JOHN A.

John A. Caviness was born in 1842 in Randolph County to Arnold Edward and Mary Craven Caviness. He was a Moore County farmer when he enlisted there at age 20 on 13 March 1863 for the war, and was assigned to Company M. He was discharged on 6 Oct. 1863 by reason of "scrufulosis, anemia cachexia." He returned home and was married Lydia F. _____ about 1876. At some point they moved to Ore Hill (now known as Bonlee) in Chatham County, where they raised their family. John A. Caviness died on 3 November 1912, and his wife survived until 1938. They are buried near their home at Providence United Methodist cemetery.

COBLE, DAVID OLIVER

David Oliver Coble was born 16 Sept. 1839 in Randolph County to Henry and Sarah Ann Campbell Coble. He enlisted in Company M at its organization on 10 June 1861 as a private. He was discharged on 28 August 1861 for unspecified reasons. He married his first wife, Martitia York, on 16 Feb. 1862. He married twice more and was survived by his third wife. He died 2 Jan. 1923 after several years of declining health and was buried at Gray's Chapel United Methodist cemetery.

COBLE, JOHN RANDOLPH

John Randolph Coble was born about 1842, probably to Henry and Sarah Ann Campbell Coble, and was most likely the brother of David O. Coble of this company. He was married to Martha J. Breedlove 12 May 1860 in Randolph County. He was 19 years of age when he enlisted in Company M at its organization on 10 June 1861. He was mustered in as 1st corporal, but was reduced to ranks before 1 Aug. 1862. He served throughout the war and was present or accounted for until he was paroled at Greensboro on 8 May 1865.

COBLE, RILEY

Riley Coble was born about 1842, probably to Abigail Coble, and farmed in Randolph County prior to enlisting at age 19 on 6 March 1862. He was hospitalized in Charlottesville, Va., 12 July 1863 with a gunshot wound. Place and date of the wound were not reported. He returned to duty 21 Sept. 1863. On 4 June 1864 he was again hospitalized, this time at Danville, Va., with a gunshot to the left hand. The place and date this wound occurred were also not documented. He reported back to duty sometime in September or October of 1864, and was paroled at Greensboro on 12 May 1865. After returning home, he was married to Betsy Ann Curtis on 16 Aug. 1866. They may have resided in Guilford County, because Riley is found in the 1870 Census living in the household of Abraham and Margaret Curtis in the Greene Township of Guilford. Betsy Anne is not listed, and may have died previous to the census.

COBLE, WILLIAM

William Coble was born 9 April 1842 in Chatham County to Eli and Keziah Lowe Coble. He worked as a carder, probably at the mill in Cedar Falls. On 10 June 1861, at the organization of Company M, he enlisted at age 19 and was mustered in as 3rd sergeant. At some point he returned home to Randolph County and died of "typhoid pneumonia" on 15 March 1862. He was buried alongside his parents at Cedar Falls Baptist cemetery. His military record states he was "a young man of fine promise."

CONLEY, JULIUS GEORGE

Julius George Conley was born about 1835, probably in Caldwell County to George Harvey Conley and resided in Caldwell County when he enlisted at age 26 in Company A 22nd Regiment on 30 April 1861. He was transferred to Company M in September 1861, and remained with them through June 1862. He was then transferred back to Company A on 1 July 1862 and deserted 28 July 1862.

COOK, WILLIAM L.

William L. Cook was born about 1827 and was married in Wake County on 27 Oct. 1848 to Fetney Terrell. He was a resident of Wake or Granville County and was by occupation a wheelwright when he enlisted in Granville County at age 36 on 22 Jan. 1863 for the war. He served for over a year, and was captured at or near Jericho Mills, Va., on or about 23 May 1864. He was then confined at Point Lookout, Md., until being released on or about 13 May 1865 after taking the Oath of Allegiance.

COX, JAMES MATTHEWS

James Matthews Cox was born 10 Sept. 1841, and was a 20-year-old resident of Randolph County when he enlisted in Company M on 10 June 1861 during its organization. He was wounded in the leg at or near Mechanicsville, Va., 26 June 1862. He returned to duty sometime after 31 Oct. 1862 and served until he was captured at Hatcher's Run, Va., 2 April 1865. He was then confined at Hart's Island, New York Harbor, until he was released on 18 June 1865 after taking the Oath of Allegiance. He drew a Confederate pension and was living in the Staley-Liberty area when he died 25 Dec. 1922. He is buried at Sandy Creek Baptist cemetery.

CRAVEN, ENOCH S.

Enoch S. Craven was born about 1839–40 in Randolph County. He resided in Randolph County and enlisted there in Company M at age 21 on 10 June 1861. He died in a hospital at Richmond, Va., 15 July or 17 Aug. 1862. The cause of his death was not reported.

CRAVEN, HENRY

Henry Craven was born about 1826 in Randolph County and was probably the son of a Sarah Craven. If this is the correct person, he was married 17 October 1857 to Delilah Scott. He resided in the Moffitt's Mills area as a farmer when he enlisted in Randolph County at age 36 on 6 March 1862. He was assigned to Company M. He was hospitalized at Richmond, Va., 30 Sept. 1862 with a gunshot wound. The place and date of the wound were not reported, but it was probably sustained at Shepherdstown Ford, Va., where action took place on 20 Sept. 1862. He was furloughed for thirty days on or about 8 Oct. 1862. He is shown still living in the Moffitt's Mills area in the 1870 Census with his wife and two daughters, Roxanna L. and Emma D. Craven. In 1880 they were living in Columbia Township with one daughter, Emma D. Craven, and with Henry's apparently unmarried sister, Nancy E. Craven, also in the household. By the 1900 Census, Emma D. and Nancy E. Craven were living in West Columbia Township with Emma listed as head of house and Nancy as aunt. Henry and Delilah were evidently deceased by this time, but no burial records have been found.

CRAVEN, JACOB FRANKLIN

Jacob Franklin Craven was born about 1842 in Randolph County possibly to Kindred and Mary Fields Craven. He was listed as an apprentice hatter in the 1860 Census, but resided as a farmer when he enlisted in Randolph County at age 20 on 25 Feb. 1862. He was assigned to Company M, 22nd Regiment. He reportedly died in a hospital in Richmond, Va., on or about 3 Sept. 1862, of "febris typhoides," or typhoid fever.

CROSS, JAMES N.

James N. Cross was born in 1839, probably in Randolph County, to Henry and Elizabeth Cross. He enlisted at Camp Holmes on 29 Jan. 1864 for the war. He was wounded at or near Wilderness, Va., in May 1864. He returned to duty on an unspecified date, and was present or accounted for through October 1864. He returned to Randolph County and remained there until his death in 1892. He is buried in Asheboro City cemetery.

CROSS, THOMAS F.

Thomas F. Cross was born about 1842, probably to Addison and Delaney Cross. He enlisted at age 18 on 10 June 1861 in Company M. He served until 7 Aug. 1862, at which time he deserted. He was returned to duty on an unspecified date and served until wounded in the head at or near Wilderness, Va., in May 1864. He deserted to the enemy on or about 24 Feb. 1865, and was confined at Washington, D.C., until released on or about 27 Feb. 1865 after taking the Oath of Allegiance.

DARR, SAMUEL

Samuel Darr was born 6 Oct. 1825 in Davidson County to Melchior and Susannah Conrad Darr. He was married to Mary Lopp on 3 Nov. 1857 in Davidson County and was a farmer there when he was conscripted at Camp Holmes on 15 March 1864 for the war. He was present or accounted for through October 1864. After the war, he returned home to his farm in northern Davidson County in Thomasville Township. He and Mary had five known children. Samuel Darr died 15 March 1896 and was buried at Mt. Pleasant United Methodist cemetery in Davidson County.

DEAL, MARCUS

Marcus Deal was born 5 September 1837 at Deal's Mill (now known as Oak Hill) in Caldwell County to William III and Catherine Smyre Deal. He was educated in a boys' school at Rutherford College. He and two of his brothers enlisted in Caldwell County in Company A 22nd Regiment on 30 April 1861. Three other brothers and their father also served during the war. Marcus was transferred to Company

Private Marcus Deal (1837–1924) enlisted in Company A, 22nd Regiment on 30 April 1861. He transferred to Company M in August or September 1861 and served with the company until transferring back to Company A in July 1862 while absent wounded. (Photograph courtesy of Robert C. Deal.)

M in August or September 1861. During his time with Company M he participated in the Yorktown Siege in Virginia and was wounded at Seven Pines, Va., on 31 May 1862. He was transferred back to Company A in July 1862 while absent wounded. He was carried as absent wounded through October 1862, and was returned to Company A and promoted to corporal during November 1862. He was wounded and captured at Gettysburg 1-4 July 1863, and hospitalized at DeCamp General Hospital, David's Island, New York Harbor. He was transferred to City Point, Va., on 28 August 1863 for exchange. He returned to duty at an unspecified date and was promoted to sergeant prior to 1 January 1864. He was then wounded in the thigh near North Anna River, Va., 22 May 1864. He returned to duty in October 1864 and was promoted to 1st sergeant in Company A sometime between November 1864 and April 1865. He was paroled in Virginia at Appomattox Court House on 9 April 1865. Marcus returned to Caldwell County and was married to Mary Adeline Bisnar on 11 March 1868. They had nine children. Marcus inherited the family businesses and ran a mill, post office and a small number of mercantile stores. He was very active in the community and his church up until his death on 26 April 1924. He was buried in his church cemetery at Cedar Valley United Methodist in Caldwell County.

DEAN, WILLIAM H.

William H. Dean was born about 1840, probably in Guilford County to Nathan and Matilda Dean. He enlisted in Company E, 22nd Regiment in Guilford County at age 21 on 23 May 1861 and was transferred to Company M between April and July of 1862. He was transferred back to Company E before 1 Aug. 1862. He was reported absent wounded in September 1862, and reported back to duty on an unspecified date. He deserted sometime before 1 Sept. 1864, but returned to duty at an unspecified date and was paroled at Greensboro 5 May 1865. He was married 12 April 1867 in Guilford County to Lydia Ann Silvey. They are not found in the 1870 Census, and may have gone west.

DOLLINGER, J. E.

J. E. Dollinger has not been identified. The name may actually be Dellinger. Several Dellingers lived in the western part of the state that could be this man. He enlisted at Camp Holmes and was assigned to Company M on 1 July 1864 for the war. He was killed at or near Reams' Station, Va., 25 Aug. 1864.

ELLINGTON, ALEX P.

Alex P. Ellington has not been identified. He enlisted at Camp Holmes on 29 Nov. 1863. No further records are found until he was paroled at Greensboro on 3 May 1865.

EULISS, GRANDISON

Grandison Euliss was born in Orange County about 1833-34 to Allen and Sarah Euliss. By 1850 Grandison, his mother and a sister were in Randolph County.

He was married 6 Feb. 1856 to Henrietta A. "Ritty" Craven in Randolph County. He and Henrietta were apparently divorced by the time of the 1860 Census. He enlisted in Company M in Randolph County on 25 February 1862 at the age of 28. He served until being captured at or near Jericho Mills, Va., 23–24 May 1864. He was confined at Point Lookout, Md., until paroled and transferred to Boulware's Wharf, James River, Va., 16 March 1865 for exchange. He returned to Randolph County and was married a second time, to Mary Elizabeth E. Staley on 17 Dec. 1868. He and his wife lived in the Pleasant Grove Township, at least until 1880.

FIELDS, ANDREW J.

Andrew J. Fields was born about 1841 in Randolph County. He resided as a farmer when he enlisted there at age 20 on 6 March 1862 and was assigned to Company M. He probably took part in the Yorktown Siege and the battle of Seven Pines, both in Virginia. He died sometime between the 20th and 24th of June 1862. The place and cause of his death were not reported.

FIELDS, JESSE

Jesse Fields was born about 1838 in Randolph County. He was a farmer there when he enlisted at age 23 on 6 March 1862 and was assigned to Company M. He was wounded in the thigh at the second battle of Manassas, Va., 29 Aug. 1862. He died at Staunton, Va., 20 Sept. or 1 Nov. 1862. Cause of death was not reported.

FIELDS, WILLIAM

William Fields was born about 1831 in Randolph County. He apparently had a wife named Elmira and resided as a farmer when he enlisted there at age 31 on 6 March 1862. He was assigned to Company M and was killed at the second battle of Manassas, Va., on or about 28 Aug. 1862.

FLINCHUM, JACOB

Jacob Flinchum was born about 6 Oct. 1847, probably in Stokes County to James and Sarah Smith Flinchum. He enlisted at Camp Holmes on 29 March 1864 for the war. He was captured at or near Jericho Mills, Va., on 23 May 1864. He was confined at Point Lookout, Md., until paroled and transferred to Boulware's Wharf, James River, Va., where he was received 16 March 1865 for exchange.

After the war he returned to Stokes County where he was married on 28 July 1867 to Rhoda Chandler. They resided in Stokes County in the Danbury area. A Danbury newspaper reported in an issue dated 11 Apr. 1895 that a Jacob Flinchum had been found dead on the bank of Camping Island Creek. It said he had been missing for about a month, and surmised that he had fallen from a foot log into the creek. This would mean that he died in early March 1895.

FOSTER, JOSEPH F.

Joseph F. Foster was born in Chatham County on 22 March 1823. His parents are unidentified. He is listed on some records as Josiah. He was married 21

April 1855 to Rebecca Melinda Staley in Chatham County. He may have resided in Randolph County just before the war as a farmer, and enlisted there in Company M on 10 June 1861 at its organization. He was reported absent without leave in July and September 1862. He returned to duty on an unspecified date. Records report he "gave up" and was captured by the enemy at Cashtown, Pa., 5 July 1863. He was confined at Fort Delaware, Del., until he was released on or about 22 Sept. 1863, after joining the U.S. Army. He was assigned to Company E, 3rd Regiment Maryland Cavalry, and served until the end of the war. He returned to Randolph County and moved his family to a new home about two miles from Asheboro. He drew a Confederate pension for several years and died 30 Sept. 1905. He is buried in Asheboro City cemetery.

FOSTER, LEVI

Levi Foster was born 4 Dec. 1841 and resided in Randolph County when he enlisted in Company M at age 19 on 10 June 1861 at the organization of the company. *Moore's Roster* states that at some point he was promoted to sergeant.

Sergeant John Turner states that "no better man than Mr. Foster ever carried a Southern musket. We fought together at Fair Oaks Farm, also together at Seven Pines at the opening of the seven days battle below Richmond; I was shot down and left in the lines of the Yankees. Foster and Calvin Allred rushed through their lines and brought me out. Next day Allred was killed at Frazier's Run. I did not see Foster again until the battle commenced. I went into the fight and saw Foster doing his duty, shooting at Yankees. I called to him, 'Levi, you are still shooting at the Blue Jackets.' 'Yes,' he replied, 'but they haven't shot me yet.' This was at Cold Harbor. Foster was wounded at Manassas and Bristow Station. He went with Lee and Jackson to Chancellorsville, Fredericksburg, Gettysburg and Petersburg."

Records indicate Foster was captured at Hatcher's Run, Va., 2 April 1865. He was confined at Hart's Island, New York Harbor, until being released 18 June 1865 after taking the Oath of Allegiance. He returned to Randolph County and was married 21 Oct. 1866 to Wincey Hardin. He drew a Confederate pension and lived in the Brunswick Community near Climax. He was in attendance at the Confederate reunion in Asheboro on 1 Sept. 1906 and became a charter member of Randolph Camp No. 1646 United Confederate Veterans. He died 23 June 1911, and was buried at Gray's Chapel United Methodist cemetery.

FOUST, CHRISTIAN

Christian Foust was born about 1831 in Randolph County probably to Conrad and Elizabeth "Betsy" Kivett Foust. He was a farmer when he enlisted there at age 30 on 6 March 1862 and was assigned to Company M. He was wounded in the side at or near Mechanicsville, Va., on or about 26 June 1862. He received his second wound, in the shoulder, at Fredericksburg, Va., on 13 Dec. 1862. He was captured at Funkstown, Md., 12 July 1863 and was confined at Point Lookout, Md., until being released on 25 Jan. 1864 after taking the Oath of Allegiance and joining the U.S. Army. He was assigned to Company B, 1st Regiment U.S. Volunteer Infantry. He is buried in McMasters family cemetery near Liberty.

FOUST, J. H.

J. H. Foust is listed in *Broadfoot's* as being a member of Company M. This is believed to be a misreading of either Jacob B. or James Madison Foust.

FOUST, JACOB B.

Jacob B. Foust was born 4 Oct. 1823 in Randolph County probably to Conrad and Elizabeth "Betsy" Kivett Foust. He was married 31 Jan. 1851 to Matilda Lineberry, who already had a daughter named Elizabeth. Together, he and Matilda had several other children. He resided as a farmer in Randolph County, where he enlisted at age 39 on 6 March 1862 and was assigned to Company M. He was reported absent without leave in July and September 1862, and was listed as a deserter in October 1862. He must have returned to duty by July 1863, because Sgt. John Turner reported that he was captured during the retreat from Gettysburg at Falling Waters by a detachment of the advanced guard of the Northern army, and was exchanged in the winter of 1863 and brought back to his company. He was wounded 5 May 1864 at Wilderness, Va., and was returned to duty by 1 Sept. 1864. Turner stated that in battle, "He loaded and shot as fast as any man in Jackson's army." He was paroled at Appomattox Court House, Va., on 9 Apr. 1865. He returned home to Randolph County where he farmed and drew a Confederate pension. He died 2 March 1913 and was buried at Mt. Pleasant Baptist cemetery.

FOUST, JAMES MADISON

James Madison Foust was born about 1839 in Randolph County probably to David and Laura Ann Wood Foust. He resided as a farmer and enlisted in Randolph County at age 23 on 25 Feb. 1862. He was hospitalized in Culpeper, Va., 10 Oct. 1862 with a gunshot wound. The place and date of the wound were not reported. He was furloughed from a hospital at Richmond, Va., on 14 Oct. 1862.

FOUST, PETER

Peter Foust was born about 1839–40 in Randolph County to Conrad and Elizabeth "Betsy" Kivett Foust. He resided as a farmer when he enlisted in Randolph County at age 21 on 6 March 1862 and was assigned to Company M. He was captured at Falling Waters, Md., 14 July 1863, and was confined at Point Lookout, Md. He was released on 25 Jan. 1864 after joining the U.S. Army, and was assigned to Company B, 1st Regiment U.S. Volunteer Infantry. His name appears on the Roll of Honor indicating he was wounded in an unspecified battle. He continued to reside in the Liberty area and is buried in the McMasters family cemetery.

FREEMAN, JAMES F.

James F. Freeman is listed in *Broadfoot's* as being a member of Company M. There was a James F. Freeman who served in Company L of this same regiment. It is believed this listing is an error, and he did not serve in Company M.

FRENCH, THOMAS P.

Thomas P. French was born about 1844 in Rockingham County to Jeremiah and Zipea French. He enlisted at Camp Holmes on 29 March 1864 for the war. He died in a hospital at Petersburg, Va., on 25 June 1864. The place and date of his wounds were not reported, but they were presumably suffered during Cold Harbor or the Petersburg Siege.

FURGERSON, JAMES

James Furgerson was born about 1827–30 in Virginia to Tunstall and Susan Furgerson, and resided in Rockingham County. He enlisted at Camp Holmes on 26 March 1864 for the war and was assigned to Company M. He was hospitalized at Richmond, Va., 24 May 1864 with a gunshot wound of the left thigh. The place and date of the wound were not reported, but this was just after the battles at Spotsylvania Court House and North Anna, Va. He was furloughed for sixty days on 10 June 1864. He was captured at Hatcher's Run, Va., 1 April 1865 and was confined at Point Lookout, Md., until being released on 26 June 1865 after taking the Oath of Allegiance.

GATEWOOD, JOHN DUDLEY

John Dudley Gatewood was born in 1841 to William and Julia Branson Gatewood. He enlisted in Company H 22nd Regiment in Stokes County 1 June 1861 at age 20. He was transferred to Company M in December 1861 and was transferred back to Company H in July 1862. He was reported absent without leave in September 1862, and returned to duty on an unspecified date. He was wounded at Jerusalem Plank Road, near Petersburg, Va., 23 June 1864. He deserted from the hospital at Richmond, Va., 10 Nov. 1864.

GENTRY, JEFFERSON

Jefferson Gentry was born on 21 April 1820, probably to Matthew Gentry, in Wilkes County. Sometime before the 1840 Census he was in Grayson County, Va., where he was married 13 Dec. 1841 to Elizabeth Rankin. Before 1850 he returned to Wilkes County and remained there at least until 1860. During the early 1860s he moved to Surry County and resided there at the time of his enlistment. The place and date of his enlistment were not reported, but he was assigned to Company M, 22nd Regiment. He was captured on the South Side Railroad near Petersburg, Va., 2 April 1865. He was then confined at Hart's Island, New York Harbor, until he was released on or about 20 June 1865 after taking the Oath of Allegiance. He returned to Surry County after the war, and at the time the 1900 Census was taken, was still living there with members of his family.

GLASGOW, JOHN W.

John W. Glasgow was born about 1841–42 in Randolph County, probably to Jesse L. and Martha Davis Glasgow. He was married in Randolph County on 21 July 1861 to Sibly Caroline Kinney. They resided there as farmers when he enlisted in Randolph County at age 20 on 6 March 1862. He deserted to the enemy on or about 12 March 1864 and was confined at Washington, D.C., until being released on or about 17 March 1864 after taking the Oath of Allegiance and joining the U.S. Army. He was assigned to the 3rd Regiment Pennsylvania Heavy Artillery.

GLASGOW, WILLIAM MONROE

William Monroe Glasgow was born 13 June 1844 in Randolph County to Jesse L. and Martha Davis Glasgow. He was by occupation a farmer or laborer when he enlisted in Randolph County at age 18 on 6 March 1862, and was assigned to Company M. He deserted on or about 5 August 1862, and was court-martialed on or about 23 January 1863. He deserted to the enemy on or about 1 March 1864 and was confined at Washington, D.C. until he was released on or about 12 March 1864 after taking the Oath of Allegiance and joining the U.S. Army. He was assigned to the 3rd Regiment Pennsylvania Heavy Artillery. After the war he returned to Randolph County and was married 6 April 1866 to Martha Jane Giles of the Giles Chapel community near Central Falls. Martha died in 1908. One source reports that William was later married to Malinda Breedlove Brown; however, I have been unable to confirm this marriage. William Monroe Glasgow died 24 January 1916 and was buried next to his wife, Martha, at Shiloh United Methodist cemetery near Julian.

GRAY, CALVIN

Calvin Gray was born about 1834 and was married in Randolph County to Sophia McDaniel on 25 December 1856. He was a resident of Randolph County when he enlisted there on 10 Aug. 1861 and was assigned to Company M. He served until being wounded in the arm at or near Mechanicsville, Va., 26 June 1862. He was reported as being absent wounded through October 1862. He was finally discharged on 21 Dec. 1864 by reason of disability. He and his wife continued to reside in Randolph County, and in 1880 his occupation was listed as blacksmith. They had at least six children. Sophia died in 1901 and was buried at Gray's Chapel United Methodist cemetery. At this writing it is unknown when Calvin died or for certain if he is buried at Gray's Chapel.

HAAS, W. F.

W. F. Haas is listed in *Broadfoot's* as being a member of Company M. This is probably William Franklin Hayes (see entry).

HARDIN, WILLIAM R.

William R. Hardin was born 29 August 1833 in Randolph County to Zimri and Lucy Routh Hardin. He resided as a farmer when he enlisted there at age 27 on 6 March 1862, and was assigned to Company M. He was reported absent sick from 26 May 1863 through October 1864; however, North Carolina pension records say that he was wounded "at Williamsburg, Va., in August 1863." He was paroled at Greensboro on 10 May 1865 and returned to Randolph County. On 12 April

1866 he was married to Elizabeth C. "Lizzie" Harlin. They farmed in the Franklinville–Gray's Chapel area and had at least three children. Lizzie died sometime after 1883, leaving Will with young children to raise. The 1900 Census shows him living as a widower in the East Franklinville Township, with two of his children in his home. He drew a Confederate pension until 1902 and registered to vote in October of 1902 at the age of 69. Several years of declining health took their toll, and he died on 26 March 1921 at the age of 87. He was buried in the family cemetery off Hardin-Ellison Road between Franklinville and Gray's Chapel, along with his wife and three children. His obituary implied that he was a man of strong Christian character.

Private James Madison Hayes (1832–1922) enlisted in Company M on 6 March 1862. (Photograph courtesy of Johnnie Ingold.)

HART, JOHN

John Hart has not been identified, due to the sparse amount of information available on him. A record bearing the date July 1862 indicates that he was transferred from Company M, 22nd Regiment at Richmond, Va., on 1 July 1862. No further records of him with this company exist. A soldier by that name is listed with Company M, *21st* Regiment, and another with Company *A*, 22nd Regiment. There are John Harts listed with other companies who served in the same battles as the "Randolph Hornets." My feeling is that he may be one of the other men by that name who was erroneously listed in Company M, 22nd Regiment on some document, or he may have been transferred briefly to this company, and then back to his original unit, as is the case with a couple of other men.

HAYES, ELIAS W.

Elias W. Hayes was born about 1842 to Anthony and Tamer York Hayes. He resided in Randolph County where he enlisted at age 20 in Company M on 10

June 1861. He was captured by the enemy in an unspecified battle and was confined at Fort Monroe, Va., until being paroled and transferred to Aiken's Landing, James River, Va., where he was received 7 Sept. 1862 for exchange. He was declared exchanged at Aiken's Landing on 21 Sept. 1862. He was returned to duty on an unspecified date and was captured a second time, at or near Falling Waters, Md., on or about 14 July 1863. He was confined at Point Lookout, Md., until being paroled and transferred to City Point, Va., where he was received on 6 March 1864 for exchange. He was then returned to duty sometime before 1 Sept. 1864. He was paroled at Greensboro on 16 May 1865. He returned to Randolph County where county records indicate he was married to Poline Leonard on 11 March 1866. They were the parents of three known children and were still living in Randolph County in the Franklinville Township in 1870, but at some point moved to Tennessee. Elias W. Hayes died in Tennessee about 1902.

HAYES, JAMES MADISON

James Madison Hayes was born 10 June 1832 in Randolph County to Samuel and Elizabeth York Hayes. He resided at Cool Springs in Randolph County as a farmer and potter, and was married 20 Nov. 1855 to Kernelia Blanchet. He enlisted in Randolph County at age 28 on 6 March 1862 and was assigned to Company M. He was captured by the enemy in an unspecified battle and was confined at Fort Monroe, Va., until he was paroled and transferred to Aiken's Landing, James River, Va., where he was received on 7 Sept. 1862 for exchange. He was declared exchanged on 21 Sept. 1862. He returned to duty sometime after 31 Oct. 1862, and was captured a second time at Falling Waters, Md., on 14 July 1863. He was confined at Point Lookout, Md., until paroled and transferred to City Point, Va., where he was received 6 March 1864 for exchange. He returned to duty on an unspecified date, and was captured a third time, at or near Hatcher's Run, Va., 2 April 1865. He was confined at Hart's Island, New York Harbor, until he was released on 18 June 1865 after taking the Oath of Allegiance. Returning home, he moved to the New Salem area about 1869 and continued working as a potter. He was in attendance at the Confederate reunion held in Asheboro on 1 Sept. 1906, and was a member of Randolph Camp No. 1646, United Confederate Veterans. He died 1 May 1922 and was buried at Mt. Lebanon United Methodist cemetery in Randleman.

HAYES, OLIVER P.

Oliver P. Hayes was born 26 March 1837 in Randolph County to Samuel and Elizabeth York Hayes. He was married 12 Sept. 1857 to Lovey Jane Allred. He resided in Randolph County as a miller when he enlisted in Company M at age 23 on 10 June 1861. He was discharged on 5 Oct. 1862 by reason of "hemiplegia of left side," or palsy of the left side. Returning home to Randolph County, he was married a second time on 3 March 1863 to Mary Jennings. They made their home in the Cedar Falls area. He died 20 April 1894 and was buried at Cedar Falls United Methodist cemetery alongside his wife and two children who preceded him.

HAYES, S. G.

S. G. Hayes is listed in *Broadfoot's* as being a member of Company M. My research has not uncovered any records for such a person in Company M, and I have not found him in any other Randolph County unit. This leads me to believe that one of the other Hayes names was misread, or a person by that name had a record incorrectly marked as "Co. M, 22nd Regiment."

HAYES, THOMAS B.

Thomas B. Hayes was born about 1842 to John and Sarah Hayes. He resided in Randolph County and enlisted there in Company M at age 19 on 10 June 1861. He was mustered in as a private and was promoted to sergeant sometime between November 1862 and August 1864. He was paroled at Greensboro on 17 May 1865 and returned to Randolph County. County marriage records show that he was married 5 March 1866 to Susan A. Baldwin.

HAYES, WILLIAM A.

William A. Hayes was born about 1846 in Randolph County to William and Nancy Johnson Hayes. He resided as a farmer when he enlisted there at age 16 on 6 March 1862 as a substitute, and was assigned to Company M. He served until 28–30 Aug. 1862, when he was killed at the second battle of Manassas, Va.

HAYES, WILLIAM FRANKLIN

William Franklin Hayes was born 19 Sept. 1835 to John and Sarah Hayes. He resided in Randolph County where he enlisted at age 25 in Company M on 10 June 1861. He was mustered in as a private. He was wounded in the right arm at Frayser's Farm, Va., 30 June 1862. He returned to duty on an unspecified date and was promoted to sergeant sometime between August 1862 and August 1864. He was paroled at Greensboro on 13 May 1865. He returned to Randolph County and was married 6 April 1866 to Margaret Isabella Williams. They resided in the Soapstone Mountain area and drew a Confederate pension. He died 30 Jan. 1916 at the home of his son in Cedar Falls. He was buried at Shady Grove Baptist cemetery. Sgt. John Turner recalled that he and Sgt. Hayes were "raised as boys together and taught by the same teacher in the same log cabin. As a soldier Mr. Hayes was as good as Lee and Jackson had under them in Virginia and did his duty as one. The writer was in some twenty odd battles with him."

HENSON, JOSEPH ALSON

Joseph Alson Henson was born 26 Dec. 1837 in Randolph County to unknown parentage. He resided as a farmer prior to enlisting in Company M in Randolph County at age 24 on 6 March 1862. He spent about a year and a half working as a teamster, driving the wagons of the regiment. He then came back to the company. He was wounded at Chancellorsville, Va., 1–3 May 1863, and was later taken prisoner at Falling Waters, Md., during the retreat from Gettysburg,

Pa. He was exchanged the following winter and returned to his command at Orange Court House, Va. He remained with Company M until being captured a second time at or near Hatcher's Run, Va., on 2 April 1865. He was then confined at Hart's Island, New York Harbor, until released on 18 June 1865 after taking the Oath of Allegiance. He returned home to Randolph County and was married to Sarah Angeline Pugh on 9 May 1867. She died in 1884, and several years later he remarried to Susan F. Burrow, who died in 1900. They are both buried at Cedar Falls United Methodist cemetery. Joseph attended the Confederate reunion in Asheboro 1 Sept. 1906 and was a charter member of Randolph Camp No. 1646 United Confederate Veterans. He was a member at Pleasant Cross Christian Church and lived until 29 June 1916. He was buried, at his request, at Bailey's Grove cemetery in North Asheboro.

HICKS, JAMES RILEY

The James R. Hix listed in the *North Carolina Troops* series is thought to be James Riley Hicks, born about 1828, probably in Randolph County to Jesse and Ruth McDaniel Hicks. He was married on 10 March 1851 to Mary Routh. He, his wife Mary and a young son, John W. S. Hicks resided in Randolph County when he enlisted there in Company M at age 33 on 10 June 1861. Records indicate that he died in a hospital at Richmond, Va., on either 27 June or 8 July 1862 of "diarrhoea."

HOLDER, LEWIS FRANKLIN

Lewis Franklin Holder was born 9 Feb. 1836, probably in Randolph County to Branson and Rebecca Caviness Holder. He may have been married in Randolph County to Sarah J. Holder on 2 Aug. 1857. He resided in Randolph County when he enlisted at age 25 in Company M on 10 June 1861. He was wounded at Seven Pines, Va., on 31 May 1862. He was reported absent without leave in September 1862 and was reported absent wounded in October 1862. The Roll of Honor states that he "deserted twice." Pension records show that he was captured at Chancellorsville, Va., in 1863, and returned home from prison in late 1864. No further military records. He was married 6 July 1865 to Lucinda (or Lousinda) Turner. They resided in the Staley area until his death on 22 Jan. 1885. He was buried at Shady Grove Baptist cemetery. His wife, Lucinda, was still living and was drawing a Confederate pension in 1909.

HULIN, NELSON KENNY

Nelson Kenny Hulin was born 25 September 1830, probably in Davidson County, to Hiram and Nancy Sexton Hulin. By 1850 his family was living in Montgomery County where he was married to Clarinda S. Crook on 15 January 1855. He resided in Montgomery County when he enlisted at Camp Holmes on 5 April 1864 for the war and was assigned to Company M. He was dropped from the company rolls on 8 July 1864 for reasons that were not reported. In January of 1865, three of his brothers, Jesse, John and William, were captured by

Confederate and Home Guard troops who were looking for outliers. They were imprisoned in Beans' Mill on Barns' Creek in Montgomery County, tried in a meeting held without their presence, and sentenced to death. The following morning, on 28 January 1865, they were marched about two miles to a place near Buck Mountain where they were lined up and shot. A messenger was sent to their family to tell them where to find the bodies. The family buried them in the Lovejoy Methodist Church cemetery. Nelson and his family moved to Brinkley, Calloway County, Kentucky, after the war, probably because much of Clarinda's family had moved there years before. They are found in the 1880 Census there, with Nelson erroneously listed as Wilson K. Hulin. He is shown with wife, Clarinda S. Hulin, and three children, all born in North Carolina: Emeline C., Linnie L. and Frank J. Hulin. There may have been other children. Nelson K. Hulin died 18 October 1895 and was buried in Trinity Cemetery, Graves County, Kentucky.

HUTSON, HENRY M.

It is difficult to identify this person, although I believe this may be the Henry Hutson listed in the Guilford County 1860 Census who was born about 1838 and was married in Guilford County on 2 April 1859 to Susan Morris. Henry M. Hutson enlisted at Camp Holmes on 1 May 1864 for the war. He was paroled at Greensboro on 11 May 1865.

IVEY, STEPHEN W.

Stephen W. Ivey was born 17 May 1826 in Richmond County and came to Randolph County around 1849–50. He was married 3 Nov. 1850 to Mary H. "Polly" York. He farmed in Randolph County until enlisting in Company M at its organization on 10 June 1861. He was discharged on 13 June 1862 by reason of being over age, at age 36. He later enlisted in 2nd Company B, 36th Regiment N.C. Troops on 29 Jan. 1863 for the war. He was present or accounted for through June 1863 when he was hospitalized. He died 24 July 1863, probably at a military hospital in Goldsboro, and is buried at Sandy Creek Baptist cemetery. His wife lived until 5 Dec. 1908.

JACKSON, JOHN

John Jackson was born about 1825 and was a resident of Moore County when he enlisted at age 38 on 13 March 1863 for the war, and was assigned to Company M. He was killed in an unspecified battle on 15 July 1863, probably in the retreat at Falling Waters, Md.

JAMES, M. R.

M. R. James is thought to be a misreading of the name Mountainville T. Jones (see entry). The only James living in Randolph County at that time who would remotely fit the description was a Marshal James, living near Asheborough, who would have been about age 38 or 39 years when the company was raised on 10 June 1861. The age of M. R. James was reported as 24, which would fit Mountainville T. Jones.

JENNINGS, PETER

Peter Jennings was born about 1841 in Randolph County to David and Mary Allred Jennings. He resided in Randolph County and enlisted there at age 20 in Company M on 10 June 1861. He died at Richmond, Va., on or about 15 June 1862 of unreported causes.

JOHNSON, JAMES

This soldier has not been identified at this writing. He may have been from Montgomery County. The place and date of his enlistment were not reported. He deserted to the enemy on or about 1 April 1865 and was confined at Washington, D.C., until he was released on or about 12 April 1865.

JOHNSON, WILLIS

Willis Johnson was born about 1842 and resided in Randolph County. In the 1850 and 1860 censuses he is shown living in the same household with Peter and Nancy Richardson. Nancy may have been his mother, older sister or other relative, because marriage records show Peter Richardson married to Nancy *Johnson* in Randolph County in 1850. Willis enlisted at age 19 in Company M on 10 June 1861. He died at Dumfries, Va., on either 17 or 31 Oct. 1861. The cause of death was not reported; however, during this period of time the regiment experienced an outbreak of measles, so this is the probable cause.

JONES, CRAVEN

Craven Jones was most likely from Lenoir County or the former Dobbs County. He enlisted at Camp Holmes on 2 July 1864 for the war. He was present or accounted for through 14 Nov. 1864.

JONES, MOUNTAINVILLE T.

Mountainville T. Jones was probably erroneously listed as M. R. James. Mountainville T. Jones was born 3 Dec. 1832 to Lewis and Elizabeth Jones. He was a resident of Randolph County when he enlisted in Company M on 10 June 1861, and was mustered in as 4th corporal. He was married to Mary C. Allred six days later while still encamped at Joshua Bain's farm near Liberty on 16 June 1861. He was discharged on 1 August 1861 for unreported reasons, and returned to his work as a blacksmith. In 1880 he was living in the Franklinville area next door to another member of Company M, William G. Stout, who was also a blacksmith. He remained in the Franklinville area until his death on 2 December 1891, and was buried at Franklinville United Methodist cemetery. His wife lived until 1934 and was buried there also.

JONES, WILLIAM C.

William C. Jones was born about 1840 in Randolph County and was probably the son of A. H. and Bethania Jones. He resided as a blacksmith prior to enlisting there at age 22 on 6 March 1862. He was assigned to Company M and mustered in as a private. He was promoted to corporal sometime during the period of October 1862 to June 1864. He was wounded in the left hand at Wilderness, Va., 5 May 1864. He was reported absent wounded until 30 Oct. 1864, when he was reported absent without leave. It is unclear whether he was married. The 1860 Census shows him in his parents' household at age 21 with possibly a wife or sister named Mary at age 18. He is not found in the 1870 Census, but there is a Mary Jones, age 34, with son William C. Jones, age 9.

KIME, W. C.

W. C. Kime is listed in *Broadfoot's* as being a member of Company M. There is no one by that name in the area who would have served in Company M. This is thought to be a misreading of "Kinne" or Kinney, and is probably the same person as Wesley Kinney of this company (see entry).

KINNEY, GEORGE

George Kinney was born about 1818 in Orange County. He was married in Randolph County on 28 Dec. 1839 to Ruth McMasters. They resided in Randolph County when he enlisted in Company M at age 43 on 10 June 1861. Records show that he died in a hospital at Petersburg, Va., on or about 20 April 1862 of pneumonia.

KINNEY, WESLEY

Wesley Kinney was born about 1829 in Orange or Randolph County. He resided in Randolph County as a farmer when he enlisted at age 33 on 6 March 1862, and was assigned to Company M. Company records indicate he died on either 7 August or 20 November 1862, but do not disclose the place and cause of death.

KIVETT, ALFRED W.

Alfred W. Kivett was born about 1838–39 in Randolph County to Eli and Anna Scotton Kivett. He was a Randolph County farmer when he enlisted there at age 22 in Company M on 10 June 1861. He served in this company in sixteen battles before being captured at or near Falling Waters, Md., on or about 14 July 1863. He was confined at Point Lookout, Md., until being released on 25 Jan. 1864 after taking the Oath of Allegiance and joining the U.S. Army. He was assigned to Company G, 1st Regiment U.S. Volunteer Infantry. Nothing further is known of him after that time. He may have gone west or he could have died in U.S. service during the remainder of the war.

KIVETT, DANIEL M.

Daniel M. Kivett was born about 1839 in Randolph County to Daniel David and Dolly Graves Kivett, and was a brother of Stanley Kivett of this company. He resided there as a farmer when he enlisted at age 22 on 6 March 1862 and was assigned to Company M. He died at Ashland, Va., either on 18 April or 6 May 1862 of unreported causes. On 18 May 1862, his brother Stanley wrote a letter home mentioning his death, and his hopes of someone coming to get the body. This letter is reprinted in its entirety elsewhere in this volume.

KIVETT, JACOB

Jacob Kivett was born about 1835–36, probably to John Alfred and Sarah "Sally" Richardson Kivett. He was a resident in the Mt. Pleasant area of Randolph County when he enlisted at age 27 in Company M, on 10 June 1861. He died less than a year later, on or about 18 May 1862, in a hospital in Richmond, Va., of typhoid fever. He was buried at Oakwood Cemetery in Richmond.

KIVETT, JAMES FRANKLIN

James Franklin Kivett was born 27 Dec. 1845 in Randolph County to Alfred Washington and Margaret Williams Kivett. Known as "Sharpe" to some friends and family, he was a farmer when he enlisted in Company M in Randolph County at age 16 on 10 June 1861. He served until 15 June 1862, when he was discharged by reason of being underage. He returned to Randolph County and was married on 12 Oct. 1866 to Rachel Isabel McDaniel. Rachel died on 28 November 1883 and was buried next to their two-year-old daughter at Mt. Pleasant Baptist Church. County records show a second marriage to Sarah Ellen Hobson on 1 Jan. 1885. He died 1 Oct. 1917 and was buried at Shady Grove Baptist cemetery, near Staley. Sarah survived until 1922 and is also buried there.

KIVETT, JAMES MURDICK

James Murdick Kivett was born about 1829–30 to Eli and Anna Scotton Kivett. He is believed to have married in 1858 to Lydia Belinda _____. They resided in Randolph County where he enlisted in Company M at age 31 on 10 June 1861. He died at Camp Holmes on 3 Oct. 1861 of typhoid fever, and became the first member of Company M to die during the war. He is buried at McMasters cemetery near Liberty, as indicated by a marker there.

KIVETT, JOEL A.

Joel A. Kivett was born 17 April 1841 to Eli and Anna Scotton Kivett in Randolph County. He enlisted in Company M at its organization on 10 June 1861 at age 20. Company records show that he was court-martialed on or about 18 Feb. 1863 for unreported reasons. He was captured at Gettysburg, Pa., 3–5 July 1863 and confined at Fort Delaware, Del., until released on 11 May 1865 after taking the Oath of Allegiance.

Joel was married in Randolph County on 24 Oct. 1869 to Nancy A. York. They were members of Mt. Pleasant Baptist Church, where he was a deacon for 50 years. Joel A. Kivett died 31 Dec. 1928, and is buried at Mt. Pleasant Baptist cemetery, near Liberty.

KIVETT, JOHN W., JR.

John W. Kivett, Jr., was born about 1837 probably to John Alfred and Sarah "Sally" Richardson Kivett. He resided in Randolph County in the Mt. Pleasant area when he enlisted in Company M at age 24 on 10 June 1861. He served until being captured at Falling Waters, Md., on 14 July 1863. He was confined at Point Lookout, Md., where he died on 8 April 1864 of "chronic diarrhoea." He was buried at Point Lookout Prison Cemetery, Scotland, Md.

KIVETT, JOHN WESLEY, SR.

John Wesley Kivett, Sr., was born about 1835 in Randolph County to Leander A. and Lucady Williams Kivett. He was married in Randolph County to Mary Jane Kirkman on 3 Feb. 1854 and resided there when he enlisted in Company M at age 26 on 10 June 1861. He served in this company until he was killed at Gaines' Mill, Va., on or about 27 June 1862. Mary Jane apparently remarried on 23 October 1863 to Zimeriah Nathanial Williams.

KIVETT, KENNETH M.

Kenneth M. Kivett was born about 1836 to Eli and Anna Scotton Kivett. He resided in Randolph County when he enlisted at age 25 in Company M, on 10 June 1861. He died in a hospital at Richmond, Va., on or about 15 June 1862 of "bronchitis." He was buried in the Oakwood Confederate Cemetery in Richmond, but a marker has been placed in the McMasters cemetery in Randolph County, raising the possibility that his remains may have been moved there at a later date, or that a memorial marker was simply placed there in remembrance of him.

KIVETT, PETER P.

Peter P. Kivett is known to have served in the 22nd Regiment, but no records have been found indicating what company he was in. Since his brothers and other relatives were in Company M, it is reasonable to assume he probably served in Company M. He was born about 1846 in Randolph County to Eli and Anna Scotton Kivett, and resided in Randolph County. The place and date of his enlistment were not reported. He deserted to the enemy on or about 12 March 1864. He was confined at Washington, D.C., until being released on or about 17 March 1864 after taking the Oath of Allegiance. There is a possibility that he may have afterwards served in Company A, 69th Pennsylvania Infantry. According to census records, Peter's wife was named Mary or May, and was born about 1840 in North Carolina. They had three children, the last of which was born in 1870 in Illinois.

KIVETT, STANLEY

Stanley Kivett was born 11 April 1833 in Randolph County to Daniel David and Dolly Graves Kivett. His family and friends knew Stanley affectionately as "Sug" Kivett. He enlisted in Company M on or about 15 Oct. 1861. According to his pension application, he was wounded at Seven Pines, Va., 31 May 1862. This was just after he had written a letter home on 18 May 1862 lamenting his brother Daniel's death, and suggesting that a hard battle was ahead of him (this letter is reprinted elsewhere in this volume). He was reported absent without leave in July and September of 1862 and was probably still recovering from his wounds. There is no further information on his service until he was paroled at Greensboro on 11 May 1865. After the war he was married in Randolph County on 6 July 1865 to Mary Wrightman. He applied for a Confederate pension and lived in the Liberty area. He died 18 Oct. 1901, and is buried at Mt. Pleasant Baptist cemetery.

KIVETT, TALTON

Talton Kivett was born about 1840 to Nathan P. and Frances Reese Kivett. He resided in Randolph County when he enlisted at age 21 in Company M on 10 June 1861. He was reported absent without leave in September 1862 and listed as a deserter in October of that year. He returned to duty on an unspecified date and was wounded at Chancellorsville, Va., 1–3 May 1863. Records say that he "gave himself up voluntarily" and was captured by the enemy at Wilderness, Va., 5–6 May 1864. He was confined at Point Lookout, Md., until being transferred to Elmira, N.Y., on 10 Aug. 1864. He died at Elmira on 16 March 1865 of "variola," otherwise known as smallpox.

Private Stanley "Sug" Kivett (1833–1901) enlisted in Company M on 15 October 1861. (Photograph courtesy of Rick Kivett and Tim Kivett.)

KIVETT, TROY THOMAS

Troy Thomas Kivett was born 20 Oct. 1842 in Randolph County to John Aldridge and Mary Welborn Kivett, and was a brother of Captain Warren B. Kivett of this company. He enlisted in Company M at its organization on 10 June 1861 at age 20. He deserted on or about 5 Aug. 1862. The Roll of Honor indicates that he deserted five times. He was married to Martha Caroline Kirkman in Randolph County on 11 Nov. 1865. Troy Thomas Kivett died on 3 February 1898 and was buried at Sandy Creek Baptist Church cemetery. Martha survived until 26 January 1924, and was also buried at Sandy Creek.

LANE, JOHN C.

John C. Lane was born about 1817 in Randolph County to _____ and Rebecca Lane. By 1860 he was living in the household of Peter Richardson. He resided in Randolph County as a farmer when he enlisted in Company M at age 44 on 10 June 1861. He was reportedly discharged on 13 June 1862 by reason of being over age. However, the Roll of Honor indicates that he died on 17 Sept. 1862. The place and cause of death were not reported, but this is the date of the battle at Sharpsburg, Maryland.

LANGLEY, BARTLEY YANCEY

Bartley Yancey Langley was born about 1824, probably to William and Mary Langley. He resided in Randolph County when he enlisted there at age 36 in Company M on 10 June 1861. He was reported absent wounded in October 1862. The place and date of his wound were not reported, but this was just after the battle at Shepherdstown Ford, Va., on 20 Sept. 1862. He was wounded a second time at Fredericksburg, Va., 13 Dec. 1862. He was listed as a deserter on 15 April 1864, but returned to duty on an unspecified date. He was captured at the Appomattox River, Va., on 3 April 1865 and confined at Hart's Island, New York Harbor, until being released on or about 20 June 1865 after taking the Oath of Allegiance.

He returned home to Randolph County and was married there on 15 Oct. 1867 to Delphina Marley. They were living in the New Salem township in Randolph County at the time of the 1880 Census.

LANGLEY, EDWARD TYSON

Edward Tyson "Tise" Langley was born 3 Jan. 1839 in Randolph County to Zimri and Nancy Warren Langley. He lived there as a farmer when he enlisted at age 20 in Company M on 10 June 1861. He was wounded in the right hand at or near Frayser's Farm, Va., on or about 30 June 1862. His pension application says that he was actually wounded at Malvern Hill, Va. His right forearm was amputated, and he was discharged on 30 July 1862 by reason of disability. He returned to his home in Randolph County and was married on 3 Sept. 1863 to Elizabeth M. "Louisa" Kivett. They lived in the Staley area and were the parents of 15 children. Louisa died in 1899, and Tise reportedly remarried to Jenny Edwards, with whom he had three more children. Tise farmed while also drawing a Confederate pension. Sgt. John Turner of Company M stated, "Since the close of the war to the time of his death, Mr. Langley followed farming and made a good living with only one hand, while there are some who can't do as well with two. While with our company he was a good soldier and did not shirk his work, and in after years he showed the same disposition." Edward Tyson Langley died 1 Nov. 1911, and was buried alongside his first wife at Shady Grove Baptist cemetery, near Staley.

LAUGHLIN, N. G.

N. G. Laughlin is listed in *Moore's Roster* as being a member of Company M, having enlisted 10 June 1861 at the formation of the company. He may have been reassigned to another unit after the reorganization of the company, or this may be a misreading of William T. Laughlin, since the enlistment date is the same.

LAUGHLIN, WILLIAM T.

William T. Laughlin was born 19 Dec. 1842 in Randolph County to Hugh and Mahala Hinshaw Laughlin. He resided in Randolph County and was employed as a carder when he enlisted in Company M at the organization of the company on 10 June 1861. He was discharged 2 Feb. 1862 by reason of disability. He came home to Randolph County and died 19 April 1862. He was buried at Mount Lebanon United Methodist cemetery in Randleman.

LINGLE, WILLIAM ALFRED

William Alfred Lingle was a farmer from Caldwell County, probably the son of John and Sarah Turnmire Lingle, who enlisted there in Company A 22nd Regiment at age 24 on 30 April 1861. He was transferred to Company M sometime after 31 Aug. 1861, and transferred back to Company A on 1 July 1862. He was reported absent wounded in July 1862, place and date of wound not reported. This was probably the wound he reported on his pension application in which a ball entered his hip and lodged in his back. He returned to duty by 13 Dec. 1862. He was wounded in the right arm at Fredericksburg, severing his arm just below the shoulder. He reported that he was hospitalized for about three months. He was discharged 16 April 1863. He was living in the Hudson community of Caldwell County when he applied for his Confederate pension on 17 July 1911.

LOVE (LOWE), W. E.

W. E. Love is listed in *Moore's Roster* as having enlisted in Company M on 6 March 1862. This is probably the same person as James P. Lowe, listed in the *N.C. Troops* series.

LOWE, JAMES P.

James P. Lowe is believed to have been born about 1847 or 1848, probably to James and Elizabeth Warren Lowe, or possibly to William and Grace Lowe. He resided in Randolph County as a farmer when he enlisted there and was assigned to Company M on 6 March 1862. He probably would have been about age 14 or 15. He served less than two months and died at Ashland, Va., on either 26 April or 6 May 1862 of unreported causes. According to Sergeant John Turner, several men from Company M were left behind at Ashland during this period of time with the measles. His death occurred while Company M was engaged in the Yorktown Siege in Virginia.

MCDANIEL, ANDERSON GREEN

Though the previous rosters give his age at enlistment as 36, Anderson Green McDaniel was born about 1836 in Randolph County to Zale and Mary Kivett McDaniel. His actual age would have been about 26 at enlistment.

He was living in Randolph County when he enlisted in Company M at its organization on 10 June 1861. He served until being reported as absent without leave in September 1862, and was listed as a deserter in October of 1862. The Roll of Honor indicates that he deserted twice during his service. He was paroled at Greensboro on 10 May 1865. He is shown living in Washington City, Daviess County, Indiana in the 1880 Census.

McLemore, Calvin D.

Calvin D. McLemore was born about 1839 in Moore County to John R. and Margaret McLemore. He resided in Moore County near Carthage as a farmer when he enlisted there on 13 March 1862 at age 22 in Company H, 46th Regiment N.C. Troops. In July of that year he was reported absent with the notation that he had failed to report for duty. He was dropped from the rolls sometime before 1 September 1862. He then enlisted a second time at Raleigh on 13 March 1863 at age 24 for the war, and was assigned to Company M, 22nd Regiment. He must have served in battle at some point, because he is named on the Roll of Honor, but he deserted on an unspecified date. His brothers also served the Confederate Army in other units. Stories have been passed down through the family and are confirmed by records about how the brothers were captured and imprisoned at Elmira, although no record is found there for Calvin. Most of the family seems to have moved to South Carolina in later years, some living near McColl.

McNeill, William

William McNeill was born 12 January 1824 and was married in Moore County on 30 November 1854 to Mahala L. Sheppard. He resided in Moore County when he enlisted at age 39 on 13 March 1863 for the war. He died on 9 March 1894 and was buried at Buffalo Cemetery, Sanford, Lee County. Mahala applied for a widow's pension on 30 June 1908 and was living in Sanford at the time of her application.

Maness, A.

Listed in *Moore's Roster* as A. Manis, there is not enough information available to identify this man with any certainty. He resided in Moore County and was one of seven men from there who enlisted on 13 March 1863 for the war. He deserted on an unspecified date.

Miller, E. P., Jr.

E. P. Miller, Jr., was born about 1842 in Caldwell County. He enlisted there at age 19 in Company A, 22nd Regiment on 30 April 1861. He was transferred to Company M sometime after 31 August 1861. He was wounded at Seven Pines, Va., on 31 May 1862. He was then transferred back to Company A sometime in July 1862. In September 1862 he was listed as absent without leave, but returned to duty by 3–5 July 1863, when he was wounded and captured at Gettysburg, Pa. He was then confined at Fort Delaware, Del., until transferred to Point Lookout, Md., 15–18 Oct. 1863. He was paroled and transferred to Boulware's and Cox's wharves, James River, Va., on 18 Feb. 1865 for exchange. He was reported present with a detachment of paroled and exchanged prisoners at Camp Lee, near Richmond, Va., on 23 Feb. 1865.

He was married at some point, because his widow, Sue Miller, applied for a Confederate pension on 5 July 1922 and was living in Lenoir, Caldwell County.

ODA, JAMES

This soldier's enlistment date and place were not reported. He was captured at or near Boonsboro, Maryland, on or about 16 September 1862, just after the battle at Harper's Ferry. He was confined at Fort Delaware, Delaware, until being transferred to Aiken's Landing, James River, Virginia, on 2 October 1862 for exchange. He was declared exchanged at Aiken's Landing on 10 November 1862.

With the limited information available, it is nearly impossible to positively identify this soldier. No one with the last name Oda is found in any census or other record anywhere in the vicinity of Company M. Having enlisted early in the war, during the period of time when all the men of Company M were enlisted in Randolph County and from the Sandy Creek area, he almost had to be from the same area as all the other men. It seems likely that the name is misspelled. My research has uncovered two possible candidates for this soldier who seem to best fit this scenario: James Alexander Odell and James Madison Odell.

James Alexander Odell was a brother of John Milton and Laban D. Odell of this company. He was born 4 November 1841 to James and Anna Trogdon Odell. He attended Middleton Academy near Cedar Falls, and subsequently taught school for a time, as did his brothers. He was married about 1865 to Mary J. Prescott and that same year went into business as a merchant. His business was moved to High Point in 1868, then to Greensboro in 1872. The business prospered and was organized as Odell Hardware Company in 1884. He also organized the first cotton mill in Durham and was involved in several other textile businesses including Odell Manufacturing Co., Kerr Bag Manufacturing Co. and J. M. Odell Manufacturing Company. Mary Prescott Odell died 26 December 1918. James Alexander Odell died 10 February 1930 in Greensboro and was buried at Green Hill Cemetery in Greensboro. They had no children.

James Madison Odell, the son of William Bedouin, Sr., and Elizabeth Forrester Odell, was also the nephew of John Milton and Laban Odell of this company. He was born 26 August 1842 in Randolph County. His family moved west sometime before the war, but it is possible he stayed behind with his grandparents and other relatives for a time or went back to visit about the time of the war. He was married on 26 October 1865 in Iowa to Rebecca Condra. He died in May, Oklahoma, on 10 May 1923.

Captain John Milton Odell was defeated for reelection and left the army due to poor health in April 1862, but came home to become superintendent of the Cedar Falls Mill. Men were generally not allowed to leave the army due only to health reasons, and his health did not appear to be so deteriorated that he could not run the mill operations. At that time during the war a soldier could, however, pay a sum of money to hire a substitute to take his place. James Oda apparently enlisted about the same period of time when Captain Odell came home. The preponderance of evidence seems to show that either James Alexander Odell or James Madison Odell joined Company M, possibly as a substitute for their relative John Milton Odell.

O'DEAR, WILLIAM

William O'Dear was born about 1826, possibly in North Carolina. The 1860 Census shows him residing in southwest Granville County in the Dutchville Township as a farmer with his wife Nancy and four children. He enlisted at age 38 on 13 March 1863 for the war, and was assigned to Company M. He served until late October or early November 1864, when he went home on furlough due to sickness. His wife reports on her application for a Confederate pension that he died seventeen days after he came home, on 21 November 1864. She was still living in Granville County in the Creedmore community when she applied for the pension on 7 July 1902.

OSELEY, W. A.

This name, listed in the *N.C. Troops* series, is believed to be the same person as William August Woosley of this company (see entry).

PEN, ALVENS

Alvens Pen is listed in the *N.C. Troops* series as a member of this company, but after researching the records, I believe his name was misread, and he is presumed to be the same person as Alpheus Pugh (see entry) of this company.

PERRY, D.

D. Perry is listed in *Broadfoot's* as having been a member of Company M. This is probably a misreading of James Perry (see entry) of this company.

PERRY, JAMES

James Perry cannot be identified with the sparse amount of information available. Several James Perrys are found who could fit his identity, especially in Chatham and Orange counties. He enlisted at Camp Holmes on 2 September 1863 for the war, and apparently served in Virginia through the Bristoe and Mine Run campaigns, the Wilderness, Spotsylvania Court House, North Anna and Cold Harbor. He died on 20 July 1864 during the Petersburg Siege, but the place and cause of death were not reported.

POUNDS, J. L.

J. L. Pounds is listed as having drawn a Confederate pension for service in Company M. He is thought to be the same person as 2nd Lieut. James M. Pounds of this company (see entry under "Lieutenants").

POUNDS, WILLIAM A.

William A. Pounds was born about 1842 in Chatham County to Archibald T. and Mourning Lowe Pounds. He was a brother to Lt. James M. Pounds of this company. He worked at the cotton factory in Cedar Falls prior to enlisting at age 18 on 10 June 1861 when Company M was organized. He was mustered in as 5th sergeant. He was captured at Fredericksburg, Va., on 13 Dec. 1862 and exchanged on 17 Dec. 1862. Returning to his company, he was once again captured at Falling Waters, Md., on 14 July 1863. He was then confined to Point Lookout, Md., until being released on 4 Feb. 1864 after taking the Oath of Allegiance and joining the U.S. Army. There, he was assigned to Company D, 1st Regiment U.S. Volunteer Infantry.

PUGH, ALPHEUS "ALVIN"

Alpheus "Alvin" Pugh was born about 1835 in Randolph County to William and Sarah Pugh. He was married in Randolph County 17 Jan. 1858 to Sarah Fields, and resided there as a farmer. He enlisted at age 26 in Randolph County on 6 March 1862 and was assigned to Company M. He was wounded and captured at Seven Pines, Va., on 1 June 1862 during a charge on the enemy breastworks. He died in the Chesapeake Hospital at Fortress Monroe, Va., on 1 July 1862 of wounds.

PULLEY, DANIEL P.

Daniel P. Pulley was born 13 Aug. 1845 in Surry County, Va., to John and Mary Ann Fuller Pulley. By the time the war began, he was residing in Granville County as a farmer. He enlisted at Camp Holmes on 1 July 1864 for the war and was assigned to Company M. A brother, Thomas Mark Pulley, also served, in Company G 47th Regiment. Daniel served with Company M in Virginia through the Petersburg Siege, and the battles at Reams' Station, Fort Harrison, Jones' Farm and Hatcher's Run. He was captured at the Appomattox River on 3 April 1865, just a few days before the surrender. He was then confined at Hart's Island, New York Harbor, until being released on 19 June 1865 after taking the Oath of Allegiance.

Daniel returned home to Granville County and was married there on 10 Dec. 1867 to Lina Fitts. They farmed and raised a family of nine children. At some point Daniel moved his family to Vance County where he remained until his death on 17 June 1931. He was buried there at the Oak Ridge Baptist Church cemetery.

RAINES, MARSHALL S.

Marshall S. Raines was born about 1842–43 in Randolph County but his parentage has not been established. In 1850 he is shown in the census as being 8 years old, and living in the home of a John and Margaret Staley. In 1860 he is listed as 17 years of age. He resided in Randolph County as a farmer when he enlisted at age 19 in Company M on 10 June 1861. He was wounded in the foot at the second battle of Manassas, Va., on 30 August 1862. He returned to duty on an unreported date, and was later captured at or near Gettysburg, Pa., 3–5 July 1863. He was then confined at Fort Delaware, Del., until being transferred to Point Lookout, Md., sometime between 15–18 October 1863. He was released on 26 January 1864 after joining the U.S. Army. He was assigned to Company B, 1st Regiment U.S. Volunteer Infantry.

REECE, JOSEPH M. D.

Joseph M. D. Reece was born 3 March 1845 in Randolph County to Joseph L. and Esther Caudle Reece. He resided in Randolph County as a farmer when he enlisted there on 4 Jan. 1862. He was assigned to Company M, where his brother was already serving. He was wounded at Seven Pines, Va., on 31 May 1862. He was discharged 15 June 1862, by reason of being under age, on the same day his brother died. His discharge certificate gives his age as 17. He returned to Randolph County to live. He died 5 April 1865 and was buried at Sandy Creek Baptist cemetery. The *Randolph County Cemetery Records* indicate that he was "Killed at Buffalo Ford." According to some family members, he was hanged for taking part in the "outlier" activity in the area.

REECE, WILLIAM D.

William D. Reece was born 8 March 1826 in Randolph County probably to Joseph L. and Esther Caudle Reece. He was married 1 July 1847 in Guilford County to Eleanor Armfield. He was living in Randolph County when he enlisted in Company M at age 35 on 10 June 1861, when the company was organized. According to the *N.C. Troops* series, he died at or near Jamestown, Va., on or about 15 June 1862. However, his wife's Confederate pension listed her as a resident of Ramseur, and states that he died of disease in Randolph County on 21 June 1862. He probably left the army sick and died at home. It is known that he is buried at Sandy Creek Baptist cemetery in Randolph County.

ROBBINS, S. M.

It is believed that this is a misreading of the name James M. Robbins (see entry under "Lieutenants"). The scant information given—that he resided in Randolph County enlisted at age 21 on 6 March 1862, and was wounded in an unspecified battle—matches that of James Robbins. Also, considering the early date of his enlistment, *Moore's Roster* only lists James M. Robbins, who began his career as a private and was promoted to 2nd lieutenant. The only other possible match that I have been able to find is a John Madison Robbins, born 9 November 1839 in Randolph County to John and Margaret Swaim Robbins, and brother to lawyer Marmaduke Swaim Robbins. He was a schoolteacher, living in the same area as many of the other men in the company, and had a brother, William Thomas Robbins, in this same company. He was married to Nettie Newby and is buried in San Diego, Calif.

My feeling is that this soldier is 2nd Lt. James M. Robbins, but I will leave it to the readers to decide.

ROBBINS, WILLIAM THOMAS

William Thomas Robbins was born 27 November 1842 in Guilford County to John and Margaret Swaim Robbins. He enlisted in Company M in Randolph County on 6 March 1862 at age 18. He served as a private in this company until he was wounded in the thigh at Chancellorsville, 1–4 May 1863. His leg was later amputated, and he died in a hospital in Richmond, Va., on 23 July 1863. He is buried at Gray's Chapel United Methodist cemetery, according to the records of a grandniece that joined the United Daughters of the Confederacy under his name.

ROUTH, AARON

Aaron Routh was born in 1844 in Randolph County to John and Nancy Hayes Routh. He resided in Randolph County as a farmer when he enlisted there at age 17 on 6 March 1862 as a substitute and was assigned to Company M. He was discharged on 3 September 1862 by reason of "rheumatism affecting the muscles of the spine and completely distorting the body."

ROUTH, GEORGE E.

George E. Routh was born about 1844 in Randolph County to Moses and Elizabeth Reitzel Routh. He was a farmer there when he enlisted at age 17 in Company M on 10 June 1861. He died at Richmond, Va., 8 or 22 July 1862 of unreported causes.

ROUTH, JAMES M.

This soldier is believed to be the James Routh born about 1838 to Isaac and Lillie Cude Routh. If this is true, he was a brother of William Clay Routh of this company, and resided with his wife Dicy in Randolph County with their young son when he enlisted in Company M at its organization on 10 June 1861. He was mustered in as corporal, and served throughout the war until deserting to the enemy on or about 23 February 1865. He was then confined at Washington, D.C., until being released on or about 26 February 1865. He was living in Indiana in 1873.

ROUTH, JESSE

Jesse Routh was born about 1819 in Randolph County to Joshua and Elizabeth Turner Routh and was a brother of William Riley Routh of this company. He never married, and resided in the Gray's Chapel area as a farmer when he joined Company M at its organization on 10 June 1861 at age 40. He died about 30 April 1862 of unreported causes at Ashland, Va.

ROUTH, JOSEPH ALSON

Joseph Alson Routh was born 31 Aug. 1838 in Randolph County to Zachariah and Agnes Spoon Routh. He resided in Randolph County and enlisted there in Company M on 6 March 1862 at the age of 23. His brother, Joshua Marion Routh, had already served in this company nearly a year when he joined. Alson suffered a gunshot wound to the arm at the battle of Gaines' Mill and was hospitalized at Richmond, Va., on 30 June 1862. He was reported absent without leave from July through September and was listed as a deserter in October 1862. He was married 28 April 1865 to Pithia Jane Pugh. They continued to reside in Randolph County.

Joseph Alson Routh died 7 Jan. 1910 and is buried at Gray's Chapel United Methodist cemetery.

ROUTH, JOSHUA MARION

Private Joshua Marion Routh (1840–1898) enlisted in Company M on 10 June 1861. (Photograph courtesy of the Routh family.)

Joshua Marion Routh was born 16 March 1840 in Randolph County to Zachariah and Agnes Spoon Routh, and was a brother of Joseph Alson Routh of this company. His family lived about two miles east of Gray's Chapel along what is now Hwy. 49. A man of small stature, he is said to have weighed about ninety pounds when he enlisted in Company M on 10 June 1861 at the age of 21. He served with this company throughout the war until 20 Feb. 1865, when he deserted to the enemy. He was then confined at Washington, D.C., until being released on 27 Feb. 1865 after taking the Oath of Allegiance. The Roll of Honor indicates he deserted twice during his service.

After the war he returned home to Randolph County and was married on 27 Oct. 1866 to Hannah Sarah "Sally" Julian. They farmed on a large acreage near Gray's Chapel, eventually owning 600 acres of farmland and timber, and were the parents of seven children. Joshua Marion Routh's death came at age 58 on 12 June 1898. He is buried at Gray's Chapel United Methodist cemetery.

ROUTH, WESLEY P.

Wesley P. Routh was born about 1846 in Randolph County probably to Sally Routh, with whom he resided as a farmer when he enlisted in Randolph County at age 16 on 25 February 1862. He was assigned to Company M and served with the unit until his death at Ashland, Va., on 15 April 1862. Cause of death was not given; however, it was reported by Sergeant John Turner that several in the company were left at Ashland at this time with the measles.

ROUTH, WILLIAM CLAY

William Clay Routh was born 4 April 1835 and was the son of Isaac and Lillie Cude Routh. He is believed to be a brother of James M. Routh of this company. He was married 12 January 1858 to Rebecca H. Nelson. He resided in Randolph County when he enlisted in Company M at age 26 on 10 June 1861. He served throughout the war in Company M, until around 31 Dec. 1864, when he deserted to the enemy. He was confined at Washington, D.C., until he was released on or about 4 Jan. 1865 after taking the Oath of Allegiance. Returning to Randolph County, he worked as a potter and farmer. He drew a Confederate pension for disease and listed his address in 1909 as "Millboro." He was in attendance at the Confederate reunion held in Asheboro on 1 Sept. 1906. He died 16 March 1910, and is buried at Gray's Chapel United Methodist cemetery.

ROUTH, WILLIAM RILEY

William Riley Routh was born about 1824 in Randolph County to Joshua and Elizabeth Turner Routh, and was a brother of Jesse Routh of this company. He resided there as a farmer when he enlisted at age 37 in Company M at its organization on 10 June 1861. He served one year and was discharged on 13 June 1862 by reason of being over age. He returned home to Randolph County and was married there on 26 December 1862 to Emily Foust.

SCOTT, ENOCH P.

Enoch P. Scott was born about 1832 in Chatham County. By the time the war had begun he was residing in Randolph County as a farmer. He enlisted there at age 29 on 6 March 1862 and was assigned to Company M. He served until his death in a hospital in Richmond, Virginia, on or about 12 August 1862 of a fever.

SCOTTEN, JAMES MARSHALL

James Marshall Scotten was born 2 April 1843 in North Carolina, to Jacob and Lucy Scotten. He resided in Randolph County when he enlisted in Company M at its organization on 10 June 1861 at the age of 18. He served as a teamster during most of the war, and was paroled at Greensboro on 10 May 1865.

Returning to Randolph County, he was married on 19 Oct. 1865 to Mary A. Staley. Their marriage produced seven known children. Sometime before 1870, the young family moved to Missouri and made their permanent residence there.

James Marshall Scotten died 20 April 1922 in Missouri, and was buried in the Green Mound cemetery in Vernon, Missouri. Mary survived him until 22 December 1923 and was buried there as well.

SHOUSE, EDWIN THOMAS

Edwin Thomas Shouse was born 16 Sept. 1830 in Stokes County to Jacob and Catharina Geiger Shouse. At some point the family moved to neighboring Forsyth County and resided there when the war began. Edwin's brothers, James Leander and Eli Augustus, along with a cousin, Wiley, joined the army early in the war. Wiley was wounded and lost a foot, Eli served through Appomattox Court House, but James died, probably somewhere in Virginia, 9 Feb. 1863.

Because his civilian job was vital to the war effort, Edwin was not required to serve until late in the war. He was enlisted at Camp Holmes on 1 July 1864 for the war, and was assigned to Company M, 22nd Regiment. He served in Virginia through the Petersburg Siege, Reams' Station, Fort Harrison, Jones' Farm and Hatcher's Run. He was captured at Five Forks, Va., 1 April 1865. He was then confined at Point Lookout, Md., until being released on 20 June 1865 after taking the Oath of Allegiance. He returned home to Forsyth County and was married 13 Feb. 1866 to Jeanette Brown. They continued to live in Forsyth County and had three children. Edwin Thomas Shouse died 23 March 1908.

SILER, H. THOMPSON

H. Thompson Siler was born 27 March 1844 in Chatham County to Joseph A. and Eliza Siler. He is listed in the *Randolph Heritage* as a member of Company M, although records of his service in Company M are sketchy. He is known to have served in the Confederate States Navy, and was sole survivor of the destruction of the naval base in Charleston, S.C. He later served in Mallet's Battalion of Camp Guards. However, he was a charter member of Randolph Camp No. 1646 United Confederate Veterans, and is listed on its records as having served in Company M, at least for some period of time. His obituary confirms that he did serve in the regular army and that he was with Lee at Appomattox, Va.

Thompson Siler was married 7 September 1876 in Guilford County to Mary E. Wood. They had six children, of whom at least four survived. They lived in the Providence Township of Randolph County and were members of Bethel Methodist Protestant Church. He was in attendance at the Confederate reunion in Asheboro 1 Sept. 1906. On 6 July 1914, he applied for his Confederate pension at age 70, and was a resident of the Climax area. Mary died at an unknown date, and about 1917 Thompson moved to Greensboro in the Morehead Township. He was last employed in the furniture business. Thompson Siler died on 5 July 1929 and was buried in the Green Hill Cemetery in Greensboro.

SILER, WESLEY C.

Wesley C. Siler was a brother to Captain Columbus F. Siler of this company. He was born, probably about 1841, to Andrew J. and Ruth Barker Siler, and was a resident of Randolph County when he enlisted at age 21 in Company M, on 10 June 1861, at its organization. He was mustered in as 3rd corporal and served as such until he was killed at Gettysburg, Pa., 1–3 July 1863.

SMITH, HENRY C.

Henry C. Smith's identity is unclear. He enlisted at Camp Holmes on 1 June 1864 for the war. He was mustered in as a private and was promoted to sergeant sometime after 31 October 1864. He was captured at Hatcher's Run, Va., on 31 March 1865 and was confined at Point Lookout, Maryland, until he was released on 3 June 1865 after taking the Oath of Allegiance.

SMITH, HOWARD E.

Howard E. Smith has not been positively identified at this point, but could be the person listed in the 1850 and 1860 censuses as Herbert P. Smith, the son of Reuben and Edith Lineberry Smith. Herbert P. Smith was living in the right location and is the correct age to be the person named as Howard E. Smith. No

Howard E. Smith fitting this description has been located in any census or other record thus far.

He was born about 1841 and was a resident of Randolph County where he enlisted on 10 June 1861 at the organization of Company M. He served one year and died at Richmond, Va., on 20 June 1862 of wounds received at Seven Pines, Va., on 31 May 1862.

SMITH, MADISON

Madison Smith was born about 1840, probably to Reuben and Edith Lineberry Smith. He resided in Randolph County, where he enlisted in at age 21 in Company M, on 10 June 1861. He was mustered in as 2nd corporal, but was reduced to ranks sometime after 31 Aug. 1861. He was listed as a deserter on 16 Nov. 1863. He went over to the enemy on an unspecified date and was released after taking the Oath of Allegiance at Washington, D.C., on 19 March 1864. He is thought to have gone west after the war.

SPINKS, JOHN D.

John D. Spinks was born about 1843–44 in Randolph County to William S. and Elizabeth Garner Spinks. He enlisted in Company M during the company's organization on 10 June 1861 at age 18. He served until he was killed at the second battle of Manassas, Va., 29 Aug. 1862.

SPRONCE, J. G.

This has been a difficult person to identify. The 1860 Census gives no one by this name. In fact, the name Spronce does not appear at all. I believe this may be a misreading of the name Sprouse or Scronce, of which several are found in the census. My guess is that he could be Jacob Scronce of Catawba County. In 1860 he is shown as being 37 years of age, with a wife and son. In the 1870 Census he is not found, but his wife is still there with the son and a daughter. They lived in the Collettsville district of Catawba County. The roster of Mallet's Battalion lists J. G. Sprouse, another possible candidate for this person.

The military record of this soldier states that he was by occupation a carpenter before enlisting at Camp Vance on 7 September 1863 for the war. He was wounded in the hand at or near Wilderness, Virginia, in May of 1864. He was shot "through great toe left foot" at Reams' Station, Virginia, on 25 August 1864. His left foot was amputated on 31 August 1864, and he was furloughed for sixty days on 13 October 1864.

STEEL, ABNER BRANSON

Abner Branson Steel was born 11 July 1842 in Randolph County to Jacob and Eunice Allridge Steel. At some point he moved to Guilford County, where he resided when the war began. He enlisted in Randolph County in Company M on 10 June 1861. He was wounded in the leg and shoulder at Seven Pines, Va., on or about 31 May 1862. He was also wounded in the leg at the second battle of

Private Charles Wesley Abner Stewart (1845–unknown) enlisted in Company M on 7 September 1863. (Photograph courtesy of Jerry Dagenhart.)

Manassas, Va., 29 Aug. 1862. He was reported absent without leave in October 1862 and returned to duty on an unspecified date. He was captured at or near Jericho Mills, Va., 21–24 May 1864 and confined at Point Lookout, Md., until transferred to Elmira, N.Y., 8 July 1864. He was released on 29 May 1865 after taking the Oath of Allegiance. He returned home to Randolph County and lived in the Franklinville area. He was in attendance at the Confederate reunion in Asheboro, 1 Sept. 1906, and was a charter member of Randolph Camp No. 1646, United Confederate Veterans. He died 19 Jan. 1915 and was buried at Franklinville Methodist cemetery.

STEWART, CHARLES WESLEY ABNER

Charles Wesley Abner Stewart was born about 1845 in Iredell County to Thomas Jackson and Mary Emily Paris Stewart. He enlisted in Company M just a few days after his father, Thomas Jackson Stewart, at Camp Vance on 7 September 1863 for the war. He was reported absent sick on furlough on 15 August 1864, and was dropped from the rolls of the company on 30 September 1864 for unreported reasons. According to family sources, he never returned home from the war, and was never heard from again.

STEWART, THOMAS JACKSON

Thomas Jackson Stewart was born about 1820 on Buffalo Shoals Creek in Iredell County to Ralph and Rebecca Johnson Stewart. He was married before

Above, left: Private Thomas Jackson Stewart (1820–1893) enlisted in Company M on 1 September 1863. (Photograph courtesy of Jerry Dagenhart.) *Right:* Private Lorenzo Dow Stout, Jr. (1831–1870), enlisted in Company M on 10 June 1861. (Photograph courtesy of L. McKay Whatley.)

1845 to Mary Emily Paris and had eight children. He enlisted at Camp Holmes on 1 September 1863 for the war and was assigned to Company M. He served until 9 July 1864, when he was dropped from the rolls for unreported reasons. After the war he returned home to Iredell County, where he ran a government distillery for many years, and was also known as a talented blacksmith and cabinetmaker. He died 26 September 1893 and is buried in the Marvin United Methodist Church cemetery in Iredell County. His wife died the following January and is also buried there.

STOUT, LORENZO DOW, JR.

Lorenzo Dow Stout, Jr., was born 29 Dec. 1831 in Randolph County to Lorenzo Dow, Sr., and Martha Hendricks Stout. He resided in Randolph County, where he was married on 3 Feb. 1857 to Eliza E. Slack. He enlisted in Company M at its organization on 10 June 1861 at age 29. He was reported on detail as a wheelwright during most of the war. He was paroled at Appomattox Court House, Va., 9 April 1865, after which he returned home to Randolph County and resided in the Franklinville area. He died 22 Feb. 1870 and was buried at Franklinville United Methodist cemetery. His wife, Eliza, filed for a Confederate pension under the 1885 pension act. She lived until 1891 and was also buried at Franklinville United Methodist cemetery.

STOUT, WILLIAM G.

William G. Stout was born in October 1833 in Randolph County probably to Lemuel and Elizabeth Stout. He resided in the Franklinville area as a blacksmith and was married on 23 September 1854 in Randolph County to Sarah E. Allred. He enlisted in Company M on 10 June 1861 at age 27 and served until being discharged on 26 November 1862 by reason of "elephantiasis of right leg." He returned to Randolph County, where he continued to work as a blacksmith. At some point after 1880, he moved to the Randleman area. His wife died in 1894, and was buried at Mt. Lebanon United Methodist cemetery in Randleman. He remained in the area until being admitted to the Confederate Soldier's Home in Raleigh on 23 May 1899. He was later discharged and was a resident of the county home near Asheboro in the 1900 Census. He drew a Confederate pension for full disability, with his "leg off above the knee" and was again living in the Randleman area until 1905, when he was reported as being deceased. He is most likely buried next to his wife at Mt. Lebanon United Methodist cemetery.

STRICKLAND, WILLIAM O.

This soldier has not been identified. He enlisted at Camp Holmes on 29 March 1864 for the war at the same time as three other men from Rockingham and Stokes counties. He served almost a year before deserting to the enemy on or about 5 March 1865. He was confined at Washington, D.C., until being released on or about 10 March 1865 after taking the Oath of Allegiance.

STROUT, W. B.

W. B. Strout is listed in the *Randolph Heritage* as being a member of Company M. I believe this to be a misspelling of W. G. Stout (see entry for William G. Stout).

SUDDERTH, WILLIAM S.

William S. Sudderth was a resident of Caldwell County in the Lenoir area, where he enlisted at age 26 in Company A 22nd Regiment on 30 April 1861. He was mustered in as sergeant. He was transferred to Company M after 31 Aug. 1861, with the rank of sergeant. He served with Company M and was wounded at Seven Pines, Va., on or about 31 May 1862. He was transferred to Company K 22nd Regiment on 1 July 1862, and back to Company A 22nd during July 1862. He was reduced to ranks before 1 Aug. 1862. He was then transferred to Company L 22nd Regiment sometime before 1 Nov. 1862. On an unspecified date he was transferred back to Company A 22nd Regiment, and was finally discharged 10 Feb. 1863 for reasons not reported.

SUMNER, JOHN R.

John R. Sumner was born about 1841 in Randolph County probably to Asa and Mary Sumner. He was married 15 Oct. 1856 to Rachel Diffee. They resided in Randolph County where he enlisted in Company M at the age of 29 on 10 June 1861. He was wounded at or near Mechanicsville, Va., 26 June 1862. He died in a hospital at Richmond, Va., 1–4 July 1862 of wounds. His burial place is unknown at this time.

THOMPSON, SPENCER D.

Spencer D. Thompson was born 30 Aug. 1829 to Samuel and Sarah Womble Thompson. He enlisted in Company M in Randolph County at the age of 31 on 10 June 1861. He deserted on 25 July 1861. He lived near the eastern border of the county, and died 10 Oct. 1899. He is buried at the old Rocky River United Methodist cemetery in Chatham County.

TROGDON, HEZEKIAH C.

Hezekiah C. Trogdon was born about 1831 in Randolph County to Emsley and Sarah "Sallie" Stout Trogdon. He resided in Randolph County, where he married Vicey Allred on 18 June 1856. He enlisted in Company M on 10 June 1861 at age 28 along with four brothers. He served until being captured at Seven Pines, Va., 31 May 1862. He was then confined at Fort Delaware, Del., until he was paroled and transferred to Aiken's Landing, James River, Va., where he was exchanged on 5 Aug. 1862. He was reported absent without leave on 24 Aug. 1864 and was dropped from the rolls of the company 24 Sept. 1864. He was paroled at Greensboro on 8 May 1865. He returned to Randolph County, then at some point moved to Tennessee, where he died sometime after 1900.

TROGDON, JEREMIAH F.

Jeremiah F. Trogdon was born about 1835 in Randolph County to Emsley and Sarah "Sallie" Stout Trogdon. He was married to Caroline A. Johnson on 8 Dec. 1855. He was 25 years old and worked as a blacksmith and farmer in Randolph County when he and his brothers enlisted in Company M on 10 June 1861. He served until being captured at Gettysburg, Pa., 1–4 July 1863. He was exchanged on an unspecified date, and returned to duty by 1 Jan. 1864. He retired from service on 8 Feb. 1865 by reason of "asthma." The last of he and Caroline's four children was born in 1868, then at some point, he and Caroline evidently separated. He moved to Kentucky, and was married a second time about 1873–74 to Jane Wagoner. By 1891 he was in Stroud, Okla., where he died when his team was struck by a train. He is buried near Stroud, Okla. His first wife, Caroline, drew a Confederate pension at Foust's Mills in 1902. She was still living in Randolph County with her son, Thomas L. Trogdon, in 1910.

TROGDON, LINDEN ALRED

Linden Alred "Lynn" Trogdon was born 24 Oct. 1837 in Randolph County to Emsley and Sarah "Sallie" Stout Trogdon. He enlisted there in Company M, along with his brothers, on 10 June 1861 at age 22. He was reported absent without leave in September 1862, and during the time of his absence, he was married in Randolph County on 1 Feb. 1863 to Susanna Kinney. He returned to duty on an unspecified date and was wounded in the left foot at Gettysburg, Pa., 3 July 1863. He was later captured at Falling Waters, Md., 14 July 1863. He was confined at Point Lookout, Md., until paroled and transferred to City Point, Va., where he was received on 6 March 1864 for exchange. He was reported as being absent without leave for "three months" but returned to duty during September or October 1864. He was paroled at Greensboro 8 May 1865. He returned to Randolph County and resumed farming. By 1880 Linden and Susanna had moved to Bear Creek in Chatham County. They remained there and had eight or nine children during their marriage. Susanna's death came sometime after 1920. Linden Trogdon died on 26 Sept. 1923, and was buried in the Edwards Hill cemetery.

TROGDON, SAMUEL

Samuel Trogdon was born about 1840 in Randolph County to Emsley and Sarah "Sallie" Stout Trogdon. He was married 2 March 1861 in Randolph County to Nancy Jennings. He enlisted, along with his brothers, in Company M on 10 June 1861 at age 21. He died 30 June 1862 of wounds received. The place and date of his wounds were not reported, but he died on the same day as the battle of Frayser's Farm in Virginia. Gaines' Mill had been fought three days earlier.

TROGDON, SOLOMON J.

Solomon J. Trogdon was born about 1827 in Randolph County to Emsley and Sarah "Sallie" Stout Trogdon, and was married to Emily Eliza Watson. He enlisted in Company M, along with his brothers, on 10 June 1861 at age 32. He served until being wounded in the face at or near Mechanicsville, Va., 26 June 1862. He was reported absent without leave in September 1862 and was listed as a deserter in October 1862. He returned to duty sometime before 16 Feb. 1864, when he was listed as being on duty as a teamster. He was wounded again, in the arm, at or near Wilderness, Va., in May 1864. He was dropped from the rolls of the company on 24 Sept. 1864 and was paroled at Greensboro on 8 May 1865. Returning to Randolph County, he lived in the Randleman area as a farmer, blacksmith and farrier. He and Emily Eliza raised nine children. He drew a Confederate pension, last receiving it in 1901. His widow was drawing a pension in 1907.

TROGDON, STEPHEN WARD

Stephen Ward Trogdon was born 24 Feb. 1837, probably in Randolph County to Daniel and Lilly Allred Trogdon. He was by trade a carpenter, and later a teamster. Known to friends as "Ward," he was married on 19 Dec. 1857 to Caroline Pugh. They resided in Randolph County when he enlisted in Company M at age 24 on 10 June 1861. He was mustered in as a private, and was promoted to corporal on 13 Dec. 1862. He was captured at Fredericksburg, Va., on 13 Dec. 1862, and was exchanged on 17 Dec. 1862. Sometime prior to 1 July 1863 he was promoted to sergeant. During the battle of Gettysburg, Pa., 1–2 July 1863, he was wounded in the right thigh and captured. His wound necessitated the amputation of his right leg. He was hospitalized at David's Island, New York Harbor, until he was paroled and transferred to City Point, Va., where he was received on 28 Oct. 1863 for exchange. He was retired to the Invalid Corps on 13 Aug. 1864.

Ward was married a second time on 1 April 1866 to Fannie Lane Kinney. They lived in the Cedar Falls area, where he drew a Confederate pension, and is remembered as one of the town fathers of Cedar Falls. He died 17 June 1897 and was buried at Cedar Falls United Methodist cemetery.

TURNER, ANDREW JACKSON

Andrew Jackson Turner was born 9 Jan. 1840 in Randolph County to Martin S. and Hannah Staley Turner. He resided in Randolph County when he enlisted in Company M at age 21 on 10 June 1861. He was reported on duty as teamster for most of the war. He was a brother of Sgt. John Tyler Turner and the son of Private Martin S. Turner of this company. He was paroled at Appomattox Court House, Va., 9 April 1865. After the war he returned to Randolph County, and was married to Malinda York on 2 Nov. 1866. They settled in the Sandy Creek area. He died 11 Dec. 1900 and is buried at Shady Grove Baptist cemetery.

TURNER, JOHN TYLER

John Tyler Turner was born 21 Feb. 1842 in Randolph County to Martin S. and Hannah Staley Turner. He resided in Randolph County in the Sandy Creek area when he enlisted in Company M at age 18 on 10 June 1861. He was mustered in as a private. He was wounded in the right arm just below the elbow at Mechanicsville, Va., 26 June 1862. He returned to duty on an unspecified date and was promoted to corporal on 1 August 1862, and at some unknown point was promoted to sergeant. He was wounded at the second battle of Manassas, Va., 28–30 Aug. 1862. He was wounded a third time, in the right shoulder, at Chancellorsville, Va., 2 May 1863. On 18 March 1864 he was examined by a doctor and recommended for a discharge, but the order did not come until 2 Aug. 1864, and he left on the 3rd. He returned home to Randolph County and on 18 Aug. 1864 he was conscripted on light duty and attached to Company B, 1st Battalion of light duty men. He was orderly sergeant for that company, and served through the rest of the war in battle at Belfield, Va., and at the Neuse River, near Goldsboro. He stated that he received twelve bullet holes in his hat at Belfield. He was paroled at Greensboro on 26 April 1865. He returned to Randolph County after the war, drew a Confederate pension, and was married 9 Nov. 1867 to Jane R. Ledman. He resided in Ramseur and was the author of several articles about the war, including "Turner's Romance," which is found elsewhere in this volume. He also wrote obituaries for many of his comrades in later years and attended several veterans' reunions. He died 1 Oct. 1923 and is buried in Sunset Knoll cemetery in Ramseur.

TURNER, MARTIN S.

Martin S. Turner was born 13 Feb. 1813 in Randolph County and was married there to Hannah Staley on 31 Jan. 1835. His wife died in 1857, and he continued to farm in the Sandy Creek area, until enlisting in Company M at Evansport, Va., 1 Dec. 1861. His two sons, Andrew and John, were already serving in this company. He was discharged on 13 June 1862 by reason of general disability, and by reason of being over age. His discharge certificate gave his age as 41. Randolph County marriage records show that after returning home he married a second time, to Hannah Holder Wright, on 27 Sept. 1862. He died 26 May 1893 and was buried next to his first wife, Hannah Staley Turner, at Sandy Creek Baptist cemetery.

TURNER, THOMAS

Thomas Turner was born about 1840 in Chatham County. He was a resident of Randolph County and was a farmer prior to enlisting at age 21 on 6 March 1862. He was wounded in the leg at or near Mechanicsville, Va., on 26 June 1862. He was reported absent wounded in July 1862, and was reported absent without leave in September 1862. The Roll of Honor indicates that he was wounded twice in unspecified battles.

WALL, WILLIAM B.

William B. Wall has not been positively identified at this writing. He may have been the son of a William and Alice Wall of Randolph County. He enlisted in Guilford County at age 18 on 23 May 1861 in Company E, 22nd Regiment. He was then transferred to Company M sometime previous to 1 July 1862 and served with this company during the action at Malvern Hill. He was then transferred back to Company E prior to 1 August 1862. The Roll of Honor indicates that he was captured at Gettysburg, but the records of the Federal Provost Marshal do not substantiate this.

WEBSTER, JAMES A.

James A. Webster was born 5 March 1844 in Randolph or Chatham county to William B. and Eliza Ellison Webster. He was living in Randolph County when he enlisted at age 19 in Company M on 10 June 1861. He was wounded in the side and captured at Fredericksburg, Va., 13 Dec. 1862, and was exchanged 17 Dec. 1862. He was court-martialed on or about 27 Dec. 1862 for unreported reasons. He deserted to the enemy on or about 12 March 1864, and was confined at Washington, D.C., until released on or about 17 March 1864 after taking the Oath of Allegiance. The Roll of Honor indicates he was wounded twice in unspecified battles. After the war he came back to Randolph County and became a minister. He was married on 4 December 1868 to Martha A. Foust. He was in attendance at the Confederate reunion held in Asheboro, 1 Sept. 1906. His wife died in 1914 and he followed on 11 Oct. 1920. They are both buried at Patterson's Grove Christian Church.

WILBURN, B. E.

B. E. Wilburn is listed in *Broadfoot's* as being a member of Company M. I have found no evidence of such a person in the company. I believe this is a misreading of some other name, or an erroneous listing in Company M, 22nd Regiment, on some lone document.

WILKERSON, DANIEL C.

Daniel C. Wilkerson was born about 1833 in Randolph County probably to James and Ellen Wilkerson. He resided as a farmer, with wife Delilah, when he enlisted in Randolph County at age 28 on 6 March 1862 and was assigned to Company M. He died on 25 June 1862. The place and cause of death were not reported. This was during the period of the Seven Days battles.

WILKERSON, JAMES M.

James M. Wilkerson was born about 1840–41 in Randolph County to James and Ellen Wilkerson. He resided as a farmer when he enlisted in Randolph County at age 20 on 6 March 1862, and was assigned to Company M. He died at Richmond or Farmville, Va., 18–19 Sept. 1862 of "erysipelas," otherwise known as St. Anthony's Fire, an acute bacterial infection of an open wound.

WILKINS, WILLIAM J.

William J. Wilkins was born 22 Nov. 1836 in Stokes County to Thomas and Delyshee Joyce Wilkins. He resided in Stokes County, where he enlisted in Company H, 22nd Regiment at the age of 24 on 1 June 1861. He was transferred to Company M in September 1861 and served through June 1862. He was then transferred back to Company H on 1 July 1862. He was present in that company through the rest of the war, and was paroled at Appomattox Court House, Va., on 9 April 1865. He returned to Stokes County and was married 28 May 1865 to Polly Ann Gann. They lived in the Sandy Ridge community on the homestead of his grandfather, John Wilkins. William died 24 Jan. 1919 and is thought to be buried in one of the Wilkins cemeteries situated in the Sandy Ridge area of Stokes County.

WILLEY, WILLIAM PARKER

William Parker Willey was born 8 Sept. 1835 to _____ and Anna Willey. It is unknown at this time where he was born. His mother was from South Carolina. He resided in Randolph County by the time of the 1850 Census. He was married on 8 May 1860 to Rebecca Jane Cheek in Randolph County.

He enlisted there at age 26 in Company M on 10 June 1861, and was mustered in as a private. He was wounded at Frayser's Farm, Va., 30 June 1862. He returned to duty on an unspecified date, and was promoted to sergeant sometime before 1 Oct. 1862. He was reported on detached service at Greensboro from 27 March through October 1864, and was reduced to ranks during this period, sometime before 1 Sept. 1864. By 1 Nov. 1864 he had reported back to Company M and was promoted to sergeant a second time. He was paroled at Greensboro on 2 May 1865. After the war he returned to Randolph County and lived in the Franklinville area, working as a carpenter, according to the 1870 Census. At some point after

1870, he moved to Guilford County and died there 22 March 1897. He and his wife are buried in the Oakwood Cemetery in High Point.

WILLIAMS, ADAM O.

Adam O. Williams was born about 1839 in Chatham County to Atha N. and Barbara Williams. He resided in Alamance County as a farmer when he enlisted in Company L, 22nd Regiment at age 22 on 18 June 1861. He was transferred to Company M in September 1861 and served through June 1862. He was then transferred back to Company L on 1 July 1862. He was wounded in the left side at the second battle of Manassas, Va., on 29 Aug. 1862. He was reported absent wounded from that date through October 1862. He was again wounded at Chancellorsville, Va., 1–3 May 1863, and deserted in August of 1863. He returned to duty sometime before 23 May 1864, when he was captured at Jericho Mills, Va. He was confined at Point Lookout, Md., until being released on or about 9 June 1864 after joining the U.S. Army. He was assigned to Company K, 1st Regiment U.S. Volunteer Infantry.

WILLIAMS, BENJAMIN

Benjamin Williams was born in 1835 in Randolph County to Jacob Sr. and Nancy Cox Williams. He was married in Randolph County on 12 Dec. 1860 to Rebecca Staley. He resided as a farmer when he enlisted there at age 26 on 6 March 1862, and was assigned to Company M. Records state that he died at Bunker Hill, Va., 20 Oct. 1862, but the cause of his death was not reported.

WILLIAMS, DAVID ENOS

David Enos Williams was born in 1842 in Randolph County to Riley and Louisa Kivett Williams. He resided in Randolph County as a farmer when he enlisted in Company M at age 19 on 10 June 1861. He served until being discharged on 15 Oct. 1862, by reason of "valvular disease of the heart." He returned to Randolph County and was married to Diannah Breedlove on 11 Feb. 1864, with whom he had two children, Lillie J. and Martha (Martitia) Williams. He never regained his health, and died about 1866 or 1869. Dianna remarried to Franklin Gardner. At this time it is unknown where David Enos Williams was buried.

WILLIAMS, JAMES MADISON

James Madison Williams was born 7 April 1827, probably in Randolph County to Jacob and Margaret Lax Williams. He was married 28 Jan. 1846 in Randolph County to Mariah Kivett, with whom he had six known children. He resided in Randolph County when he enlisted in Company M at age 35 on 10 June 1861. He served until being captured at or near Jericho Mills, Va., 23 May 1864. He was confined at Point Lookout, Md., until he was paroled and transferred to Bouleware's Wharf, James River, Va., where he was received 19 March 1865 for exchange. The Roll of Honor shows that he was wounded in an unspecified battle. After the war he may have gone west, as did at least one of his children.

WILLIAMS, JOEL

Joel Williams was born about 1838 in Randolph County. His parentage is uncertain at this time; however, he is found in the 1860 Census listed in the household of Jane Aldredge/Allred as a mechanic or blacksmith along with several others, including Joshua C. Bain, who would later host Company M at his barn for their first camp.

Joel Williams still resided there as a blacksmith when he enlisted on 6 March 1862 at age 24, and was assigned to Company M. He served from that time until 7 October 1864, when he was reported under arrest. The Roll of Honor indicates that he was wounded in an unspecified battle.

WILLIAMS, JOHN RANDOLPH

John Randolph Williams was born in 1844 in Randolph County to Riley and Louisa Kivett Williams. He resided in Randolph County when he enlisted in Company M at age 19 on 10 June 1861. He served in twelve battles, including the battle in which he was killed, at Shepherdstown Ford, Va., on 20 Sept. 1862.

WILLIAMS, LINDSEY

Lindsey Williams was born about 1826 and was a resident of Moore County where he was married to Sophia Kelly 29 May 1859. He enlisted at age 37 in Moore County for the war on 13 March 1863 and was assigned to Company M. He served with this company until he died the next year on 21 May 1864. The cause and place of death were not reported, but he died during the time of the battles around Spotsylvania Court House, Va.

WILLIAMS, MARTINE

Martine Williams is listed in the *Randolph Heritage* as being a member of Company M. He is presumed to be the same person as William Martin Williams (see entry).

WILLIAMS, WILLIAM MARTIN

William Martin Williams was born 5 Jan. 1846 in Randolph County to Jacob and Malvina Kivett Williams. He enlisted at Camp Holmes at the age of 18 on September 20 1864 for the war, and was assigned to Company M. He was paroled at Greensboro on 17 May 1865. He returned to Randolph County, where he was married on 9 June 1867 to Isabella Kivett. According to the 1910 Census, they had at least four children: John L. Williams, Henry S. Williams, America M. Williams and Etta Williams. William Martin Williams died 16 Oct. 1900 and was buried at Shady Grove Baptist cemetery. Isabella survived him by about ten years, and was also buried at Shady Grove.

WOOSLEY, WILLIAM AUGUST

William August Woosley was born 13 June 1845 in Friedburg, Davidson County to Joseph and Lavinia Krouse Woosley. By the time of the 1860 Census, he resided in Forsyth County. He was still a resident there when he enlisted at Camp Holmes on 1 July 1864 for the war and was assigned to Company M. He was captured by the enemy at Petersburg, Va., subsequent to 21 October 1864 and was confined at Hart's Island, New York Harbor, until being released on 20 June 1865 after taking the Oath of Allegiance.

Following the war his family moved to the vicinity of Knob Noster, Missouri, and later to Kansas, finally settling in Chanute, Kan., about 1898. He was married on 22 April 1866 to Nellie Mahalia Snipes, a Sioux Indian, said to be the daughter or niece of Chief Red Cloud and his wife Ayala, and raised by a white family named Snipes. August became blind soon after the birth of his fourth child, probably the latent result of war injuries, and made his living keeping bees and grinding sorghum. The family also relates that during the war he pulled a bad tooth himself, filling the hole with a bit of tobacco and a whittled piece of hickory wood. The wooden "tooth" remained in his mouth up until his death, which occurred on 23 July 1906 in Chanute, Neosho County, Kan. He was buried there in Elmwood Cemetery. Mahalia lived until 1912 and was also buried at Elmwood.

WRIGHT, DAVID

David Wright was born 28 July 1836 in Randolph County to Abraham and Anna Barbara Kivett Wright, and was the son of a Primitive Baptist minister. Residing in the Sandy Creek area, he enlisted in Company M at age 23 on 10 June 1861 with his brothers Darius and Isaac as the company was being organized. He was reported absent wounded in July 1862. The place and date of the wound were not reported, but this was during the time that Company M was engaged at Malvern Hill. He was reported absent without leave in September 1862 and listed as a deserter in October of that year. However, Sgt. John Turner indicates that Wright was wounded in Virginia in August 1862 at 2nd Manassas and again in September at Shepherdstown, so he may have actually been absent wounded. He returned to duty on an unspecified date and was wounded again at Chancellorsville, Va., 1–3 May 1863. He returned to duty on an unspecified date. Sgt. Turner indicates that he may have been slightly wounded again at Spotsylvania Court House, Va., in May 1864. He was paroled at Appomattox Court House, Va., 9 April 1865. He returned to Randolph County and was married 31 July 1866 to Judith Emily "Juda" Curtis, with whom he had two children: Augusta A. Wright and Jacob R. Wright. He remained in the Sandy Creek area until his death on 4 May 1915. He is buried at Sandy Creek Baptist cemetery. His wife lived about ten years longer.

WRIGHT, ISAAC

Isaac Wright was born about 1827 in Randolph County to Abraham and Anna Barbara Kivett Wright, and was a brother of David and Darius Wright of this company. He was married 20 June 1847 in Randolph County to Elizabeth Langley, with whom he had four children before Elizabeth died in 1853: Alfred Spinks Wright, Barbara A. Wright, John Wright and Eli Wright. He enlisted there in Company M at its organization at age 35 on 10 June 1861 and probably served in the early Virginia engagements at Yorktown and the Seven Days battles before he died at Richmond, Va., on 4 Aug. 1862 of disease.

WRIGHT, JOHN DARIUS

John Darius Wright (sometimes listed as Doris) was born about 1828 in Randolph County to Abraham and Anna Barbara Kivett Wright. He was a brother of David and Isaac Wright of this company. He was married 12 Dec. 1852 in Randolph County to Emily Jones, and was a shoemaker by occupation when he enlisted there at age 33 in Company M on 10 June 1861. He was reported absent without leave in July and September 1862, and was listed as a deserter in October 1862. The Roll of Honor states that he was wounded once in an unspecified battle and deserted twice. After the war, he and his family apparently moved to Surry County where they are found in the 1880 Census. He and Emily are shown there with five children and a probable daughter-in-law.

YEARGIN, DANIEL

Daniel Yeargin was born 5 Jan. 1832 in Randolph County to Isaac and Millicent Coble Yeargin. He resided in Randolph County with his parents in the Liberty area, where he enlisted in Company M at age 29 on 10 June 1861 at the organization of the company. He served until he was reported absent without leave in September 1862. He then returned to duty on an unspecified date. He was wounded at Chancellorsville, Va., on 4 May 1863. He returned to duty sometime before 5 July 1863, when he was captured at or near Gettysburg, Pa. He was confined at Fort Delaware, Del., until released on 3 May 1865 after taking the Oath of Allegiance. He then returned home to live with his parents. He never married, and continued to live in the Liberty area. He drew a Confederate pension for "disease" and went to live in the Confederate Old Soldier's Home in Raleigh on 28 Feb. 1906. He died there 14 Nov. 1910, and was buried in the Oakwood Confederate Cemetery in Raleigh.

YORK, BRAXTON

Braxton York was born about 1844 in the Moffitt's Mill community of Randolph County to Pleasant and Mary Henson York, and was a brother of Joseph York of this company. He resided there as a farmer when he enlisted in Company M at Cedar Falls at age 18 on 6 March 1862. He was wounded at Frayser's Farm, Va., on 30 June 1862, and died on 1 July 1862. The place of his death was not reported.

YORK, DARIUS

Darius York was born about 1829 in Surry County to Jeremiah and Sarah York. He was a resident of Randolph County and was a farmer when he enlisted there in Company M at age 31 on 10 June 1861. He was wounded at Seven Pines, Va., on 31 May 1862, and was reported absent wounded in July 1862. He was subsequently reported as absent without leave in September of 1862, but had returned to duty by 14 July 1863 when he was captured at Falling Waters, Maryland. He was confined at Point Lookout, Md., until he was released on 24 January 1864 after joining the U.S. Army. He was assigned to Company C, 1st Regiment U.S. Volunteer Infantry.

Following the war, he returned to Randolph County and was married there to Sarah J. Cross on 7 September 1867.

YORK, JABEZ LINDSAY

Jabez Lindsay York was born 20 July 1844, probably in Randolph County to Jabez and Sarah Julian York. He resided there with his parents when he enlisted on an unknown date, and was assigned to Company M. He was first listed in company records on 23 December 1864. He served through the end of the war and was paroled at Appomattox Court House, Va., on 9 April 1865.

Returning to Randolph County, he was married on 26 April 1866 to Mary Ann E. Jones. They had no children born to their marriage and resided as farmers in the Franklinville Township. Jabez died on 20 January 1910, and was buried at Gray's Chapel United Methodist cemetery. His wife Mary lived until 1919 and was also buried at Gray's Chapel.

YORK, LARKIN CULBERSON, JR.

Larkin Culberson York, Jr., was born 30 Dec. 1844 in Randolph County to Larkin Culberson, Sr., and Sophia "Tilly" Kivett York. His father died the same year he was born, and his guardian stepfather, Pinkney Davenport, taught him the trade of distilling. He was helping his stepfather in that business at Soapstone Mountain near Mt. Pleasant Creek at the time of the 1860 Census. He was married to Barbary Lousina Pugh, probably just before enlisting for the war.

He enlisted in Company M at the age of 17 on 10 June 1861 at Cedar Falls in Randolph County, and was enlisted by his third cousin once removed, John M. Odell, who was captain of the company. He served until 13 June 1862, when he was discharged by reason of being under age. He was also deaf following the war, attesting to the hard service he endured at Evansport, Va., the Yorktown Siege, and the battle of Seven Pines, Va. He returned home to his log cabin in Randolph County, his wife and three month old son.

He and his wife tended an 88-acre farm in Columbia Township, and had a total of six children. They were members of White's Chapel Methodist Church. Larkin C. York, Jr., died 24 Dec. 1924. He and his wife are buried at White's Chapel United Methodist cemetery.

YORK, SAMUEL CLARKSON

Samuel Clarkson York was born 22 July 1841 in Randolph County to Semore and Martha "Patsy" Bray York. He resided there as a farmer when he enlisted at age 20 on 6 March 1862 and was assigned to Company M. He was wounded in the scalp and neck at or near Mechanicsville, Va., on or about 26 June 1862 and was hospitalized at Richmond, Va. He was reported as absent wounded through October 1862.

He may have later enlisted in Kinston, Lenoir County on 17 Jan. 1863 at the age of 21 in Company K, 5th Regiment N.C. Cavalry, 63rd N.C. State Troops, known as the "Partisan Rangers." A man named Samuel Clarkson York joined the unit on that date, and his older brother, Spencer Donald York, had previously joined this same regiment. On 4 May 1863 his unit was on patrol in Carteret County near Beaufort when they and several other Confederates were captured by the Union troops that had penetrated the area. They were held as prisoners of war in Beaufort until 24 May 1863. On that date York and 230 other prisoners were transferred to Fort Monroe, Va., for release or exchange. They were received at City Point, Va., on 28 May 1863. He served until being paroled at Camp Stokes in north Greensboro on 14 May 1865.

After returning to Randolph County, he was married on 24 March 1867 to Rebecca D. Webb. They made their home in eastern Randolph County, and raised two sons and three daughters. Samuel Clarkson York was disabled due to his wounds and drew a Confederate pension until his death on 31 August 1921. He and his wife are buried at Kildee Wesleyan Church cemetery, east of Ramseur.

YORK, WILLIAM J.

William J. York was born in Randolph County. He resided there as a farmer when he enlisted at age 18 on 10 June 1861. He was discharged on 9 January 1862 due to "indigestion" and "a weak back." This William J. York is unidentified at this time, but may be a William Jasper York, born about 1845 to Leander and Eliza Ward York. He was married on 6 Aug. 1864 in Randolph County to Martitia Curtis.

Another possibility is that this is the same person as William Joseph York (see entry). If this is true, he may have enlisted in the company a second time.

YORK, WILLIAM JOSEPH

William Joseph York was born 7 February 1846 in Randolph County to Pleasant and Mary Henson York, and was a brother of Braxton York of this company. He resided here as a farmer when he enlisted on 25 February 1862 and was assigned to Company M. He was wounded in an unnamed battle (probably Harper's Ferry or Shepherdstown Ford, Va.) in September 1862. He was reported on duty as a teamster during most of the war, probably because of his Quaker convictions. He was paroled at Appomattox Court House, Va., on 9 April 1865. It may be possible that he served previously in this company (see entry for William J. York).

After returning to Randolph County he was married on 25 March 1866 to Sarah Martha Spinks. They lived in the Pleasant Grove area where he worked as a wagon maker and wheelwright after the war. Sarah Martha York died on 15 October 1897, and William Joseph York followed on 11 June 1900. They were buried at Holly Springs Friends Meeting.

5. Old Times There Are Not Forgotten

During the war, the South was hard-pressed to provide everything its people needed. They made do. Most of the time, they did without. And many times that included even such simple things as paper to write on. When the war came to an end, many documents were destroyed, either by enemy troops who burned as they went, or by Southerners who didn't want to give anything to their captors to implicate people or to be used as evidence against them. Many records were simply lost or never even existed to begin with.

Thankfully, many of the leaders and soldiers alike penned their memories so that they would not be forgotten. They provide an important record of this pivotal time in American history.

A few letters and diaries also remain. In the case of Company M, Sergeant John T. Turner took it upon himself to record his remembrances and write many obituaries for his fellow soldiers, so people would know what his men fought for and how they sacrificed. Other such documentation about Company M is not to be found as far as we know, so I would like to share each of the ones I have found.

Ramseur Confederate Veterans circa 1903. Left to right: Capt. Y. M. C. Johnson of Company L, 22nd Regiment; Sgt. John Tyler Turner of Company M, 22nd Regiment; Pvt. Daniel Burgess of Confederate States Navy, crew member on the steamer *North Carolina*; Pvt. Aubrey Covington, unknown; Pvt. Robert Tate McIntyre of Company E, 27th Regiment; and Pvt. Murphy Burris of 16th Battalion and Company A, 15th Regiment. (Photograph courtesy of Randolph Room, Asheboro Public Library.)

The Records and Remembrances of Old Soldiers

OLD SOLDIERS GREW YOUNG. [Undated newspaper clipping from unknown paper, thought to be from around 1913]

Upon invitation from Capt. Y. M. C. Johnson a few of the veterans met with him at his home the 30th of January last for the purpose of celebrating his 73rd birthday and relating our experience in war under Lee and Jackson.

A delicious dinner, in marked contrast with hardtack and Nassau bacon, the usual fare of the soldier of '61–'65, was prepared and served by Mrs. M. E. Johnson and Miss Irene Johnson.

After dinner we assembled in the sitting room and began relating our varied experiences. Capt. Johnson and I had served in the same company during the war while the others were each of different companies. I objected at first to telling of my courtship but, being called upon the second time, related the following which the readers of this sketch may call romance or courtship whichever they choose.

I was wounded below Richmond and carried to a hospital there. Shortly, I along with two or three hundred others was transferred to Petersburg, from which place, I wearing nothing but my hospital gown, set out to find a North Carolina hospital. Before going far I became weak and sat down. Shortly, a colored woman approached me and asked me whether I was a man or a woman. I replied that I was a wounded North Carolina soldier. This being her native state, she was so glad to see me that she kissed me all over the face at one stroke. Upon learning that I was in search of a North Carolina hospital she assisted me to walk but we had not gone far before I became weak and sat down. At length we tried again, but with the same result. I was so sick by this time that she held me in her lap. There was no laughter from the passing people as there would be now-a-days.

Two gentlemen came up, one of them remarking that I was a wounded soldier and upon ascertaining that I was a North Carolinian, he replied that this was his good old state, too. I recognized Governor Vance and told him that I was one of his supporters in the election. He thanked me and said that he would like to talk with me but saw that I was too weak. Under Gov. Vance's instructions the Negro woman carried me to the hospital and upon leaving me there requested that I not forget her, which I never have.

One day about two weeks later Gov. Vance came into the hospital and talked and shook hands with the wounded men, many of whom had served under him before he became governor. In reply to his inquiry I replied that I was still weak.

I noticed that as the old soldiers came in that morning they were using canes to assist them in walking, but when they left the canes were being carried under their arms. They had grown young. The army was well represented by infantry, heavy artillery and buttermilk drinkers. All old veterans know who these were.

John T. Turner
Sgt. Company M, 22nd Regt.[1]

THE CONFEDERATE MONUMENT
[Clipping from unidentified newspaper]

MR. EDITOR: I notice in your issue of August 31st, a gentleman from Franklinville wrote favorably of a monument at Asheboro in memory of our Confederate dead, although the correspondent says he was too young for service in the civil war.

I also see in your issue of September 28th, that a gentleman from Ohio says he was a Randolph boy, and loves them yet, although he wore the "Blue" at Gettysburg, and is ready to send a dollar as a donation.

I wore the "Gray" from 1861 to 1865, and am not ashamed of the suit. I am glad the young soldier remembers '61 to '65, and is willing to help us.

Now, let us help ourselves some. I say to the brothers who wore my color let us go to work and have the monument raised at the Court House. I know there are many who fell in battle and not a mark to show where they fell. Many have children living that are anxious about perpetuating the names of their fathers in some permanent way. All could help, and in this way every soldier, who fell in battle, could have his name, regiment, etc., engraved on the monument.

Let us see what can be done to erect it, and have it unveiled at our reunion next year. Brothers, let us hear what you have to say about it.

John T. Turner
Ramseur, N. C., Oct. 2, 1899[2]

AN ACTIVE VETERAN [*The Asheboro Courier*—July 21, 1910]

There are in Ramseur 7 Confederate Veterans, and one of them, John T. Turner, was a member of the famous 26th (22nd) North Carolina Regiment and is 68 years of age. He owns a mule 38 years old, with which he cultivates a farm several miles out in the country. This year, he made 64 bushels of wheat and other crops in proportion, all by his labor. He is still hale and hearty.[3]

OLD SOLDIER WRITES OF REUNION.

[Undated clipping from unidentified newspaper]

Mr. Editor:

I am back from the Reunion at Winston, and will say a few words concerning it. I have attended a great many but never before saw so many "Rebs" at a state reunion.

I never before saw a more sober crowd. All were quiet and well pleased with their trip. I am well pleased with it. Our sleeping quarters were neat and clean, just suited to the weather. Our mess hall was well arranged and well furnished. I was well pleased with Winston.

I met three old vets I had not seen since August, 1864, when we were near Petersburg, and we knew each other. They were Mr. Crouch, who was our drummer boy, and Mr. Harper Poe, both of whom were from Guilford County and belonged to Company E, 22nd Regiment; and Mr. W. A. Elliott, of Company M, 21st Regiment. Mr. Elliott now lives in Orange County. No doubt there were more of my old friends but we are old and look different from the young men we were in the sixties.

All of us who attend these reunions should wear some kind of badge showing our company and regiment and all could see who we are. I would like to see all of the old 22nd regiment now living, but never will in any other way.

I shook hands with Judge Clark. He used to drill with our regiment back in '62. He was a boy then. I hope he will be in the front ranks next November.

John T. Turner
Sergeant Company M, 22nd North Carolina Regiment.[4]

[*Note:* A similar article was written in a different paper, also unidentified, in which he ends with the following poem.]

BRAVE MEN WHO WORE THE GRAY.

By John T. Turner, Sergeant Co. M, 22nd North Carolina Regiment

A sad but lovely sight to see
　Old soldiers in their gray,
And hear them tell what used to be
　On every battle day.

They left their native home to aid,
    To gain or get defeat,
And keep the honor that was made
    At the battle of Chancellorsville.

Those Yankees with joy to take our Richmond town,
    Were bravely met by Carolina boys, who completely broke their plans
Then came in Hooker with his Yankees
    To push our Carolina boys from their stand;

He was met by Jackson and his boys who completely broke their lines.
    Here Jackson was a noted general, he with Carolina boys did fight;
He met Hooker's crowd at Chancellorsville
    And put them all to flight.

These are our heroes too,
    These men we look upon this day
Who fought so bravely in their gray,
    And kept the honor due.

We had more men in the Civil War,
    More wounded, killed outright,
Than any other state by far.
    The boys in gray could fight.

At Bethel, she was first, you know,
    And bravely took her stand;
The farthest at Gettysburg to go,
    They stood by their command.

Their heads are almost white,
    Their faces show careworn;
'Twill not be long till they will be,
    In a brighter, better home.

So let them live a quiet life,
    So honored and so brave;
And throw aside all grudge and strife,
    To meet beyond the grave.

I wish you all that life can give,
    Extend to you my love and hope
That I may meet you far above.

Veterans, please consider the last two verses of the above, as we will soon all be gone from this earth.[5]

REUNION AT RICHMOND: RANDOLPH VETERAN WRITES OF MANY POINTS OF INTEREST VISITED
[Undated clipping from an unknown newspaper]

    Mr. Editor: The Veterans are back from the Reunion at Richmond, but a sketch of what was seen will be of interest to those who could not attend. Many of us visited many of the roads we traveled with the army, bringing back many sad memories which nevertheless gave much pleasure.

We visited the battle field of Fair Oaks and Seven Pines; crossed the Chickahominy river where began the seven days fight in front of Richmond. We also visited Mechanicsville battle field, Frazier's Farm, Gaines Mill, Cold Harbor, and found all looking very much like it did back in the sixties.

Another interesting place was at Petersburg, where the enemy placed a mine under our lines and killed hundreds of our soldiers.

I think all the boys who wore the gray had a grand time at Richmond. Many of us spent only a short time in Richmond, the remainder of the time we were visiting old scenes.

Comrades, we used to have to answer the roll call three times a day, but we will never have to do this again, but we must answer one more call sooner or later, so let us all live so that we will be ready when that last call comes.

John T. Turner
Co. M, 22nd, N. C. Reg., Ramseur, N. C.[6]

RAMSEUR, N. C., JUNE 17TH, 1907 [The following is similar to the above article, and is dated, but is from another newspaper, *The Bulletin*, published 20 June 1907.]

Editor Bulletin:—I am back from the Confederate reunion at Richmond, will say first that the old soldiers had a jolly old time from what I could see of them. I was in town one day only. I first looked over Fair Oaks famous battle field; then to Seven Pines. Both fields look very much like they did when we were fighting there. I visited the grounds at Oak Wood where thirteen thousand Confederate dead were buried, killed and died in hospitals. I also visited Holly Wood where eighteen thousand of the men who wore the gray are sleeping. I then journeyed north to the Chickahominy river and crossed where A. P. Hill's troop crossed to open the seven day fight in front of Richmond; thence down the north side one mile to McCanick's mill where we got into 'hot water' right. The battle field is now owned by Mr. Joseph Brooks who runs a vegetable farm. The field that I saw strewn with dead and wounded and drenched in blood, now produces cabbage, onions, tomatoes, water melons, etc. I went to the Ellerson mill from where I was wounded by a soldier from the 4th Michigan regiment. This place looks very natural. I visited the Blowup below Petersburg which makes old soldiers feel young to see. I was on the north side of Appomattox river in sight when it took place in July 1864. I was in the mine and find it to be about 80 ft. long, 40 ft. wide and 15 ft. deep. I went into the tunnel where it has not yet fallen in. I suppose it is four hundred yards long, four feet wide and six feet high.

I would have been glad to have had some of the 22nd regiment with me in my travels.

Back again to Richmond with my old brother soldiers to hear them talk if Lee or Jackson had been there to command them, Grant could not march into Richmond or Petersburg. Where are all the boys of the 22nd regiment? I saw one that I have not seen since the war closed. His name is J. M. May of Company E from Guilford Co.

Brothers, we are growing old; our ranks are thinning fast. A few more years and we will answer to the last roll call. Let us all live the life that when we meet the last time we will have a greater season of rejoicing than at Richmond. Comrades, if I have misrepresented anything in these lines I beg your pardon. If any of you ever go to McCanicks mill, visit Joseph Brooks and wife. I shall never forget their kind treatment toward me.

With best wishes to all.

John T. Turner
Company M, 22nd N. C. Reg.[7]

A CONFEDERATE VETERAN WRITES CONCERNING
THE CIVIL WAR [Undated and unnamed newspaper]
Mr. Editor:

I belonged to Co. M, 22nd North Carolina Regiment. I volunteered in the spring of 1861 and served in Virginia under Lee and Jackson, only being excused from duty one day while in that state, and went through 32 days of battle and never lost a drop of blood until I was wounded in the right arm, below Richmond. I was discharged in 1864 below Petersburg, and after having been at home eight days, was conscribed and became 1st Lieutenant in Co. B, 1st Battalion of light infantry to do guard duty on the train from Wilmington to Weldon. When Johnson surrendered the City of Wilmington I became guard on the train from Weldon to Raleigh; and later on the run from Raleigh to Salisbury. At the close of the war I returned home.

I have attended three general reunions of the soldiers, one at Charlestown, S. C., two at Richmond, Va., the State reunion seven times and all the county reunions.

Now the monument to the memory of the Confederate veterans is to be unveiled soon. I hope to meet every soldier living in this county on that day. Come one and all who wore the gray in the sixties and see how many of us can be there. I think it is credit to us to see this shaft at the county site if we did fight for the lost cause. I am glad I was a soldier and to attend these reunions.

Jno. T. Turner
Sergeant Co. M, 22 N. C. Reg., Ramseur, N. C.[8]

Letter Written Home by Stanley "Sug" Kivett to His Family Concerning the Death of His Brother, Daniel M. Kivett

State of Va   Richmond   May the 18 1862

Dear father   Mother   Brother and Sisters   I take the oppertunity of Riting you a few lines to let you know that I am well at this time and hope these few lines may find you all well and Doing well   I have know good news to Rite to you we have hard times hear we have Bin marchin for amonth or more through Rain and mud Sometimes knee Deep and Sometimes all knight We have aheep of Sickness hear I have never had the chance to Rite to you Since I heard that D M Kivet was Dead I never heard that he was Dead till afew days a go I heard that J R Bowman was coming after him I would Be glad to hear of his Coming after him and would Be glad to see him I Dont know what ailded him I want you to Rite to me as Soon as you get these few lines for I want to know if John has come after him I would like to come and see you all we havent Bin in any fight yet But I exspect we will have the hardest Battle hear that ever was Red of we are in two miles of Richmond we came hear last knight I think we will Stay hear till the fight Comes on I cant tell when I will have the Chance to Come home when I get the Chance I will come I Shall look for answer before long Sow you must Rite to me Soon and fail not for I want to hear from you all very Bad

                        This from Stanly Kivett
                        to Daniel Kivet
                        Direct your letter to Richmond Va[9]

Obituaries Written by John T. Turner

[Sergeant John T. Turner was faithful in writing obituaries for his comrades when he knew about their passing. The following are some examples found in local papers. Some are undated, so I have inserted dates of death for those that are not dated.]

ANOTHER OLD VETERAN PASSES AWAY
[*The Courier*—Died 2 March 1913]
To the Editor of The Courier.

I write for my old comrade veteran who belonged to my company and fought side by side with me during the sanguinary struggle of the war between the States. His name was Jacob Foust. He joined our company in the spring of 1862 near the little town of Fredericksburg, Va., where a few months later one of the great battles of the war was fought.

He was a good soldier and faithfully performed every duty that fell to his lot. I was in several battles with him, to-wit, Seven Days Battle around Richmond, two days at Sharpsburg, two days at Manassas, three days at Chancellorsville and three days at Gettysburg. In these gigantic struggles he proved himself to be a vigilant soldier and one who was willing if necessary to sacrifice his life for the good of his country.

During the famous retreat from that frightful field of Gettysburg he was captured at Falling Water by a detachment of the advanced guard of the northern army. He was exchanged in the winter of 1863 and was back with his company.

In the spring of 1864 he lay around in front of Petersburg. In the aforesaid battles he loaded and shot as fast as any one in Jackson's army.

When the war was over he returned home and made his support by holding the plow handles. He continued a hardworking man as long as he was able. As he was a good soldier in time of war, so was he a good citizen in time of peace.

I could say more about Mr. Foust but it is sufficient to say that he has passed over the river and it won't be long before all of our old vets will cross the river never to return.

John T. Turner
Co. M, 22nd N. C. Regiment, Ramseur, N. C.[10]

A TRIBUTE [*The Courier*—16 November 1911]

Ramseur, N. C., Nov. 11, 1911.
Editor Courier, Asheboro, N. C.
Dear Sir:

Another Confederate soldier of Company M, 22nd N. C. Regiment, answered to the last roll call on November 4th. This was Private E. Tyson Langley, who volunteered in '61 and went from this county with M, the Odell Company, to the Army of Virginia and served there two years.

He went through the Battle of Seven Pines, but in the second day's battle of the seven days' fighting below Richmond he lost his right hand and received his honorable discharge from the service. Since the close of the war to the time of his death, Mr. Langley followed farming and made a good living with only one hand, while there are some who can't do as well with two. While with our company he was a good soldier and did not shirk his work, and in after years he showed the same disposition.

Of all the 132 members of our company who went off at the outbreak of the war, I know of but 8 or 10 now living, the rest died in battle, in the hospitals, or like Mr. Langley, in a well-earned peace. Who next of Company M will answer the last roll? God knows and we don't. We have but a short time to wait until, let us hope, we shall meet some of the members of our old camp army, who have been mustered out before us for a peace which is eternal.

John T. Turner, Serg't Co. M,
22nd N. C. Troops, C. S. A.[11]

ANOTHER CONFEDERATE SOLDIER GONE [Died 30 January 1916]

Mr. Editor:

The many friends of W. Franklin Hayes regretted to hear of this death which occurred January 30 at the home of his son near Cedar Falls. He was buried in the Shady Grove cemetery the 21st [actually 31st].

The writer of this sketch and Mr. Hayes were raised as boys together and taught by the same teacher in the same log cabin.

As a soldier Mr. Hayes was as good as Lee and Jackson had under them in Virginia and did his duty as one. The writer was in some twenty odd battles with him. He was one of my messmates for about three and one-half years. During those days when Lee moved his army around Richmond and Petersburg in 1864, the writer was transferred to North Carolina on light duty and lost sight of Mr. Hayes until the end of the war. He was wounded only once during the war.

After the surrender he married Miss Isabel Williams and settled down to farming and made a fair living. He was raised a Primitive Baptist and lived in that faith until he died.

The writer looks back to his youthful days and recalls those with whom he went off to war and to the number about whom he has written a sketch of their travels together. Their ranks are growing thinner every day and there are but few of those who went to war together left. I could say a great deal about Mr. Hayes for the better, but it will do him no good as he has passed over the river. Who will come next?

John T. Turner
Co. M. 22nd Reg. N. C. Troops[12]

ANOTHER CONFEDERATE VETERAN GONE
[Undated clipping from unidentified newspaper]

As I write for all the old soldiers that die that I was acquainted with before and after the war, it is now my lot to write concerning the death of Joseph A. Henson which occurred June 29, 1916. He volunteered in the spring of '61 in Co. M, 22nd North Carolina Regiment, the same company that I was a member of. We went to Virginia at the start and were under Lee and Jackson. For the first year and a half he was not with the company, but was detailed as a driver. Then, the number of teams being reduced, he came back to the company and took up his musket with the rest of us boys, and was with us through all the fighting that the regiment engaged in until the retreat from Gettysburg when he was cut away from us as a prisoner at Falling Water. This was in '63. He was exchanged the following winter and returned to his command at Orange Court House, and remained with us until the armies were all drawn around Richmond and Petersburg. On August 2, 1864, I was transferred from Virginia to this State, and I can't say any more about Mr. Henson until after the war, but from the way he acted as a soldier while I was with him, I'm sure he stuck to his duty as a soldier. After the war, he returned home and was married to Angeline Pugh. Several years after her death he was married to Susan Burrow, who died some 15 years ago. By occupation he was a carpenter and farmer, and made a good living as he did a soldier. He was a member of Pleasant Cross Christian church and did a great deal of Sunday School work at various places. He was buried at Bailey's Grove in compliance with his request. He was a good, pious man, attended to his own business and let other people's alone. He leaves the following children by his first wife: Messrs. J. G., R. C. and H. A. Henson and Mrs. J. D. Leonard. Mrs. W. I. Carpenter, another daughter, preceded him to the Better Land a few years ago. In addition to the children named there are 20 grandchildren and one great-grandson.

I could say a great deal more about Mr. Henson as a soldier, but he has answered the last roll call which we must all soon do, so let us all live the life that Mr. Henson did and be ready to respond to the call when it comes to us. Mr. Henson was 79 years, six months and two days old.

      John T. Turner,
      Sergeant Co. M, 22nd N. C. Regiment[13]

ANOTHER OLD SOLDIER GONE [*The Courier*—13 May 1915]

  Here is another one of my neighbor boys who has crossed over the river and is waiting for me. David Wright, who volunteered in the spring of 1861, and served in my company and went through all of the battles my regiment was in under Lee and Jackson in Virginia, and answered to his name at Appomattox, the 9th day of April, 1865, went to his last resting place the 5th instant, at old Sandy Creek cemetery.

  I will say for Mr. Wright, as a citizen and soldier, he was among the best of each. I cannot say too much concerning him, for I had all chances to know him. We were raised near each other and lived near together all of our lives up to the time the war broke out between the states, when both volunteered and went off in the same company for over four years, and then lived as neighbors till near the time of his death, when I left that neighborhood. I am satisfied Mr. Wright lived as he did before I left those parts.

  He was a son of Abraham Wright, a Primitive Baptist minister. David followed his father in that respect, except that he was not a preacher. I am satisfied he has gone well.

  He was wounded four times: first, at Malvern Hill; second, at Spottsylvania Courthouse, Virginia; third, at Shepherd Town, Maryland; and fourth, at Manassas; but at no time badly enough for a furlough. He stayed with his company and was always ready to answer to his name for duty, let come what would. He was ready to do his part and more if he could.

  I could write a great deal more about Mr. Wright as a good Confederate soldier; but he is gone, and it will do him no good now.

      John T. Turner,
      Co. M, 22nd Reg. N. C. Troops.[14]

LETTER FROM CONFEDERATE VETERAN [*The Courier*—5 July 1911]

    Interesting Reminiscences of the Civil War.

Mr. Editor:

  I notice in your issue of the 29th ult. the death of Levi Foster. I will write a few lines for you to print of our ups and downs through the war between the states.

  Mr. Foster and I volunteered in Capt. J. M. Odell's Company M, 22nd N. C. Regiment, the 10th day of June, 1861, and served under Lee and Jackson in Virginia, and no better man than Mr. Foster ever carried a Southern musket. We fought together at Fair Oaks Farm, also together at Seven Pines at the opening of the seven days battle below Richmond. I was shot down and left in the lines of the

Yankees. Foster and Calvin Allred rushed through their lines and brought me out. Next day, Allred was killed at Frazier's Run. I did not see Foster again until the battle commenced. I went into the fight and saw Foster doing his duty, shooting at the Yankees. I called to him, "Levi, you are still shooting at the Blue Jackets." "Yes," he replied, "but they haven't shot me yet." This was in Cold Harbor, Md.

Foster was wounded at Manassas and Bristow Station. He went with Lee and Jackson to Chancellorsville, Fredericksburg, Gettysburg and Petersburg.

After the war was over Foster returned home and settled down to farming. He was a good farmer and a good Christian man.

It may be interesting to The Courier readers to know the names of a few of the first volunteers who are still living out of the 130 men who first went off with Capt. Odell: W. F. Hayes, Joe Kivett, Joseph Hinson, David Wright, Simon Allen, J. F. Kivett, Larkin York, J. M. Cox, John T. Turner, sergeant. The rest have crossed over the river, and we are waiting to go.

I would like to hear from someone of the old company if they feel like writing. Yours as ever,

John T. Turner
Co. M, 22nd Reg. N. C. T.[15]

John Turner's Obituary

[I find it only fitting to include the obituary of John Tyler Turner here, as he did this for so many others.]

Mr. John T. Turner, Aged Citizen of Ramseur, Dies Monday
[From *The Courier*—4 October 1923]

Ramseur, Oct. 3.—John T. Turner, aged 81 years, a resident of Ramseur for thirty odd years, one of her most respected citizens and a brave Confederate Veteran died Monday after three weeks illness from paralysis. Mr. Turner had been in good health until three years ago when he suffered a stroke of paralysis since which time he has been incapacitated for his regular work, but able to do home chores and go about town to some extent. But when becoming suddenly sick about three weeks ago he failed to recover strength and grew weaker until the end came.

Mr. Turner served in more than a score of battles in the Civil War and was wounded once and suffered many hardships in the bravest manner for the sake of his country. He took great delight in telling about his many experiences in the war, and wrote interesting letters in the Courier some years ago. He had many firm friends among the old soldiers, most of them having preceded him to the beyond. He goes to again join the ranks of the faithful ones who believed in their Great Captain.

Opposite: **Gravesite of Sergeant John Tyler Turner at Sunset Knoll Cemetery in Ramseur, N.C.**

Mr. Turner was a faithful member of the M. E. Church, South, for more than fifty years. He loved his brothers in the church and was ready to help in the work of the church. He was also a member of the Masonic fraternity since young manhood.

He leaves a widow, three sons, P. P. Turner of Greensboro, Walter Turner of Columbia, S. C., and Ernest Turner of Ramseur and four daughters, Mrs. G. H. Jones of Franklinville, Mrs. Ella McMath and Miss Maggie Turner of Ramseur and Mrs. Morris of Greensboro, many other relatives and friends at this and surrounding places.

Funeral services were conducted by his pastor, Rev. W. L. Scott Tuesday at three o'clock and interment by his brother Masons in the city cemetery. The throng that attended his funeral and the many beautiful flowers that covered his grave showed the love and great esteem felt for this good man. His family and friends have our deepest sympathy.[16]

The Confederate Veterans Reunion

[The 9 August 1906 edition of *The Courier* announced a Confederate Veterans reunion to be "held this summer at Asheboro, for the purpose of organizing camps of veterans and their sons and a chapter of Daughters of the Confederacy." It was to include a picnic dinner, speakers and brass bands. It also stated that, "Federal soldiers present will be entertained as guests of the Confederacy." The reunion took place 1 September 1906, with seven members of Co. M attending, and was reported as follows in the 6 September 1906 edition of *The Courier*:]

CONFEDERATE REUNION.

104 Veterans of the Civil War Registered for Membership.

RANDOLPH CAMP WILL BE ORGANIZED.

Senator Overman Was Headed Off By
Wreck But The "Experience Meeting"
Was Enjoyed—Sumptuous
Dinner Served on Academy
Grounds—Many Impromptu
Speeches and Music
Formed the Program.

Saturday was an ideal day for the Reunion of Confederate Veterans of Randolph held at Asheboro. The weeks of rain ceased Friday and Saturday the mud had disappeared. Hundreds of people began arriving early Saturday morning and the warmth of the sun seemed to penetrate the souls of both old and young, causing a mingled pathetic joy to beam from every face. The Confederate veterans met at the courthouse in the morning to enter their names for membership in the retired army of Confederate warriors, whose ranks is rapidly thinning but whose glory will live in the hearts of true Americans forever.

A hundred and four, many bearing marks of battle, many tottering with age, while others were still active as youths, applied for membership in the camp, and at 11 o'clock formed in line of march in front of the courthouse under command of Capt. G. V. Lamb, the oldest officer present. He was assisted by Capt. W. S. Lineberry, Lieutenant J. A. Rush and Privates P. H. Morris and W. S. Crowson. At 11:10 Capt. Lamb called the camp to attention, and at his command, led by the Asheboro Nightingale Band, the body moved toward the Academy campus where more than 800 men and women and children had gathered to welcome the camp and provide entertainment for the day. The program of the day opened with prayer by Rev. H. A. Albright, of Moffitt, followed by a short welcome address by Rev. N. R. Richardson, pastor of the M. E. Church of Asheboro. It was expected that Senator Overman of Salisbury, would address the assembly but a telegram from him about 11 o'clock announced his regrets, saying he was unable to pass the wreck on the High Point and Asheboro road in time to fill his appointment. This was a great disappointment to our people, but throwing the meeting open for impromptu speeches and camp experiences the minds of the veterans were soon turned toward the vivid camp fire scenes, both happy and pathetic which made the day wear rapidly away. Speeches were made by Veterans C. Presnell, T. B. Tysor, W. S. Lineberry, H. C. Ingram, P. H. Morris and W. P. Wood. These were interspersed, with music, lead by Miss Nannie Bulla at the piano, consisting of pathetic airs enthusiastically participated in by the audience and solos, "Around the Camp Fire" by Mrs. E. E. Kephart and "Tenting On the Old Camp Ground" by Henry B. Martin. It was indeed a pathetic scene to look at the large concourse of veterans, who in younger days would have shouted for joy at the sound of those stirring strains, but can now find relief from their choaking patriotism and enthusiasm in silent tears.

About (12) o'clock dinner was served on the campus and it was truly sumptuous. The ladies of the county had provided well filled baskets, the contents of which were spread on long tables, which were presided over by a committee consisting of a member of each family presenting a basket. The reunion closed about four o'clock, all declaring it one of the most pleasant and interesting ever attended. The veterans who registered were:

F. L. Johnson, A 10th Bat., Artillery; J. W. Pugh, F, 2nd Battalion; A. J. Woodell, F, 2nd Battalion; A. M. Moore, G, 2nd Battalion; J. A. Hinson, M, 22nd Regiment; A. B. Steele, M, 22nd Regiment; A. S. Williams, B, 52nd Regiment; W. B. Scott, E, 52nd Regiment; E. D. Tucker, F, 46th Regiment; Duncan Davis, F, 46th Regiment; W. M. Mitchell, I, 22nd Regiment; E. M. Overman, G, 6th Regiment; D. N. Owen, I, 22nd Regiment; H. M. Lamb, H, 2nd Battalion, W. M. Stephenson, I, 36th Regiment; Capt. G. V. Lamb, I, 22nd Regiment; Nixon Presnell, I, 22nd Regiment; W. C. Routh, M, 22nd Regiment; W. D.

5. Old Times There Are Not Forgotten

Brower, K, 5th Cavalry; Dr. T. C. Dowd, 61st Regiment; A. G. Murdock, H, 58th Regiment; Dr. F. E. Asbury, A, Chew's Bat., P. H. Morris, E, 70th Regiment; J. H. Kirkman, H, 3rd Regiment; John W. Hancock, F, 46th Regiment; John R. Brown, State Militia; W. S. Crowson, F, 1st Regiment Junior Reserves; Ransom Johnson, A, 10th Battalion; W. W. Caviness, E, 26th Regiment; T. L. Russell, H, 38th Regiment;

W. D. Cross, I, 22nd Regiment; J. T. Shaw, H, 38th Regiment; Z. A. Cranford, H, 38th Regiment; B. F. Parrish, I, 42nd Regiment; N. C. Allred, I, 18th Regiment; Z. A. Lewallen, F, 2nd Battalion; M. C. Cross, I, 40th Regiment; W. C. Hooker, F, 2nd Battalion; Ab Smith, F, 2nd Battalion; R. L. Causey, I, 22nd Regiment; W. F. McCrary, H, 48th Regiment; Sam'l Aldridge, E, 10th Battalion; E. K. Moffitt, F, 2nd Battalion; A. J. Rush, B, 52nd Regiment; W. M. Miller, B, 52nd Regiment; S. F. Pugh, H, 16th Battalion; Lemuel Spencer, F, 46th Regiment; M. Thomas, E, 26th Regiment; Soloman York, L, 22nd Regiment; Patrick Lowder, D, 21st Regiment; Alex O'Brien, L, 22nd Regiment; D. A. Sikes, H, 3rd Regiment; J. R. Frazier, D, 44th Tennessee; W. S. Lineberry, F, 70th Regiment; Col. A. C. McAlister, 46th Regiment; A. M. McCollum, I, 22nd Regiment; D. G. McMasters, H, 38th Regiment; W. W. Brady, D, 48th Regiment; A. C. Rush, K, 54th Regiment; M. H. Moffitt, F, 2nd Battalion; W. P. Wood, I, 22nd Regiment; J. W. Holder, G, 46th Regiment; J. C. Frazier, F, 70th Regiment; J. M. Fields, F, 70th Regiment; J. A. Webster, M, 22nd Regiment; W. D. Ingram, H, 38th Regiment; J. M. Hayes, M, 22nd Regiment; J. C. Hanner, I, 22nd Regiment; W. R. Ashworth, F, 70th Regiment; John Heilig, I, 22nd Regiment; H. C. Presnell, K, 52nd Regiment; Levi Foster, M, 22nd Regiment; J. M Brown, L, 22nd Regiment; H. T. Siler, Confederate Battery, Navy; Z. N. Williams, H, 3rd Regiment; Wm. Skillicorn, Riley's Battery; H. H. Nelson, B, 3rd Regiment; C. M. Vestal, L, 22nd Regiment; Ruben Swaney, B, 48th Regiment; W. D. Siler, B, 40th Regiment; T. W. Andrews, F, 2nd Battalion; S. E. Allen, M, 22nd Regiment; Dan'l Chrisco, F, 70th Regiment; Ruben Cameron, K, 5th Cavalry; Iredell Robbins, I, 22nd Regiment; T. B. Tysor, I, 32nd Regiment; Sam'l Spoon, E, 1st Regiment; J. C. Cornelison, H, 44th Regiment; Elkanah Walls, I, 33rd Regiment; Alex Freeman, Junior Battalion; Z. Ellison, A, 10th Battalion; Nathan Morgan, B, 48th Regiment; J. M. Morgan, F, 3rd Regiment; J. A. McCaskill, C, 14th Regiment; W. H. McPherson, I, 26th Regiment; Absolom Fields, H, 30th Regiment; Kirb Bean, I, 42nd Regiment; L. O. Sugg, B, 2nd Battalion; H. C. Ingram, H, 38th Regiment; Sam'l Morrison, Raleigh Guard; H. C. Causey, F, 70th Regiment; H. A. Albright, C, 10th Regiment; N. T. Adams, I, 22nd Regiment; J. W. Jolly, I, 22nd Regiment.[17]

Opposite: **Confederate statue dedicated 2 September 1911 at Randolph County Courthouse in honor of the county's veterans. It was nicknamed "Hugo" after being damaged during the hurricane of that name. Strangely, Company M was omitted from the list of troops engraved on the monument. (Photograph courtesy of Randolph Room, Asheboro Public Library.)**

Captain John M. Odell's Expenses in Equipping Company M

One interesting set of documents in existence is the expense account records of Captain John M. Odell, which he presented to the county for payment. Though incomplete, these records give some insight into how the company was equipped as it left for the war. Among other things, it contains such information as where the material for uniforms for Company M was made. The records seem to show that much of the material came from "F. Fries." This would indicate Francis Fries of the Salem Manufacturing Cotton Mill in Salem, N.C. His mill produced a great deal of uniform material for the state throughout the war. Records still exist documenting how his fabrics were made.

The account records of John M. Odell are now held by the North Carolina State Archives in Raleigh. In addition, I have included a requisition to the army, dated 21 March 1862, for additional equipment needed for new recruits brought in during the first Conscript Act. The first document is a cover note explaining the expenses to the County Finance Committee.

[No date]

The inclosed Bills will explain the articles Bought and used by the Randolph Hornets more fully than I can do—And the amount charged for provisions was used by the Company while encamped in Randolph County and on their way to Raleigh and the expenses charged in Bill No. 1 was incurred Purchasing Goods for uniforms for the Company and the amount set opposite each article of Clothing will cover all the cost of same, I think.

J. M. Odell, Capt.
Randolph Hornets

Randolph Hornets

1st.   There was no donations in the acct.

2nd.   List of Equipment for Soldiers

80	Pair Pants of Salem Jeans	@ 3.15	$172.00
80	" " " " "	@ 2.40	192.00
80	Fatigue Shirts (Plaid Linsey)	@ 1.05	84.00
80	" Jackets (Salem Jeans)	@ 2.85	228.00
80	Cloth Caps	@ 75	60.00
80	pair Shoes(average	@ 1.75	140.00
80	Canteens & Straps	@ 55	44.00
80	Knapsacks & Straps	@ 1.50	120.00
80	Leather Belts(average)	@ 20	16.00
15	Tents (of Osnaburg)	@ 87½	& rope
11	Chopping Axes		

7	Hatchets
12	Spades
6	Mattocks
12	Frying Pans
12	Tea Kettles
6	Skillets & 7 Buckets
14	Coffee Pots
17	Camp & Mess Chests
14	Sets Knives & Forks
80	Pint Tins
80	Plates
6	Camp Kettles
14	Tin Pans

Amt. used by Commissioned Officers $ 56.00

I certify that the above is a true statement to the best of my Knowledge.
    J. M. Odell, Capt. Co. (M)
    Randolph Hornets

                                                   Cedar Falls   July 9, 1861

Randolph County
                In a/c with J. M. Odell

1861

June 11		To	Expense of J. M. Odell to Raleigh	10.90
		"	Amt. paid for Coat Buttons	14.50
		"	4 Hand Axes @1.00	4.00
		"	Freight on goods	1.00
		"	Amt. paid for Liquors	4.00
		"	Amt. pd. for Oil Cloth	65.00
		"	11 Chopping Axes & 2 Tea Cans	12.95
"	15	"	Expenses to Salem & Raleigh	16.50
		"	Canteens & Camp Kettles	33.75
		"	Freight	.75
		"	73 Belts of Kivett	12.41
		"	Beef of L. Leonard	10.71
		"	Potatoes &c.	3.15
July 1		"	Amt. pd. J. R. Cole for services in drilling	28.00
	6	"	Expenses in carting Drill Master to N.C. R.R.	2.00
		"	Amt. pd. for Onions, Potatoes & Beans	3.50

"		20 pr. Shoes for sundry volunteers			
				@1.75	35.00
"		200 pr. Socks		@25	50.00
"		6 Mattocks		@1.00	6.00
" 8	"	Amt. pd. John Brower for Drilling			15.00
"		50 Tin cups		@10	5.00
"		60 Tin Plates		@12½	7.50
"		4 Spiders		@1.25	5.00
"		5 Camp Kettles		@1.25	6.25
"		8 Belts		@30	2.40
"		48 Pint Tins		@8½	4.08
					$410.02
		Cr. By Cash Rec'd			189.00
					$221.02

[Bill No. 1]

Randolph Hornets
Capt. J. M. Odell

In account with Cedar Falls Co.

1861

July	To	Paying	J. M. Odell's		Bill No. 1	410.02
"	"	"	Lyndsay & Campbell's		" No. 2	36.30
"	"	"	Seborn Perry's		" No. 3	25.20
"	"	"	Sarah C. Julian's		" No. 4	66.00
"	"	"	E. L. Crowson's		" No. 5	7.41
"	Paid A. Creech for Pant Goods					136.43
"	"	F. Fries " " "				300.50
"	To	498¾ yds. Osnaburg		@10		49.87
"	"	495½ " "		@11		54.51
"	"	23 " Plaid Linsy		@25		5.75
"	"	24 " " "		@16⅔		4.00
"	"	111½ " " "		@25		27.87
"	"	Cotton thread & twine				2.44
"	"	27½ yds. Plaid Linsy		@27½		9.35
"	"	70 dz. Buttons		@4		2.85
"	"	¾ yd. Statian [Satin?] Cloth				.35
"	"	11 pr. Shoes		@1.65		17.71
"	"	23 " "		@1.50		34.50
"	"	3 " "		@1.85		5.55
"	"	7 " "		@1.60		11.20
"	"	1 " "		@1.35		1.35

5. Old Times There Are Not Forgotten   151

"	"	9½ lb. Flax Thread	@1.25		11.87
"	"	18½ lb. Pieces Shirting	@16⅔		3.13
"	"	26 lb. Coffee	@25		6.50
"	"	47 " Sugar	@12½		5.87
"	"	4 lb. 6 oz. Butter	@69 and		
		4 " 11 oz. do.	@70		1.39
"	"	383 lb. Bacon	@15		57.45
"	"	5 Sacks Flour	@3.75		35.75
"	"	4 do.	@3.50		14.00
"	"	192 lb. Meal	@2		3.84
"	"	50 dz. Buckels	@5		2.65
					1,340.56

1861		Account Brot Over			1,340.56
"	"	1 Hand Axe			.75
"	"	1 do.			.88
"	"	1 do.			1.00
"		1¼ yds. Jeanes			.75
"	"	¼ yds. do.			.20
"	"	9 yds. Salem Geans	@85		7.65
"	"	6 " " "	@1.00		6.00
"	"	1¼ yd. " "	@75		.94
"	"	4 pr. Socks	@30		1.20
"	"	2 pr. do.	@75		1.50
"	"	9 Bonnet Braids			.44
"	"	24 yds. Cambric	@10		2.40
"	"	4 lbs. Powder	@1.00		4.00
"	"	4 lbs. Shot	@12½		.50
"	"	11¾ yds. Worsted Twine (?)	@52		5.88
"	"	12½ lb. Nails	@7		.86
"	"	12 " Soap	@4		.48
"	"	87½ " Rope	@28		22.78
"	"	1 Cake Beeswax	@30/lb.		.69
"	"	3 Sets Knives & Forks		@75	2.25
"	"	1 " " " "		@1.50	1.50
"	"	1 " " " "		@1.75	1.75
"	"	91 yds. Sheeting	@10		9.10
"	"	2 Sets Plates	@35		.70
"	"	2 lbs. Candles	@30		.60
"	"	1 Candle Stick to 38 Skeins Silk 1.90			2.05
"	Paid Glasgow for cutting 55 pr. Pants		@20		11.00
"	"	" " Extra Work on same			.64

"	To	18 yds. Velvet Trimming @12½	2.25
"	"	3 yds. Silk Twist @15 1 Plug of Tobacco @15	.60
"	"	6 yds. Stripes @12½ (Pattern ?) Ribbon @38	1.23
"	"	3 Pans @35 4 @ 40 1 pr. Blankets 3.50	6.15
"	"	6¾ yds. Satinett @1.00 16 Pad Locks 2.80	8.75
"	"	Steel Pens .25 Paper .20 Envelopes .20	.65
"	"	6 Sacks @12½ 6 Tea Kettles @60	4.35
"	"	3 Coffee Pots @50 6 Shovels @1.25	9.00
"	"	7 Buckets @50 Teaming Lumber 40	3.90
			1,465.13

1861		Amount Brot Over		1,465.13
"	To	11¾ yds. Tweeds	@40	5.28
"	"	14 Provision Boxes	@86	12.00
"	"	Putting Helves in Axes		1.75
"	Paid for Making 62 Coats		@75	46.50
"	" " " 75 Pants		@25	18.75
"	" " " 90 Caps		@25	22.50
"	Paid for Making 40 Shirts		@15	6.00
"	" " " 88 Haver Sacks		@4	3.52
"	" " " 10 Tents		@2.00	20.00
"	" " " 88 Knap Sacks		@6	5.28
				1,605.71

Rec. payt. in full

Geo. Makepeace Agt.
Cedar Fall Co.

[Bill No. 2]

Franklinsville   July 8, 1861

J. M. Odell

Capt., Randolph Hornets
Bought of Cedar Falls Co.:

17½	yds	Flax Cloth @25	4.37½
23¾	"	Marlboro Checks @16	3.80
1	Gal.	Molasses	.50
2	lb.	Coffee @25	.50
1¼	yds	Col'd Cambric	.12½
6	pr.	Woolen Half Hose	1.50
7	pr.	Shoes @1.60	11.20
12	pr.	Shoes @1.75	21.00

1		Goat Skin	1.40
27		Tin Cups 1 Pt.	1.68
2		Tin Pans @15	.30
2		Bars Soap	.10
1	set	Edged Plates	.37½
8	lb.	Coffee	2.00
½	bu	Salt	.62½
2	bu.	Soda @15	.30
156½	lb.	Bacon @15	23.47½
1	pr.	Shoes	1.75
44	yds.	Marlboro stripes @15	6.60
4	hanks	Flax Thread	.70
2		Tin Pans 6 qt.	1.00
3		Coffee Pots 4 qt. @50	1.50
3	yds.	Spotted Flannel	1.20
2	lb.	Coffee	.50
Paid for Making		36 Fateugue Jackets	5.40
" " "		31 Towels	.15½
" " "		10 pr. Pants	2.50
" " "		24 pr. Coats @75	18.00
" " "		7 Large Boxes @2.25	15.75
" " "		Teaming Bacon, Flour &c.	1.00
			128.81

I certify that the within list is correct and that the articles was for the use of the Randolph Hornets.

July 22d 1861.

     John M. Odell Capt.
     Randolph Hornets

[Bill No. 9]

    J. M. Odell   Capt.
     Randolph Hornets

To Cedar Falls Co.

To Payt. for making 15 pr. pants @25	3.75
To Making 8 Coats @75	6.00
" " 4 Shirts @20	.80
	$10.55

Rec. payt.
  George Makepeace, Agt.
  Cedar Fall Co.

Capt. J. M. Odell, in acct.
    with Randolph Hornets

Cedar Falls Co.	Bill No. 1	1605.71
" " "	" " 2	128.81
J. H. & J. S. Steed	" " 3	37.57
Leander York	" " 4	34.25
B. Moffitt	" " 5	14.70
Moring & Byrns	" " 6	29.55
Coffin Foust & Co.	" " 7	34.51
		1885.10
J. W. Brower	" " 8	81.43
Cedar Falls Co.	" " 9	10.55
		$1977.08

We the undersigned Committee of Finance for the County of Randolph certify that we have examined the foregoing accounts and find them Correct and recommend the County to pay the same.

Augt. 7, 1861

     A. S. Horney}
         }Finance Committee
     Danl. Bulla }

North Carolina
Randolph County

I, J. M. Worth, County Trustee of said County, do hereby certify that I have paid the above sum of nineteen hundred seventy seven and 08/100 Dollars under the orders of the County Court of said County.

Oct. 1st 1861

     J. M. Worth

I, Joseph H. Brower, Clerk of the County Court of said County do hereby certify that A. S. Horney and Daniel Bulla are two of the three members of the committee [of finance of said county.]

     [Joseph H. Brower]

Received of Capt. Odell fifty six dollars the amount used by the Commissioned Officers in the inclosed account.

Oct. 24, 1861

     A. S. Horney, one of the Committee
     of Finance for Randolph County.

No. 40

SPECIAL REQUISITION

    44   Uniform Coats
    44   Pair Pants
    44   Caps
    44   Knapsacks & Straps
    44   Canteens & Straps
    44   Haversacks

I certify that the above requisition is discreet; and that the articles specified are absolutely requisite for the public service, required so by the following circumstances:

    They are for recruits who have not been supplied.

W. M. Pearce ? . . . .
. . . . Quarter Master North Carolina Army, will issue the articles specified in the above requisition.

                                Jno. M. Odell
                                      Commanding

   RECEIVED AT   Raleigh   the   21st   day of   March   1862
of   W. M. Pearce ?   Quartermaster of North Carolina Army,

    All the above specified articles.

In full of the above requisition.

    [SIGNED DUPLICATES]   Jno. M. Odell
                                    Capt. Co. M, 22nd R, NCT[18]

Request for Furlough for Private Thomas Arnold

A copy of a request for furlough for Pvt. Thomas Arnold was found in the Civil War clipping files of the Randolph Room of Asheboro Public Library. I do not know the original document's location, but I felt it needed to be included to give an insight into other service rendered by men from Company M. It was written by Alexander S. Horney, a local justice of the peace and one of the founders of the Cedar Falls Company, to Colonel A. C. McAlister. The Major Harris referred to in the document was Major James G. Harris of the 7th N.C. Infantry Regiment, who had been brought to Randolph County from Petersburg, Va., with a detachment of men to work under Col. McAlister in arresting deserters and absentees from the army in the Randolph-Moore-Chatham area. Evidently, Thomas Arnold was helping to find these deserters.

> Franklinsville March 20, 1865
> Col. McAlister
> Dear Sir,
> Thomas Arnold who belongs to Co. M 22 Regt. was at home upon furlough and his furlow has run out he has been acting as guide & spy for Maj. Harris ever since he has been in this neighborhood. he is still willing to act as such he would like to remain at home a few days as his family are all down with the measles & he wishes you to give him something to show to protect him.
> Yours Truly,
> A. S. Horney[19]

Death Notices of Company M Soldiers Written by Someone Other Than Sgt. John Turner

The following obituaries of Company M soldiers were found in various local papers and may or may not mention their Confederate service during the war, but give information on family connections, burial, etc.

MR. J. M. ODELL DEAD [*The Courier*—28 July 1910]

Mr. J. M. Odell, one of North Carolina's prominent cotton mill men, died at his home in Concord, last Thursday night after a lingering illness of several months. The funeral was conducted Saturday afternoon followed by interment in the family mausoleum. Bishop John C. Kilgo, of Durham, preached the funeral sermon.

Mr. Odell was a native of Randolph County. For several years he and a brother conducted the Cedar Falls manufacturing plant. After the war, he went to Greensboro and engaged in the mercantile business and later moved to Concord, where he established the Odell Manufacturing Company.

Mr. Odell is survived by one brother, Mr. J. A. Odell, of Greensboro; two sisters, Mrs. Deritta Swaim of Millboro, Randolph County; and Mrs. Tabitha Ellison of Franklinville; one son, Mr. W. R. Odell of Concord; and one daughter, Mrs. S. P. Durham, of Bessemer City.[20]

5. Old Times There Are Not Forgotten

Gravesite of Captain Columbus Frank Siler in Oakwood Cemetery, Raleigh, N.C.

CAPT. C. F. SILER [*The Courier*—5 August 1909]

The Courier regrets to learn of the death of Capt. C. F. Siler which occurred at the Soldier's Home in Raleigh on Wednesday of last week.[21]

D. O. COBLE DEAD [*The Courier*—11 January 1923]

Mr. D. O. Coble, an old Confederate veteran died at his home near Millboro January 2. He had been in feeble health for a number of years having a cancer on his face and a complication of troubles. Mr. Coble had been married three times. The last wife survives him. Also the following children, Mrs. J. C. Coltrane, Greensboro; Mrs. James Nelson, Millboro; Mrs. Lou Staley, Randleman; Mr. J. R. Coble, Gray's Chapel; John Coble; Clem Coble, Ramseur; W. M. Coble; and one son, Randolph Coble, who lives in the west. Deceased was 83 years of age. Rev. W. F. Ashburn conducted the funeral of deceased at Grays Chapel. Burial followed.[22]

TRAIN KILLS JOE BREEDLOVE [*The Courier*—25 November 1915]

Joe Breedlove was killed by the northbound passenger train north of Liberty yesterday. Mr. Breedlove cannot hear well and it is believed he was walking on the track. He was 75 or 80 years old.[23]

J. M. POUNDS [*The Courier*—28 March 1929]

J. M. Pounds, aged 88 years, 4 months and 6 days, died at his home at Cedar Falls Monday after declining health of nearly two years and confinement of about one week. He had been a loyal member of Cedar Falls Baptist church for 60 years, and was one of the most substantial and highly respected citizens in his community. Funeral services were held Tuesday afternoon at the Cedar Falls Baptist church by P. D. Buck, assisted by Rev. George Loflin, pastor of M. E. church at Cedar Falls. Mr. Pounds is survived by his wife, and three children, Miss Minnie Belle Pounds and Randolph Pounds of Cedar Falls, and J. L. Pounds of Asheboro.[24]

S. E. ALLEN DEAD [*The Courier*—13 March 1924]

After years of ill health, S. E. Allen, of Ramseur suffered a second stroke of paralysis this week, resulting in his death Tuesday. Mr. Allen was a well known man of the county and is a Confederate Veteran, having gone through the four years of the war without being wounded. He was 80 years old. His wife, who was Miss Ursula Masten and three sons survive. The sons are W. H. Allen, of Rockingham; M. E. and C. E. Allen, of Asheboro. The funeral and burial services were conducted by Rev. T. G. Green and Rev. John Allred, at Pleasant Ridge church Wednesday. Mr. Allen had a great many staunch friends who mourn his death.[25]

PETER BROWN DIES [*The Courier*—24 January 1929]

Peter Brown, 82, prominent farmer of the Julian community, died Wednesday afternoon following an illness lasting ten days. Funeral will be conducted at Shiloh church Friday morning by Rev. W. F. Ashburn, of Greensboro. Surviving are two daughters, Mrs. Mollie Staley, of Julian, and Mrs. J. C. Wicker, of Liberty; and two sons, J. F. Brown, of Julian, and W. A. Brown, of Charlotte.[26]

DEATH OF MR. CAMPBELL—FUNERAL CONDUCTED AT FORMER HOME AT CEDAR FALLS LAST WEEK [*The Courier*—13 June 1907]

J. E. Campbell, father of Wm. Campbell, of Ramseur, who left Cedar Falls two years ago, and has since been employed at the Southside cotton mills at Winston-Salem, died last week. He was buried at Cedar Falls Tuesday of last week. Mr. Campbell was 67 years old and leaves a wife and several children. He had been a member of the Baptist church for many years and was esteemed by all who knew him.[27]

JOSEPH FOSTER [*The Courier*—5 October 1905]

Mr. Joseph Foster died on October 1st at his home of neuralgia of the heart, about two miles from Asheboro. He was an old soldier having served four years in the Civil War, two first years on the confederate side and two last years on the Union side. He has drawn a pension for a number of years. Mr. Foster was born and raised in Chatham county and moved to his home near Asheboro soon after the war. He had been a remarkably strong man never having had a spell of sickness. About a year ago he professed religion and expressed himself as ready to go to the Great Beyond. Deceased was 78 years old and leaves a wife and seven children.[28]

5. Old Times There Are Not Forgotten   159

Soldier's Home in Raleigh—At least three men from Company M spent their last days here. The home's longtime superintendent was Captain Winfield Scott Lineberry of Randolph County.

Thompson Siler, 85, Dies After Brief Illness
[*Greensboro Daily News*—6 July 1929]

Thompson Siler, aged 85, died at his home, 1114 Oakland avenue, yesterday morning at 3:35 o'clock. He had been in his usual health until Wednesday. He was a member of Bethel Methodist Protestant church in Randolph County, and had made many friends since coming here from Randolph 12 years ago.

Mr. Siler enlisted in the Confederate navy at the age of 17, and is said to have been the sole survivor after the naval base at Charleston was blown up. He then enlisted in the army, and was with Lee at Appomattox. He is survived by two sons, G. W. and P. T. Siler of Greensboro; and two daughters, Mrs. W. A. Kime of Greensboro and Mrs. C. M. Coble of Rutherford College. Services will be held from his home tomorrow morning at 11 o'clock by Rev. R. H. Melvin. Interment will be in Green Hill cemetery.[29]

Another of the Old Guard Gone
[*The Courier*—8 December 1910]

One of the North Carolina soldiers who laid down their arms at the command of "Marse" Robert has obeyed orders to lay down his arms forever at the command of Jehovah.

William Alridge's last stand at the end of seventy years of battles was against consumption which defeated him at 3 o'clock a. m. Dec. 4.

Since January 17th 1905, he had been an inmate of the Soldier's Home in

Raleigh, and for some time the only inmate from Randolph county. He belonged to Co. M, 22nd North Carolina, and served throughout the war. He leaves no immediate family, which accounts for his presence in Raleigh. Randolph seldom allows even the State to care for her veterans, only 5 ever having entered the Soldier's Home from her confines.[30]

Wounds of Capt. C. F. Siler, Taken From His Pension Application Dated 6 July 1903

Wounds: (1) Right Femur, ball entered upper ⅓ bursting bone & ranged to hip joint causing pain & stiffness. (2) Ball entered middle of left thigh in & through limb. (3) Right Humorous bone broken at upper ⅓ by ball. (4) Also Olecron Process (point of the elbow) broken by another ball causing stiffness of joint. (5) Left Shoulder torn & scarred by bursting shell leaving ugly scar & stiffness. (6) One flesh wound on right side of chest & one on neck—neither of these give trouble.
      Applicant's disabilities amounts to ¾ ths.
      A. F. Thompson, MD[31]

Members of Company M Who Were Members of Randolph Camp No. 1646, United Confederate Veterans

James Madison Hayes	Lieut. James M. Pounds	H. Thompson Siler*
Joseph Alson Henson*	Capt. Columbus Franklin Siler	Abner Branson Steel*

*Indicates Charter Members

The Letters of Stephen Ward Trogdon

Stephen Ward Trogdon of Company M, 22nd Regiment, wrote the following letters during the first two years of the war. He enlisted with the company at its organization on 10 June 1861 and served until being wounded and captured at Gettysburg, Pa., in July 1863. He was promoted to sergeant sometime prior to the battle. His right leg was amputated due to his wound and he was paroled and exchanged in October 1863. Finally, he was retired to the invalid corps on 13 August 1864. The letters appear here courtesy of Mrs. Fawnie Poupore, a descendant of Ward Trogdon's sister, Susan Trogdon Burrow.

 The first letter reprinted here is written to his sister, Susan Trogdon Burrow, who was married to Charles Wesley Burrow. It is undated, but is evidently an early letter, since it mentions

Randolph County Courthouse (1835–1909)—The rear portion of this building was the courthouse used during the war. In later years, many veterans came to the courthouse as pictured here to fill out their pension applications. (Photograph courtesy of Randolph Room, Asheboro Public Library.)

that his men had captured two boats. This indicates it was written during the latter part of the time at Evansport, Va. Most of the other letters written by Ward Trogdon were addressed to his brother-in-law, C. W. Burrow, some with an additional letter on the back addressed to Emsley Allred, another brother-in-law, who married Ward's sister Anna Trogdon. I have endeavored to leave the original spelling of the letters intact as much as possible. There are a few exceptions, noted by brackets to clarify some of the sentence structures.

TO HIS SISTER, SUSAN TROGDON BURROW

Dear Sister
I take my Seate to drop you afew lines to let you know that I have not for goten you yet   I am well at presant and I hope when these few line come to hand they will find you in the Saim health   I would like to See you the best in this world but I do not know when I will   I haven't much to write you at presant only we captured two boats the other day   they was worth Severl thousan dolars but I do not know how much and they did not hurt any of us   them letters you worked on my things is the very thing   I can tell my things now with out any trubel and I am very much oblige to you for working them   I must close by Saying write Soon as you git this and let me know how you are A giten along
From S. W. Trogdon
To Susan Burrow[32]

TO HIS BROTHER-IN-LAW, C. W. BURROW, AND HIS SISTER, SUSAN TROGDON BURROW

Camp Holmes Va. Dec. the 16 1861
Mr. C. W. Burrow

Dear Brother and Sister   it is one more time I Seate my self to drop you afew lines to inform you that I am well at present Since hopeing that when these few lines comes to hand they will find you all injoying the Saim health. I recived your kind letter and was so very glad to hear that you had got back home once more A live, for guess you had A rite Serious time of it at Washington. I would like to go to Washington but not like you did for I would guess it was not very pleasant to haft to Stay in prison four months. dear Brother I have nothing of any importance to write at present only that we haven't had any fight yet but we are exSpecting one here ever day but it may be that we wont have arey one   but if we do I think we can whip the yankies very bad at this place but I may be fooled but I do not think I am   I can say that the yankies throwed a bum Shell over the river and wounded two of our men but not Searious   they will get well   the men belongs to A Virginia regiment   they had charge of the battery   So I will conclude my letter by saying write as Soon as you get this   So I still remain yours truly
To C. W. Burrow   from S. W. Trogdon[33]

5. Old Times There Are Not Forgotten

[On the back]

TO HIS BROTHER-IN-LAW, EMSLEY ALLRED

A few lines to Mr. E. Allred
Dear Brother and Sister   it is with grate pleasure I take the present opportunity of droping you afew lines to inform you that [I] received your kind letter and was very glad to hear from you all and hear that you was well   I haven anything of importance to write at present only that I am well at present and have ben well for Some time and I am in hopes that I will remain So untill my time is out   I would like to come home about Chrismass but it is out of my power but you must get along the best you can with out me   I would like to be thare to beat you A Shooting and if I could be thare that would be very easey to do and if I cant beate you A Shooting at A paper I can beate you A Shooting at yankies that one thing Sirten   you Sead that Cedar Falls was coming out in the way of fighting and you Seaid that they was A fight thare the knight before your letter was wrote   I am like the duchman was   I would like to know hwo in the devil fough[t]   So I will bring my letter to A close by Saying write as Soon as you get this   So I still remain your true and affectionate Brother untill death   this
From   S. W. Trogdon
to Emsley Allred[34]

TO HIS BROTHER-IN-LAW, C. W. BURROW

Head Quarters
22 Reg NC troops
Camp Holmes Va   Feb the 2 1862

Dear Brother
    it is with pleasure I take the present opportunity of droping you afew lines to inform you that I recived your kind letter and was very happy to hear from you once more and to hear that you was all well and doing well and this leaves me well and very well sadisfied Considern the drauth for the mud is about half leg deep here and it has ben raining about two weeks an it looks like it would Snow befour morning and I think it will and I would rather it would Snow than to rain for it is So muddy now we cant hardly get about   well C. W. I haven't any thing of importance to write you at present only our boys is all well   not a man on the Sick list and you know that is Something very uncomon   our Regiment is Said to be the healthy Regiment in the field and I think if they will give them a chance they can do Some of as good fighting as any of them for we have got as good A Colonel as they ever was if not the best and as Smart A one as any of them if not the Smartest I must Say Somthing about them tories as you call them   I want you to keep them under untill we get back and then we will tend to them   we heard that Some of them had ben talking about raseing A union flag   I can just Say to you I defie any man or any Set of men to rase A union flag after we get home for we will hunt them as Same as hunting rabbits   but just lay low and let the hair grow untill the Randolph Volunteerse get home and then they will Settle all of that

[On back]

times is pretty Still on the potomac now but I think they will fight hear towards Spring So I conclude my Short note by Saying write Soon and ofting So I Still remain your Brother untill death   S. W. Trogdon[35]

TO HIS BROTHER-IN-LAW, EMSLEY ALLRED
[Also on back of letter to C. W. Burrow]

Afew lines to Emsley Allred
    Dear Brother   it is with pleasure I take the present opportunity of droping you afew lines to inform you that I recived your very kind letter and was happy to hear from you and hear that you was all well and doing well and I am well at present and as well sadisfied as could be exspected for a man of my age   for I am A geting very old and febel   I would like to See you all very well and I think I will befour Six months longer   You Said in your letter that it was out of any man power to beat you A Shooting   if you are Such a good marksman I don't See why you don't kill Some of them tories about in your naborhood   I think if [I] was thair and they got to talking about raseing A union flag and I was as good a marksman as you Say you are I would pop one over once in A while to Show them that they was Some Suthern men in [the] South yet   but just lay low untill we get back and we will Settle all Such as that   So I will quit for this time and I will write you A big letter befour long   I would A wrote you A big letter this time but my canel has burnt out and I though[t] I would put afew lines in Wese [Charles Wesley Burrows'] letter for you   So no more only write as Soon as you get this to your Brother S. W. Trogdon[36]

FROM C. W. BURROW IN CEDAR FALLS, N.C.,
TO STEPHEN WARD TROGDON

                    Cedar Falls   ~~April~~ May the 8th 1862
                                        Dear Brother
    I take opportunity of trying to communicate to you a few lines to let you now that we are well at hoping these will reach you well or doing well   received your letter yesturday and was glad to hear from you and hear that you was well and doing well as could be expected although you said that you had saw hard times sense you got back to old Va   that I don't dispute and ward your cant imagine the tales that is aflote about your regiment   the nuse come hear last week that 15 of cap Odell co had goined the yankees and that the reg was cut all to peices and then we heard that you were all Taken prisoners and that is the kind of nuse that is going dayley   then your pa heard tuesday at coart our men cut all to peices and all that did get away did so by clean running   this com by a solgier that was in the engagment so it was pretty true as we thought but as for my part think the nuse must of com in the wind   but gust to tell the plain truth about the mater it is gust done to flusterate the women that is left   your pa and ma was the gladest to hear from you that I ever saw in my life   I haven't spoke to them to day but

did last evening   your pa was complaining of his head   he said he wanted me to write and tell you that he would write be fore long but not wait for him to write   your ma sends her best respects to you and wants you to write often   this is all the satisfaction that we have now a days   give my love to Mr. E Allred and tell that Buck is very unwell but is so as to be up to day   the rest of his family is well   tell Capt. Odell that go [Joe?] sold for a hundred and ninty dollars but perhaps he has heard of it before now   you have heard about the fall of New orleans   this has raised grat confusion amonsk the people   it is bad but then we mus not give up at that   so will write no more at present

You will pleas write as soon as this comes to hand for I am very ankcious to hear from you if it was every day or at least every week but write gust as soon as posable to your Brother at Cedar Falls   C. W. Burrow
Tell Em [Emsley Allred] to write to me if he pleases[37]

To his brother-in-law, C. W. Burrow

          Camp near Richmond Va

Dear Brother   June the 13 1862

    it is with pleasure I Seate my Self to drop you afew lines to inform you that I received your kind letter and was glad to hear from you and hear that you was all well and doing well and this leaves me well but I have ben Sick   but I have got back to the regiment and A Seeing hard times for we have bin on picket ever Since the fite and that on the [front?] post two   our pickets and the yankies pickets is Shooting at each other all the time and they kill one once and while   I am Sorry to Say that Emsley Allred was killed or wonded and taken prisner and I do not know witch but he is gone and three more with him   H. C. Trogdon A. Pugh and L. F. Mcmasters   they are all gone Some wher but I do not no wher and they was A good maney of our boys wonded but I think the most of them is gone home now   I think we will have Another fite here before long   our men is throwing up breast works ever day and I think if they will give us A fair chance we can whip them worse than we did at the Seven pine battle   I would like to See you all very well but I cant See you untill the yankies is whipped   So I will close for this time and write the more when I have time   So write Soon as you get this and give me all of the newes   So I Still remain yours as ever
                                S. W. Trogdon[38]

To his brother-in-law, C. W. Burrow

          Camp below Richmond VA   July the 20 1862
                    Mr. C. W. Burrow

Dear Brother,   it is with grate Sadisfaction I take the present opportunity of writing you a few lines to inform you that I reived your kind letter dated June the 25 this morning and was very glad to heare from you once more and that you was all well but I am not very well but I keep going about and doing duty   I haven't anything of importance to write you at present only our boys is all Sick or at least they ant many but what is Sick   it ant worth while for me to write any

thing about the battles for I guess you have herd all about them before now   I can Say to you that we are in camp below Richmond and we drill Some and go on picket once and while but the yankies is about 20 miles from this plase but I think we will fight them Some where before longe but I cant tell wher   I thinke our men aimes to drive them out of virginia if they can but I think it will be hard to do   but if they try hard A nuff they will do it   the yankies Sayes that the North Carolinaines will charge hell with A Barlow knife for A canteen and haversack   I will tell you Something about the crops a bout here   wheat was very good but they was lots of it wasted   corn wher they have worked it is very good but they weeds hids Some of it   I must close by Saying give my love to all inquiring frinds   So write Soon and oftin to your loveing Brother
                                                                            S W Trogdon[39]

To his brother-in-law, C. W. Burrow

                        Camp Near Martinsburg Va. Oct. 22, /62
Dear Brother
    it is with grate pleasure I take the present opportunity of writing you afew lines to inform you that I am well at present and I hope when these few lines comes to hand they will find you all in the Saim health and doing well   Dear Brother I haven't any thing of importance to write you at present only we march to this plase the other day and exspected to fight the yankies but they took the hint and Crossed the river and I was not Sarey of it for I have fought the yank as much as I want two   we have ben tareing up the Rale road for the last two day   I exspect we will go back to wards [towards] Stauton [Staunton, Va.] when we get the Rale road tore up as much as they want it and we have burnt up Martinsburg   I think the yankies is A fraid of us A little   we may have A fight here yet before we leave this plase

[Inside folded letter]

Dear Brother   Oct. the 29 /62
    I Started to write you A letter on the 22d but we had marching orders and I did not get to finish it untill now   you will learn from the first Page wher I was then and I Can tell you wher I am now   I am on the Roade that leads from Harpers Ferry to Winchester and I tell you it is Cold Weather in this part of the Country and keeps getting Colder   I think if we don't get out of this part of the Country we will all freese to death but I Still think we will leave here before longe at least I am in hopes   So Dear Brother I haven't time to write much this time for the Capt is a going to Start home in about ten minnetts   I would be glad if I could write more and I would be very glad in deed to Come home about 30 days but as it is I cant until they get reddy for me two
    Please tell Maw that I got them things that She Sent to me by J. M. Lawr. and I am very much Oblige to her for them   Please tell Anna Allred that I recived her letter and I will write to her in A day or two   I would write now if I had time but I have not   So I will close by Saying give my respect to all of fathers famley

and tell them to write to me and write your Self as Soon as you get this to your loveing Brother   S W Trogdon[40]

TO HIS BROTHER-IN-LAW, C. W. BURROW

                                            Camp Near Fredericksburg Va
                                            Dec the 7 1862

Dear Brother
   it is with pleasure I take the present opportunity of droping you afew lines to inform you that I recived your kind letter and was happy to hear from you and hear that you was all well and doing well but Sarey to hear that you had to come back to the army for you wont find it like it was when you was in the Army before I Saw Some of the Boys that belongs to your Regiment the other days as I was coming from the vally   they was in Camp about 4 miles from this plase and I allso Saw A good many more Boys that I was acquanted with that belonged to the 46 Regt   Sir I would be very glad if you would get transfurd to this Regt and this Company if you haft to come out again   the weather is very cold in this part of the country at present and no tents yet and only one Blanket A pice   our Boxes has not got here yet   we are A looking for them to day   Dear Brother we had A very hard march coming from the valley to this place   we March from Winchester to this plase in twelve days   A distance of about two hundred miles and they was Snow on the Blue Ridge when we Crossed it and they was none on the other side nor on this Side but plenty on the top of it and they is A plenty here at this place now   I will Close for this time By Saying write as Soon as you get this to your   Brother S W Trogdon[41]

Letter of Solomon York to His Future Wife

   I have included this letter from Solomon York to his future bride, Delphina Cox, even though he was not a member of Company M. He was, however, a member of Company L, 22nd Regiment, and was part of the same regiment as Company M. He would have been in the same camps and battles as Company M, so this gives some additional insight on life early in the war.

                                            January the 18, 1862
                                            Camp Holmes Near Evans Port, Va.

Dear Miss,
   I embrace this present opportunity of writting you a few lines informing you that I received yours of the 3rd of this inst., which afforded me much satisfaction.
   Yes I was more than glad to hear that you was well. These few lines leaves

me well and I truly hope they will find you in the possession of all that is needful for your happiness. I have nothing verry interesting to write. Though if I could tell you more than I can write and it would be more satisfaction to talk with you than to write.

    I will tell you something about our fair. We fair tolerable well. We have plenty to eat and have tolerable good tents to stay in. The weather is verry disagreeable, it has been raining, snowing & hailing for the last week. The ground is verry muddy at present. Though we don't have much to do we have to stand Picket every fourth night which is tolerable disagreeable. We have to get wood and work every fifth day in the batteries. We have had no fight here yet though. They say that the Yankeys are going to attact us here by land and water though. Things have been verry quiet for several days with some cannonading on the River.

    There was heavy firing last night at a steam tug as it passed up the River. There was ninty that fired at it. It was thought that some of them took effect. It is nothing strange to hear the Cannons Roaring and hear the balls whistling over us though. Their is none of us boys been hurt yet and I hope they will all get home safe for I long to see the day that I can return home to the armes of my friends and most especially the armes of thee, my dearest dear, for theirs nothing that affords me the satisfaction than the prospect of my returning to old Randolph again. Though I am far from thee my hart is with you and I hope you will still want it. Though I can't say that it is worthy of your favor I would be happy to be their to be at some of your parties or quilting to see the Girls flying around the Boys, for I haven't seen a Girl for the last two months, though they say there is some Girls in Va. Though if their was some Girls here they would not seem like my darling one that I left behind.

> When on these lines thou cas an eye
> Please to Remember me.
> For as a friend most surely I
> Will long remember thee.
>
> Forget thee I shall never
> Although it was hard to part
> Thy love shall for ever be
> Stamped upon my hart.
>
> Although our acquaintance has been short
> Our friendship has been Strong
> Our pleasant moments together past
> Will be remembered long.
>
> When this thou dost see
> Think of thy absent friend
> And every opportunity
> To me a letter send.

Being that I am tired and it is getting late, I will close. Give my love and respects to enquiring friends. If there be any reserve, a large portion for your self. Write soon. I still remain your sincere friend and true Love until Death.

S. York

to Miss Delphina Cox

P. S. Tell Hannah that I still remember her and would like to see her, and I will come over and get some of them potatoes, for we have none here. If I don't get their in time to get them I will be their next fall in time for them.

S. York   to Miss Delphina Cox[42]

6. Company M, 22nd Regiment N.C. Troops "Randolph Hornets" (Reactivated)

In 1994 Mike Richardson, Fred Schoenberger, Jeff Haithcock and Roger Johnson set up a Civil War display during a public event at the old Cedar Falls mill. After several such events, this group of local history buffs and reenactors evolved into an organized unit for the purpose of portraying living history. Richardson and Johnson were veteran Civil War reenactors, having been involved in the hobby for several years with the 26th N.C. Regiment, while Schoenberger and Haithcock had long held an interest in the Civil War and soon developed their own interpretations.

They felt that something needed to be done locally to promote an interest in the war, give people with similar interests a place to meet and to educate area people on the way their ancestors lived. The group became known as the "Randolph Living Historians." The idea was to allow each member to create their own identity and portray whatever role they chose, without being limited to a completely Southern or Northern viewpoint. The important thing was to create an accurate portrayal of how a local person lived during the Civil War period.

Over the years the group has experienced name changes, first as the "Piedmont Historical Society of the 1860s" and finally as "Company M, 22nd Regiment, N.C. Troops, 'Randolph Hornets'." The latter change came about as a way to give the group a military designation and allow greater participation in larger events. It also gave the group a tie to those who served during the war. The "Randolph Hornets" portray both infantry and artillery impressions, since the original 22nd Regiment was an infantry unit, but also had men who performed as artillery on at least a couple of occasions. One of the men in Company M had also previously served in the Confederate Navy. Members are, however, still free to portray

Reactivated Company M, 22nd Regiment N.C. Troops, "Randolph Hornets"—A Civil War reenactment and living history organization, photographed in July 2002 at Cedar Falls Mill. *Front row:* Mark Waisner, Kyle Routh, Terry Waisner, Andy Shores, Jeff Stapleton. *Back row:* Darrell Cagle, Fred Schoenberger, Terry Routh, Wally Jarrell, Alan Lamb, Matt Waisner, Jeff Haithcock, Mike Richardson, Brad Thomas, Joshua Haithcock. (Photograph courtesy of Henry Bowers.)

6. "Randolph Hornets" (Reactivated)

Reactivated Company M, 22nd Regiment N.C. Troops, "Randolph Hornets," photographed July 2002 at Cedar Falls Post Office. *Front row:* Mark Waisner, Kyle Routh, Jeff Stapleton, Terry Routh, Matt Waisner, Terry Waisner. *Back row:* Andy Shores, Darrell Cagle, Fred Schoenberger, Alan Lamb, Brad Thomas, Wally Jarrell, Mike Richardson, Jeff Haithcock, Joshua Haithcock. (Photograph courtesy of Henry Bowers.)

an alternate role, or an additional role to their military character. Women have been and still are an important part of the group in illustrating home life during the 1860s.

Over the years, the group has participated in a wide variety of events, such as the annual Veteran's Day Parade in Asheboro, living history encampments in various locations, town festivals, memorial services in remembrance of Civil War veterans, the re-dedication of the Confederate Monument at the Randolph County Court House and large scale battle reenactments. In July 1998 the group took part in the 135th Anniversary reenactment of the battle of Gettysburg, Pa., the largest event of its kind ever held, with some 23,000 participants. For a number of years the group has held weekend encampments at state-owned historical sites such as Bennett Place in Durham and Bentonville Battleground in Johnston County, providing living history to those visiting the parks. Some of the members are certified by the state parks to demonstrate firearms. Company M has also participated each year in the annual Pottery Festival at Seagrove, N.C., providing visitors from around the nation, and perhaps the world, a bit of local history.

Probably the most rewarding events we have conducted, however, are school programs. Company M has been invited to many of the local schools to share our knowledge and expertise on the Civil War with the children. It is a humbling experience to see interest in history awaken in the kids as they view us in our authentic period clothing with an array of artifacts and equipment that make the past become tangible to them.

Appendix: Burial Sites of Company M Soldiers

Asterisk (*) indicates *probable* burial site

ASHEBORO CITY CEMETERY
    James N. Cross
    Joseph F. Foster
BAILEY'S GROVE BAPTIST CEMETERY—RANDOLPH CO., N.C.
    Joseph Alson Henson
BENSALEM CEMETERY—MOORE COUNTY, N.C.
    Henry Brewer
BUFFALO CEMETERY—SANFORD, LEE COUNTY, N.C.
    William McNeill
CEDAR FALLS BAPTIST CHURCH CEMETERY—RANDOLPH CO., N.C.
    2nd Lieutenant James M. Pounds
    James E. Campbell
    William Coble
CEDAR FALLS UNITED METHODIST CHURCH CEMETERY—RANDOLPH CO., N.C.
    Oliver P. Hayes
    Stephen Ward Trogdon
CEDAR VALLEY UNITED METHODIST CHURCH CEMETERY—CALDWELL CO., N.C.
    Marcus Deal
EBENEZER UNITED METHODIST CEMETERY—RANDOLPH CO., N.C.
    James Robbins
EDWARDS HILL CEMETERY—CHATHAM CO., N.C.
    Linden Alred Trogdon
ELMWOOD CEMETERY—CHANUTE, KAN.
    William August Woosley
FRANKLINVILLE UNITED METHODIST CHURCH CEMETERY—RANDOLPH CO., N.C.
    Mountainville T. Jones
    Abner Branson Steel
    Lorenzo Dow Stout, Jr.

GRAY'S CHAPEL UNITED METHODIST CHURCH CEMETERY—RANDOLPH CO., N.C.
    David Oliver Coble
    Levi Foster
    Calvin Gray*
    Major Laban D. Odell
    William Thomas Robbins
    Joseph Alson Routh
    Joshua Marion Routh
    William Clay Routh
    Jabez Lindsay York

GREEN HILL CEMETERY—GREENSBORO, N.C.
    H. Thompson Siler

GREEN MOUND CEMETERY—VERNON, MO.
    James Marshall Scotten

HARDIN FAMILY CEMETERY—RANDOLPH CO., N.C.
    William R. Hardin

HOLLY SPRING FRIENDS MEETING—RANDOLPH CO., N.C.
    William Joseph York

KILDEE WESLEYAN CHURCH CEMETERY—RANDOLPH CO., N.C.
    Samuel Clarkson York

MCMASTERS' CEMETERY—RANDOLPH CO., N.C.
    Captain Warren B. Kivett*
    Christian Foust
    Peter Foust
    James Murdick Kivett*
    Kenneth M. Kivett*
    1st Lieutenant Lewis Franklin McMasters*

MT. LEBANON UNITED METHODIST CHURCH CEMETERY—RANDOLPH CO., N.C.
    James Madison Hayes
    William T. Laughlin
    William G. Stout*

MT. PLEASANT BAPTIST CHURCH CEMETERY—RANDOLPH CO., N.C.
    Jacob B. Foust
    Joel A. Kivett
    Stanley Kivett

MT. PLEASANT UNITED METHODIST CHURCH CEMETERY—DAVIDSON CO., N.C.
    Samuel Darr

MARVIN UNITED METHODIST CHURCH CEMETERY—IREDELL CO., N.C.
    Thomas Jackson Stewart

OAKWOOD CEMETERY—CONCORD, N.C.
    Captain John Milton Odell

OAKWOOD CEMETERY—HIGH POINT, N.C.
    William Parker Willey

OAKWOOD CEMETERY—RICHMOND, VA.
    Jacob Kivett

Gravesite of Major Laban Odell at Gray's Chapel United Methodist Church in Randolph County, N.C.

OAKWOOD CONFEDERATE CEMETERY—RALEIGH, N.C.
    Captain Columbus Frank Siler
    William Allridge
    Daniel Yeargin
OAK RIDGE BAPTIST CHURCH CEMETERY—VANCE CO., N.C.
    Daniel P. Pulley
PATTERSON'S GROVE CHRISTIAN CHURCH—RANDOLPH CO., N.C.
    James A. Webster
PHILADELPHIA NATIONAL CEMETERY—PHILADELPHIA, PA.
    Nathan David Barker
PLEASANT RIDGE CHRISTIAN CHURCH CEMETERY—RANDOLPH CO., N.C.
    Simon Elwood Allen
POINT LOOKOUT CEMETERY—SCOTLAND, MD.
    Newman C. Breedlove
    James Cannon
    John W. Kivett, Jr.
PROVIDENCE UNITED METHODIST CHURCH CEMETERY—CHATHAM CO., N.C.
    John A. Caviness
ROCKY RIVER UNITED METHODIST CEMETERY—CHATHAM CO., N.C.
    Spencer D. Thompson
SANDY CREEK BAPTIST CHURCH CEMETERY—RANDOLPH CO., N.C.
    James Matthews Cox
    Stephen W. Ivey
    Troy Thomas Kivett
    Joseph M. D. Reece
    William D. Reece
    Martin S. Turner
    David Wright
SHADY GROVE BAPTIST CHURCH CEMETERY—RANDOLPH CO., N.C.
    William Franklin Hayes
    Lewis Franklin Holder
    James Franklin Kivett
    Edward Tyson Langley
    Andrew Jackson Turner
    William Martin Williams
SHILOH UNITED METHODIST CHURCH CEMETERY—JULIAN, N.C.
    Joseph Madison Breedlove
    Peter P. Brown
    William Monroe Glasgow
SUNSET KNOLL (RAMSEUR) CEMETERY—RANDOLPH CO., N.C.
    John Tyler Turner
TRINITY CEMETERY—GRAVES CO., KY.
    Nelson Kenny Hulin
WHITE'S CHAPEL UNITED METHODIST CHURCH—RANDOLPH CO., N.C.
    Larkin Culberson York, Jr.
WILKINS CEMETERY (SANDY RIDGE AREA)—STOKES CO., N.C.
    William J. Wilkins*

Notes

Chapter 1. Onward to Victory

1. Purefoy, Elder George W. *A History of the Sandy Creek Baptist Association.* New York: Sheldon, 1858.
2. Trotter, William R. *Silk Flags and Cold Steel.* Winston-Salem: Blair, 1988.
3. Letters of Private Stephen Ward Trogdon. Courtesy of Mrs. Fawnie Poupore.
4. Hamilton, J. G. de Roulhac, Ph. D. (Editor) *The Correspondence of Jonathan Worth.* Vol. 1, p. 143. Raleigh: Edwards, 1909. 4 volumes.
5. Papers of Captain John Ritter. Manuscript Department of the William R. Perkins Library, Duke University.
6. *North Carolina Bulletin.* Asheborough, 27 June 1859.
7. *The Courier.* Asheboro, 27 March 1924.
8. Turner, John T. "Turner's Romance." *The Courier.* Asheboro, 29 January–2 July 1914.
9. *Ibid.*
10. *The Semi-Weekly Patriot.* Greensboro. May 1861.
11. Turner, John T. "Turner's Romance." *The Courier.* Asheboro, 29 January–2 July 1914.
12. *Ibid.*
13. *Ibid.*
14. *Ibid.*
15. *Ibid.*
16. *The Times.* Greensboro. 1861.
17. Letter of Solomon York to Delphina Cox, 18 January 1862. Courtesy of Mr. Jimmy York.
18. Letters of Private Stephen Ward Trogdon. Courtesy of Mrs. Fawnie Poupore.
19. Letter of C. W. Burrow of Cedar Falls, N.C., to Private Stephen Ward Trogdon. Courtesy of Mrs. Fawnie Poupore.
20. Letter of Private Stanley Kivett to his parents. 18 May 1862. Courtesy of Mr. William Ivey.
21. Turner, John T. "Turner's Romance." *The Courier.* Asheboro, 29 January–2 July 1914.
22. *Ibid.*
23. *Official Records.* Series I, Vol. XI, pt. 2, p. 900.
24. Letters of Private Stephen Ward Trogdon. Courtesy of Mrs. Fawnie Poupore.
25. Turner, John T. "Turner's Romance." *The Courier.* Asheboro, 29 January–2 July 1914.
26. *Official Records.* Series I, Vol. XIX, pt. 1.
27. Letters of Private Stephen Ward Trogdon. Courtesy of Mrs. Fawnie Poupore.
28. *Ibid.*
29. Turner, John T. "Turner's Romance." *The Courier.* Asheboro. 29 January–2 July 1914.
30. *Ibid.*
31. *Official Records.* Series I, Vol. XXVII, pt. 2, p. 669–672.
32. *The Courier.* Asheboro. 29 January–2 July 1914.
33. *Official Records.* Series I, Vol. XXVII, pt. 2, p. 669–672.
34. Clark, Walter. (Editor). *Histories of the Several Regiments and Battalions from North Carolina in the Great War, 1861–1865.* Raleigh: Nash, 1901. 5 volumes.
35. Turner, John T. "Turner's Romance." *The Courier.* Asheboro. 29 January–2 July 1914.
36. Clark, Walter. (Editor). *Histories of the Several Regiments and Battalions from North Carolina in the Great War, 1861–1865.* Raleigh: Nash, 1901. 5 volumes.
37. Turner, John T. "Turner's Romance." *The Courier.* Asheboro. 29 January–2 July 1914.

38. Wood, Hon. W. P. (1907, Feb.). "Capt. C. Frank Siler, Hero of Heroes." *Confederate Veteran*. p. 90.
39. Turner, John T. "Turner's Romance." *The Courier*. Asheboro. 29 January–2 July 1914.
40. Clark, Walter. (Editor). *Histories of the Several Regiments and Battalions from North Carolina in the Great War, 1861–1865*. Raleigh: Nash, 1901. 5 volumes.
41. Wood, Hon. W. P. (1907, February), "Capt. C. Frank Siler, Hero of Heroes." *Confederate Veteran*. p. 90.
42. *Ibid.*
43. Kennedy, Frances H. (Editor). *The Civil War Battlefield Guide*. Boston: Houghton. pp. 285–286.
44. *Ibid.*

Chapter 2. Turner's Romance

1. Turner, John T. "Turner's Romance." *The Courier*. Asheboro. 29 January–2 July 1914.

Chapter 3. That Tattered Old Flag

1. Letter of Solomon York to Delphina Cox, 18 January 1862. Courtesy of Mr. Jimmy York.
2. Flag.
3. Cooper, Oliver C. "Annals of the War, Chapters of Unwritten History, Blockading the Potomac." *The Weekly Times*. Philadelphia. 20 December 1879.
4. Suggs, Joseph R. (1969, May), "The Battle Flag Comes Home." *The State*. p. 12.
5. *Ibid.*

Chapter 4. Roster of Company M, 22nd Regiment

1. Moore, John W. (Editor). *Roster of North Carolina Troops in the War Between the States*. Raleigh: Ashe, 1882. 4 volumes.
2. Hewett, Janet B. (Editor). *North Carolina Confederate Soldiers 1861–1865*. Wilmington: Broadfoot, 3 volumes.
3. Manarin, Lewis A. (Editor). *North Carolina Troops 1861–1865: A Roster*. Raleigh: State Department of Archives and History, 1966–1998. 14 volumes.
4. State Auditor, Pension Office, Confederate Pension Records, Applications for Pension, Acts of 1885 and 1901, State Archives, Division of Historical Resources, Raleigh, N.C.
5. Martin, Cheryl L. (Editor). *The Heritage of Randolph County North Carolina, Volume 1*. Charlotte: Randolph County Heritage Book Committee, 1993.
6. Manarin, Lewis A. (Editor). *North Carolina Troops 1861–1865: A Roster*. Raleigh: State Department of Archives and History, 1966–1998. 14 volumes.
7. Unidentified Salisbury, N.C., newspaper clipping dated 10 August 1899. Courtesy of Phyllis Phillips.

Chapter 5. Old Times There Are Not Forgotten

1. Unidentified and undated newspaper clipping believed to be around 1913. Collection of Wally Jarrell.
2. Unidentified and undated newspaper clipping from about October 1899. Collection of Wally Jarrell.
3. *The Courier*. Asheboro. 21 July 1910.
4. Unidentified and undated newspaper clipping. Collection of Wally Jarrell.
5. *Ibid.*
6. *Ibid.*
7. *The Bulletin*. Asheboro. 20 June 1907.
8. Unidentified and undated newspaper clipping. Collection of Wally Jarrell.
9. Letter of Private Stanley Kivett to his parents. 18 May 1862. Courtesy of Mr. William Ivey.
10. *The Courier*. Asheboro. Undated clipping, probably March 1913. Collection of Wally Jarrell.
11. *The Courier*. Asheboro. 16 November 1911.
12. *The Courier*. Asheboro. Undated clipping, probably February 1916. Collection of Wally Jarrell.
13. Unidentified and undated newspaper clipping. Probably July 1916. Collection of Wally Jarrell.
14. *The Courier*. Asheboro. 13 May 1915.
15. *The Courier*. Asheboro. 5 July 1911.
16. *The Courier*. Asheboro. 4 October 1923.
17. *The Courier*. Asheboro. 6 September 1906.
18. Compiled Service Records of Confederate Soldiers Who Served During the Civil War, Record Group 109, National Archives, Washington, D. C. (microfilm, State Archives, Division of Archives and History, Raleigh, N.C).
19. Photocopy of unidentified document found in Civil War clipping files of the Randolph Room. Asheboro Public Library.
20. *The Courier*. Asheboro. 28 July 1910.
21. *The Courier*. Asheboro. 5 August 1909.
22. *The Courier*. Asheboro. 11 January 1923.
23. *The Courier*. Asheboro. 25 November 1915.
24. *The Courier*. Asheboro. 28 March 1929.
25. *The Courier*. Asheboro. 13 March 1924.
26. *The Courier*. Asheboro. 24 January 1929.
27. *The Courier*. Asheboro. 13 June 1907.

28. *The Courier*. Asheboro. 5 October 1905.
29. *Greensboro Daily News*. Greensboro. 6 July 1929.
30. *The Courier*. Asheboro. 8 December 1910.
31. Civil War Pension Application of Capt. C. F. Siler, State Auditor, Pension Office, Confederate Pension Records, Applications for Pension, Act of 1901, State Archives, Division of Historical Resources, Raleigh, N.C.
32. Letters of Private Stephen Ward Trogdon. Courtesy of Mrs. Fawnie Poupore.
33. *Ibid.*
34. *Ibid.*
35. *Ibid.*
36. *Ibid.*
37. *Ibid.*
38. *Ibid.*
39. *Ibid.*
40. *Ibid.*
41. *Ibid.*
42. Letter of Private Solomon York to Delphina Cox. 18 January 1862. Courtesy of Mr. Jimmy York.

Bibliography

Adams, Norma. E-mail interview, 25 June 2002 (Gentry family).
Allen, Lester M. *The Allen Family—Descendants of John and Amy Cox Allen with Allied Lines.* Self-published, 1987 (Allen family).
Allred, Don. "Allred Family Roster." 22 March 2001. *Allred Family Organization.* 12 July 2002. http://www.allredfamily.org/roster_page.htm
Barrett, Jocelyn Brabham. (Editor). *Randolph County Cemetery Records—Volume IV.* Asheboro: Randolph County Genealogical Society, 1996.
Barrett, Jocelyn Brabham. (Editor). *Randolph County Cemetery Records—Volume VII.* Asheboro: Randolph County Genealogical Society, 2000.
Brewer, Doris Myers. (Editor). *Randolph County Cemetery Records—Volume II.* Asheboro: Randolph County Genealogical Society, 1997.
Burge, Warren. E-mail interviews, 17–27 March 2002 (Woosley family).
Cannada, Scott. E-mail interview, 25 June 2001 (Pulley family).
Cates, Larry W. E-mail interview, May 2002 (Williams family).
Church of Jesus Christ of Latter Day Saints. *Family Search Internet Genealogy Service.* 1 Dec. 2002. http://www.familysearch.org/
Cooper, Linda Allred. E-mail interview, May 2002 (Allred family).
Costello, Beulah. *Trogdon: William One and His Seed.* Marceline: Walsworth, 1983 (Trogdon family).
Dagenhart, Jerry. E-mail interviews, correspondence, 28 January 2003–4 February 2003 (Stewart family).
Davis, Laverne Brady. (Editor). *Randolph County Cemetery Records—Volume I.* Asheboro: Randolph County Genealogical Society, 1996.
Davis, Laverne Brady. (Editor). *Randolph County Cemetery Records—Volume V.* Asheboro: Randolph County Genealogical Society, 1999.
Davis, Laverne Brady. (Editor). *Randolph County Cemetery Records—Volume VIII.* Asheboro: Randolph County Genealogical Society, 2001.
Davis, Laverne Brady. (Editor). *Randolph County Cemetery Records—Volume X.* Asheboro: Randolph County Genealogical Society, 2002.
Doty, Linda. E-mail interview, 16 October 2001 (Euliss family).
Federal Census of Chatham County, N.C.: 1850, 1860, 1870, 1880.
Federal Census of Guilford County, N.C.: 1850, 1860, 1870, 1880, 1900.
Federal Census of Montgomery County, N.C.: 1850, 1860, 1870, 1880.
Federal Census of North Carolina: 1840, 1850.
Federal Census of Randolph County, N.C.: 1850, 1860, 1870, 1880, 1900, 1910, 1920.

Federal Census of Surry, County, NC: 1900, 1910.
Federal Census of Virginia: 1840, 1850.
Gardner, Sandra Wilkins. E-mail interview, 15 June 2001 (Wilkins family).
Gentry, Bill. E-mail interview, June 2001 (Gentry family).
Hewett, Janet B. (Editor). *North Carolina Confederate Soldiers 1861–1865*. Wilmington: Broadfoot, 1999. 3 volumes.
Kivett, William D. E-mail interviews, 23 May 2002–2 August 2002 (Kivett and related families).
Kivett, William D. *The Kivett Family*. March 1998 edition. Self-published (Kivett and related families).
Lednum, Shirley. E-mail interview, 17 July 2002 (Samuel M. Burgess family).
Lockey, Nelson. E-mail interviews, 14 February 2002 (McLemore family).
McMasters, Phyllis D. *McMasterpiece, the Story of James McMasters and His Descendants Through the Fifth Generation*. Compiled 1986. Albany, Oregon.
Manarin, Lewis A. (Editor). *North Carolina Troops 1861–1865: A Roster*. Raleigh: State Department of Archives and History, 1966–1998. 14 volumes.
Martin, Cheryl L. (Editor). *The Heritage of Randolph County North Carolina, Vol. 1*. Charlotte: Randolph County Heritage Book Committee, 1993.
Mefford, Clifford. "Descendants of Peter Kivett." *Personal Ancestral File*. 28 Dec. 2001. *The Church of Jesus Christ of Latter Day Saints*. 28 July 2002. http://www.webpak.net/~cdm2/kivett/index.htm
Moore, John W. (Editor). *Roster of North Carolina Troops in the War Between the States*. Raleigh: Ashe, 1882. 4 volumes.
Nash, John T. E-mail interview, 3 August 2002 (Breedlove family).
Parker, Anthony E. *A Guide to Moore County Cemeteries*. Southern Pines: The Moore County Historical Association, ca. 1976.
Phillips, Phyllis. E-mail interviews, letters, 29 September 2001–13 October 2001 (Odell family).
Register of Deaths, Guilford County, N.C.
Register of Deaths, Randolph County, N.C.
Register of Marriages, Guilford County, N.C.
Register of Marriages, Randolph County, N.C.
Reprint of D. A. R. Cemetery Records in Randolph County, North Carolina. Asheboro: Randolph County Genealogical Society, 1995.
Routh, Lawrence W. *The Rouths of Randolph County, N.C.* Self published. Undated—ca. 1978 (Routh Family).
Spence, Carolyn. E-mail interview, 7 August 2001 (Willey family).
State Auditor, Pension Office, Confederate Pension Records, Application for Pension, Act of 1885, State Archives, Division of Historical Resources, Raleigh, N.C.
State Auditor, Pension Office, Confederate Pension Records, Application for Pension, Act of 1901, State Archives, Division of Historical Resources, Raleigh, N.C.
Stevens, Agnes Hussey. (Editor). *Randolph County Cemetery Records—Volume III*. Asheboro: Randolph County Genealogical Society, 1996.
Stevens, Agnes Hussey. (Editor). *Randolph County Cemetery Records—Volume VI*. Asheboro: Randolph County Genealogical Society, 2000.
Stevens, Agnes Hussey. (Editor). *Randolph County Cemetery Records—Volume IX*. Asheboro: Randolph County Genealogical Society, 2001.
Weller, Nelson A. L. E-mail interview, 8 June 2001 (Shouse family).
Wilburn, Peggy. E-mail interviews, letters, 28 September 2001–10 March 2002 (Odell family).
Woosley, Dale. E-mail interview, 7 June 2001 (Woosley family).
York, Dennis R. E-mail interviews, conversations, September 2002 (York family).
York, Mike. E-mail interview, 22 January 2002 (Joshua Marion Routh family).

Index

Adams, N. T. 147
Adkerson, Martha J. 76
Adkerson, Stephen 76
Aiken's Landing, James River, Va. 75, 95, 107, 119
Alamance County, N.C. 124
Albright, the Rev. H. A. 145, 147
Aldredge/Allred, Jane 125
Aldridge, Samuel 147
Alleghany County, N.C. 47
Allen, Amy Cox 77
Allen, Braxton Nathaniel 77
Allen, C. E. 158
Allen, Edith Henson 76
Allen, Henry Milton 77
Allen, John 77
Allen, Joseph James 77
Allen, Lester M. 77
Allen, M. E. 158
Allen, Samuel 76
Allen, Simon Elwood 76, 77, 143, 147, 158, 178
Allen, Ursula A. Masten 76, 158
Allen, W. H. 158
Allred, Abigail Trogdon 78
Allred, Anna 166
Allred, Anna Trogdon 78
Allred, Benjamin F. 76
Allred, Calvin C. 22, 77, 90, 143
Allred, Caroline Rose 77
Allred, Emsley 5, 20, 21, 50, 78, 162, 163, 164, 165
Allred, Fanny Johnson 78
Allred, Henry C. 12, 46, 74
Allred, James A. 78
Allred, Jeremiah 78
Allred, the Rev. John 158
Allred, John "Tennessee" 77, 78

Allred, Lemuel 77
Allred, Lovey Jane 95
Allred, Mary C. 99
Allred, Mary Routh 76
Allred, N. C. 147
Allred, Polly York 77, 78
Allred, Reuben 74
Allred, Samuel Hogan 78
Allred, Sarah 77
Allred, Sarah E. 118
Allred, Sarah Spoon 74
Allred, Vicey 119
Allred, William 76
Allred, William F. 78
Allridge, Satha 79
Allridge, William 41, 79, 159, 178
Amelia Court House, Va. 40
Anacosta, Union gunboat 63
Anderson, Gen. Richard H. 29, 33, 36
Andrews, T. W. 147
Andrews' Battery, R. S. 22
Appomattox Court House, Va. 27, 41, 42, 72, 79, 88, 91, 113, 114, 117, 121, 123, 126, 128, 129, 141, 159
Appomattox River, Va., 37, 56, 136; action at 104, 109
Aquia Creek, Va. 15
Archer, General 25, 31
Arkansas 65
Armfield, Eleanor 110
Army of Northern Virginia 8, 21, 28, 32, 41, 50, 139
Army of the Potomac 27
Arnold, Alfred Norman 25, 79
Arnold, Elizabeth 79
Arnold, Martitia Hutton 79

Arnold, Thomas 79, 155, 156
Around the Campfire 145
Asbury, Dr. F. E. 147
Ashburn, Rev. W. F. 157, 158
Asheboro (Asheborough), N.C. 5, 6, 7, 8, 45, 72, 90, 95, 97, 98, 113, 114, 116, 118, 122, 133, 139, 144, 158
Asheboro City Cemetery 86, 90, 175
The Asheboro Courier 9, 43, 50, 72, 134
Asheboro Female Academy 7
Asheboro Male Academy 7, 145
Asheboro M. E. Church 145
Asheboro Nightingale Band 145
Asheboro Public Library 63, 66
Asheboro Veteran's Day Parade 173
Asheborough Guards 7
Ashland, Va. 19, 20, 49, 100, 105, 111, 112
Ashworth, W. R. 147
Aunty 52
Austin, Col. John S. 65
Ayala (wife of Chief Red Cloud) 126
Aycock, Governor C. B. 72

Bailey's Grove Baptist Church cemetery 97, 140, 175
Bain, Joshua C. 10, 11, 12, 46, 99, 125
Baker, Elizabeth Harvell 79
Baker, John Henry 79
Baldwin, Susan A. 96
Baltimore & Ohio Railroad 25, 27, 54

Index

Baptist churches 4, 158
Barker, Nathan David 32, 79, 178
Barns' Creek 98
Barton, Gen. Seth M. 41
Battery 45, Petersburg, Va. 38, 39
Bean, Kirb 147
Bean's Mill 98
Bear Creek, N.C. 120
Beaufort, N.C. 129
Beauregard, Gen. P. G. T. 53
Beaverdam Creek 21, 35, 51
Belfield, Va. 38; battle of 57, 121
Bennett Place, Durham, N.C. 173
Benning, Brig. Gen. Henry L. 37
Bensalem Cemetery, Moore Co., N.C. 81, 175
Bentonville, N.C., battle of 58
Bentonville Battleground, Johnston County, N.C. 173
Bessemer City, N.C. 156
Bethel, Va. 135
Bethel Methodist Protestant Church 114, 159
Bethesda Church, Va., action at 35
Birne, William C. 80
Biscoe, N.C. 73
Bisnar, Mary Adeline 88
Blanchet, Kernelia 95
Blue Ridge Mountains, Va. 167
Bolivar Heights 24
Bonlee, N.C. 84
Boonsboro, Md. 107
Boulware's Wharf, James River, Va. 89, 106, 124
Bowers, Henry 172, 173
Bowman, John R. 138
Brady, W. W. 147
Brandy Station, Va., battle of 29, 54
Breckinridge, Maj. Gen. John C. 36, 49
Breedlove, Abraham 80
Breedlove, Diannah 124
Breedlove, Henry 35, 80
Breedlove, John 80
Breedlove, Joseph Madison "Joe" 80, 157, 173, 178
Breedlove, Julia Ann Wrenn 80
Breedlove, Levi, Sr. 80
Breedlove, Martha J. 84
Breedlove, Mary Jane McMasters Wood 80
Breedlove, Newman C. 42, 80, 178

Breedlove, Quenette Hesley Chappell 80
Breedlove, Sarah 80
Breedlove, Sarah Wheeler 80
Breedlove, Wesley 80
Brewer, Henry 81, 175
Brewer, 1st Lt. R. H. 25
Brewer, Talitha A. 81
Brinkley, Calloway County, Ky. 98
Bristoe Station, Va., battle of 33, 90, 108, 143
Brooke's Station, Va. 15, 47, 65
Brooks, Joseph 136, 137
Brooks Turnpike 19
Brower, J. W. 154
Brower, John 11, 150
Brower, Joseph H. 154
Brower, W. D. 145, 147
Brown, Adam 81
Brown, J. F. 158
Brown, J. M. 147
Brown, James B. 81
Brown, Jeanette 114
Brown, John R. 147
Brown, Malinda Breedlove 93
Brown, Mary 81
Brown, Peter P. 81, 158, 178
Brown, Riley J. 81
Brown, Rosannah H. Coble 81
Brown, S. P. 81
Brown, W. A. 158
Brown Township, Morgan County, Ind. 79
Brunswick community 90
Bryant, W. P. 82
Buck 165
Buck, P. D. 158
Buck Mountain 98
Buckland, Va. 33
Buffalo Cemetery, Lee County, N.C. 106, 175
Buffalo Ford, N.C. 110
Buffalo Shoals Creek 116
Buford, Gen. John 32
Bulla, Daniel 154
Bulla, Miss Nannie 145
The Bulletin 136
Bunker Hill, Va. 25, 32, 55, 124
Burgess, Catherine L. Craven 82
Burgess, Daniel 132
Burgess, Edward Clinton "Clint" 82
Burgess, Franklin F. 82
Burgess, James Austin "Jim" 82
Burgess, John P. 82
Burgess, Lovie Ellen 82
Burgess, Mary Elizabeth "Lizzie" 82

Burgess, Matilda Elizabeth York 82
Burgess, Robert Stevenson "Bob" 82
Burgess, Samuel M. "Sam" 23, 82
Burgess, W. 83
Burgis, W. 83
Burlington, N.C. 58
Burris, Murphy 132
Burrow, Charles Wesley 19, 22, 160, 162, 163, 164, 165, 166, 167
Burrow, Susan F. 97, 140
Burrow, Susan Trogdon 18, 160, 162
Burus' Shop 8
Butler, Maj. Gen. Benjamin 38
Byrns, Catherine Beckerdite 80
Byrns, Enoch 80
Byrns, William 80

C. & O. R. R. 21, 50, 52
Cagle, Darrell 172, 173
Caldwell County, NC 46, 85, 87, 88, 105, 106, 118
Cameron, Ruben 147
Camp Bee 15
Camp Carolina 14
Camp Crabtree 14, 46
Camp Gregg 26, 27, 28, 54
Camp Holmes 17, 42, 76, 78, 79, 80, 81, 83, 86, 87, 88, 89, 92, 97, 98, 99, 101, 108, 109, 113, 114, 117, 118, 125, 126, 163, 167
Camp Lee 106
Camp Stokes 129
Camp Vance 115, 116
Camp Washington 48
Campbell, Isaac 83
Campbell, James E. 83, 158, 175
Campbell, Martha E. Pugh 83
Campbell, Nancy Williams 83
Campbell, William 158
Camping Island Creek 89
Candor, N.C. 73
Cannon, Jackson 83
Cannon, James 35, 83, 178
Cannon, Johnnie 83
Cannon, Sarah F. 83
Cannon Manufacturing Company 69
Cape Fear River, N.C. 57
Carlisle, Pa. 29, 54
Carpenter, Mrs. W. I. 140
Carr, Gen. J. S. 72
Carroll, Edward W. 83
Carroll, H. Spain 28, 83
Carroll, Nancy 83
Carter, W. B. 84

Index

Carteret County, N.C. 129
Carthage, N.C. 7, 106
Cashtown, Pa. 29, 90
Caswell County, N.C. 47
Catawba County, N.C. 115
Caudle, L. M. 72
Caudle, Sarah M. Lane 84
Caudle, Wesley E. 84
Causey, H. C. 147
Causey, R. L. 147
Caviness, Arnold Edward 84
Caviness, John A. 84, 178
Caviness, Lydia F. 84
Caviness, Mary Craven 84
Caviness, W. W. 147
Cedar Falls, N.C. 5, 9, 12, 19, 46, 68, 69, 75, 78, 85, 95, 96, 107, 121, 127, 128, 139, 149, 158, 163, 164, 165, 171, 172, 173
Cedar Falls Baptist Church 75, 158; cemetery 75, 83, 85, 175
Cedar Falls Company 9, 12, 14, 15, 68, 69, 74, 107, 108, 150, 152, 153, 154, 156
Cedar Falls Company Store 12, 13, 68
Cedar Falls Historical Society 13
Cedar Falls M. E. Church 158
Cedar Falls United Methodist Church cemetery 95, 97, 121, 175
Cedar Mountain (Cedar Run), Va., battle of 23, 53, 69
Cedar Valley United Methodist Church cemetery, Caldwell Co., N.C. 88, 175
Cemetery Ridge 55
Centerville, Va. 23, 33
Central Falls, N.C. 93
Chamberlain, Brig. Gen. Joshua 41
Chambersburg, Pa. 29
Chambersburg Pike 29
Chancellorsville, Va. 54, 56; battle of 8, 9, 27, 28, 33, 70, 71, 72, 74, 76, 78, 84, 90, 96, 97, 103, 111, 121, 124, 126, 127, 135, 138, 143
Chandler, Rhoda 89
Chanute, Kan. 126, 175
Charleston, S.C. 114, 137, 159
Charlotte, N.C. 158
Charlottesville, Va. 85
Chatham County, N.C. 72, 75, 84, 85, 89, 90, 108, 113, 114, 120, 122, 124, 156, 158, 175, 178
Cheek, Rebecca Jane 123
Chesapeake Hospital, Fortress Monroe, Va. 109

Chesson, Ms. Mary 2
Chester, Pa. 32, 75, 79, 83
Chewning Plateau 33
Chew's Battery: Company A 147
Chickahominy River 20, 21, 22, 36, 50, 56, 136
Chrisco, Dan'l 147
City Point, Va. 81, 83, 88, 95, 120, 121, 129
Clark, John W. 10
Clark, Lt. Col. Walter 10, 134
Climax, N.C. 90, 114
Coble, Abigail 85
Coble, Betsy Ann Curtis 85
Coble, Mrs. C. M. 159
Coble, Clem 157
Coble, David Oliver 84, 157, 176
Coble, Eli 85
Coble, Henry 84
Coble, J. R. 157
Coble, John 157
Coble, John Randolph 84
Coble, Keziah Lowe 85
Coble, Martha J. Breedlove 84
Coble, Martitia York 84
Coble, Randolph 157
Coble, Riley 85
Coble, Rosannah H. 81
Coble, Sarah Ann Campbell 84
Coble, W. M. 157
Coble, William 85, 175
Coffin Foust & Co. 154
Cold Harbor, Va., battle of 36, 56, 76, 78, 82, 90, 92, 108, 136, 143
Cole, Maj. (Lt. Col.) C. C. 25, 28, 70, 71
Cole, J. R. 11, 149
Coleridge, N.C. 5
Collettsville, N.C. 115
Coltrane, Mrs. J. C. 157
Coltrane, Rosanna 76
Columbia, S.C. 144
Columbia Township 128
Company M, 22nd Regiment N.C. Troops "Randolph Hornets" (Reactivated) 2, 171, 172, 173
Concord, N.C. 69, 72, 156, 176
Condra, Rebecca 107
Confederate Battery, Navy 147
Confederate monument, "Hugo" 135, 137, 146, 147, 173
Confederate Reunion 76, 90, 95, 97, 113, 114, 116, 122, 144
Confederate Soldier's Home, Raleigh, N.C. 73, 74, 79, 118, 127, 157, 159, 160
Confederate States Navy 114, 132, 159, 171

Confederate States of America 4, 52, 61
Confederate Veteran magazine 73
Conley, George Harvey 85
Conley, Julius George 85
Connecticut 66
Connor, Col. James 21, 50
Conscript Act 18, 47, 49, 148
Cook, Fetney Terrell 85
Cook, William L. 85
Cooke, Brig. Gen. John R. 40, 73
Cool Springs, N.C. 95
Cooper, Oliver C. 62
Cornelison, J. C. 147
Corse, Brig. Gen. Montgomery 41
The Courier 1, 8, 138, 139, 141, 142, 143, 144, 156, 157, 158, 159
Covington, Aubrey 132
Cox, Delphina 18, 167, 169
Cox, James Matthews 85, 143, 178
Cox, Col. Jesse D. 8
Cox's Landing, James River, Va. 74, 106
Cranford, Z. A. 147
Craven, Catherine L. "Katie" 82
Craven, Delilah Scott 86
Craven, Emma D. 86
Craven, Enoch S. 86
Craven, Henrietta A. "Ritty" 89
Craven, Henry 86
Craven, Jacob Franklin 86
Craven, Kindred 86
Craven, Mary 69
Craven, Mary Fields 86
Craven, Nancy E. 86
Craven, Roxanna L. 86
Craven, Sarah 86
Creech, A. 150
Creedmore, N.C. 108
Crook, Clarinda S. 97
Cross, Addison 87
Cross, Delaney 87
Cross, Elizabeth 86
Cross, Henry 86
Cross, James N. 86, 175
Cross, M. C. 147
Cross, Sarah J. 128
Cross, Thomas F. 87
Cross, W. D. 147
Crouch, Mr. 134
Crowson, E. L. 150
Crowson, Private W. S. 8, 145, 147
Culpepper, Va. 23, 26, 27, 29, 53, 54, 91
Cumberland County, N.C. 79
Curtis, Abraham 85

Index

Curtis, Betsy Ann 85
Curtis, Judith Emily "Juda" 126
Curtis, Margaret 85
Curtis, Martitia 129

Dagenhart, Jerry 116, 117
Danbury, N.C. 89
Danville, Va. 85
Darbytown Road 22
Darr, Mary Lopp 87
Darr, Melchior 87
Darr, Samuel 87, 176
Darr, Susannah Conrad 87
Davenport, Pinkney 128
Daves, Col. Graham 31, 32, 37
David's Island, New York Harbor 121
Davidson County, N.C. 87, 97, 125, 176
Davis, Duncan 145
Davis, President Jefferson 40
Davis, Major 72
Davis, Mary Martitia Allen 77
Deal, Catherine Smyre 87
Deal, Marcus 87, 175
Deal, Mary Adeline Bisnar 88
Deal, Robert C. 87
Deal, William III 87
Deal's Mill, N.C. 87
Dean, Lydia Ann Silvey 88
Dean, Matilda 88
Dean, Nathan 88
Dean, William H. 88
DeCamp General Hospital, David's Island, New York Harbor 88
Deep Run Creek 26
Dellinger family 88
Diffee, Rachel 118
Dinwiddie Court House, Va. 39
Dobbs County, N.C. 99
Dollinger, J. E. 38, 88
Dowd, Dr. T. C. 147
Doyleston, Pa. 66
Drewry's Bluff, Va. 37, 56
Dubose, Gen. Dudley M. 41
Dumfries, Va. 99
Durham, Mrs. S. P. 156
Durham, N.C. 58, 72, 107, 156
Dutchville Township 108

Early, Gen. Jubal 34
East Franklinville Township 94
Ebenezer United Methodist Cemetery, Randolph County, N.C. 175
Edwards, Jenny 104
Edwards Hill Cemetery, Chatham County, N.C. 120, 175

18th Regiment N.C. Troops: Company I 147
11th Massachusetts Infantry 63
Ellington, Alex P. 88
Elliott, W. A. 134
Ellis, Gov. John W. 4
Ellison, Pvt. David Perry 37
Ellison, Tabitha Odell 156
Ellison, Z. 147
Ellison's Mill, Va., battle of 69, 136
Elmira Prison, N.Y. 34, 103, 106, 116
Elmwood Cemetery, Chanute, Kan. 126, 175
Empire P. O., Randolph County, N.C. 76
England 65
Erect, N.C. 73
Euliss, Allen 88
Euliss, Grandison 88
Euliss, Henrietta A. Craven 89
Euliss, Mary Elizabeth E. Staley 89
Euliss, Sarah 88
Evansport, Va. 15, 16, 17, 18, 19, 47, 48, 50, 61, 62, 63, 68, 72, 75, 122, 128, 162, 167
Ewell, Gen. Richard S. 28, 29, 32, 33, 34, 35, 41

Fair Oaks, Va., battle of 20, 50, 69, 90, 136, 141
Falling Waters, Md. 32, 55, 91, 95, 96, 98, 100, 102, 109, 120, 128, 138, 140
Farmville, (Cumberland Church), Va., battle of 41, 123
Federal II Corps 39, 40, 41
Federal V Corps 21, 35, 39, 40
Federal VI Corps 40
Federal Provost Marshal 122
Field, Gen. Charles W. 22
Fields, Absolom 147
Fields, Andrew J. 89
Fields, Elmira 89
Fields, J. M. 147
Fields, Jesse 89
Fields, Sarah 109
Fields, William 23, 89
15th Regiment N.C. Troops: Company A 132
5th Regiment N.C. Cavalry: Company K 129, 147
58th Regiment N.C. Troops: Company H 147
54th Regiment N.C. Troops: Company K 147
52nd Regiment N.C. Troops: Company B 9, 145, 147; Company E 145; Company K 147
1st Massachusetts Infantry 62, 63, 64
1st N.C. Battalion: Company B 43, 47, 56, 121, 137
1st N.C. Regiment Junior Reserves: Company F 147
1st Regiment Arkansas Infantry 16, 47
1st Regiment N.C. Troops: Company E 147
1st Regiment U. S. Volunteer Infantry: Company B 91, 109; Company C 128; Company D 109; Company G 100; Company I 78; Company K 76, 124
Fitts, Lina 109
Five Forks, Va., battle of 39, 113
Flinchum, Jacob 89
Flinchum, James 89
Flinchum, Rhoda Chandler 89
Flinchum, Sarah Smith 89
Forsyth County, N.C. 113, 114, 126
Fort Delaware, Del. 74, 75, 81, 90, 101, 106, 107, 109, 119, 127
Fort Fisher, N.C. 57
Fort Harrison, Va., action at 38, 109, 113
Fort Monroe, Va. 21, 95, 129
Fort Sumter, S.C. 4
40th Regiment N.C. Troops: Company B 147; Company I 147
48th Regiment N.C. Troops: Company B 147; Company D 147; Company H 147
44th Regiment N.C. Troops: Company H 147
44th Tennessee Regiment: Company D 147
42nd N.Y. "Tammany" Regiment 31, 32
42nd Regiment N.C. Troops: Company I 147
47th Regiment N.C. Troops: Company G 109
47th Virginia Infantry 16, 47
46th Regiment N.C. Troops 147, 167; Company F 9, 145, 147; Company G 9, 82, 147; Company H 106
Foster, Joseph F. 89, 158, 175
Foster, Josiah 89
Foster, Levi 90, 141, 143, 147, 176
Foster, Rebecca Melinda Staley 90
Foster, Wincey Hardin 90

Index

14th Regiment N.C. Troops: Company C 147
4th Michigan Regiment 21, 51, 136
Foust, Christian 90, 176
Foust, Conrad 90, 91
Foust, David 91
Foust, Elizabeth "Betsy" Kivett 90, 91
Foust, Emily 113
Foust, J. H. 91
Foust, Jacob B. 41, 91, 138, 139, 176
Foust, James Madison 91
Foust, Laura Ann Wood 91
Foust, Martha A. 122
Foust, Matilda Lineberry 91
Foust, Peter 91, 176
Foust's Mills, N.C. 119
Franklinsville (Franklinville), N.C. 9, 10, 12, 45, 46, 72, 78, 79, 94, 99, 116, 117, 118, 123, 133, 152, 156
Franklinville Manufacturing Company 14
Franklinville Township 95, 128
Franklinville United Methodist Church cemetery 99, 116, 117, 118, 175
Frayser's (Frazier's) Farm, Va., battle of 22, 69, 72, 77, 82, 90, 96, 104, 120, 123, 127, 136, 143, 144
Frazier, J. C. 147
Frazier, J. R. 147
Fredericksburg, Va. 9, 10, 19, 26, 27, 28, 49, 54, 69, 82, 138, 167; battle of 26, 54, 69, 78, 90, 104, 105, 109, 120, 122, 143
Fredericksburg & Potomac Railroad 15, 47
Fredericksburg Road 35
Freeman, Alex 147
Freeman, James F. 91
Freeman's Ford, Va., skirmish at 82
Freemasons 144
French, Jeremiah 92
French, Gen. Samuel G. 16
French, Thomas P. 92
French, Zipea 92
Friedburg, N.C. 125
Friend's House 21
Fries, Francis 148, 150
Funkstown, Md. 90
Furgerson, James 42, 92
Furgerson, Susan 92
Furgerson, Tunstall 92

Gaines' Mill, Va., battle of 21, 22, 69, 102, 111, 120, 136

Galloway, Col. T. S., Jr. 14, 40, 72, 73
Gann, Polly Ann 123
Gardner, Diannah Breedlove Williams 124
Gardner, Franklin 124
Garysburg, N.C. 14, 47
Gatewood, John Dudley 92
Gatewood, Julia Branson 92
Gatewood, William 92
Gentry, Elizabeth Rankin 92
Gentry, Jefferson 92
Gentry, Matthew 92
German's Ford, Va., action at 32, 55
Gettysburg, Pa. 28, 29, 55; battle of 8, 9, 29, 30, 31, 32, 54, 55, 74, 79, 81, 83, 88, 90, 91, 96, 101, 106, 109, 114, 119, 120, 122, 127, 133, 135, 138, 140, 143, 160, 173
Giles, Martha Jane 93
Giles Chapel community 93
Glasgow, Jesse L. 92, 93
Glasgow, John W. 92
Glasgow, Malinda Breedlove Brown 93
Glasgow, Martha Davis 92, 93
Glasgow, Martha Jane Giles 93
Glasgow, Sibly Caroline Kinney 92
Glasgow, William Monroe 93, 178
Glasgow family 151
Globe Tavern, Va., action at 37
Goldsboro, N.C. 57, 58, 98, 121
Gorden's Mill, Winchester, Va. 51
Gordon, Gen. John B. 41
Gordonsville, Va. 23, 33, 52, 54, 76
Grant, Gen. Ulysses S. 33, 34, 35, 36, 37, 38, 39, 136
Granville County, N.C. 85, 107, 109
Grapevine Bridge 22
Gray, Calvin 93, 176
Gray, Mattie Horney 9, 10
Gray, Lt. Col. Robert Harper 9, 10
Gray, Sophia McDaniel 93
Gray's Chapel, N.C. 94, 111, 112, 157
Gray's Chapel United Methodist Church cemetery 70, 90, 93, 111, 112, 113, 128, 157, 176, 177
Grayson County, Va. 92
Green, the Rev. T. G. 158
Green Hill Cemetery, Greensboro, N.C. 107, 114, 159, 176

Green Mound Cemetery, Vernon, Mo. 113, 176
Greensboro, N.C. 17, 42, 52, 57, 58, 69, 78, 80, 82, 83, 84, 85, 88, 93, 95, 96, 98, 103, 105, 107, 113, 114, 119, 120, 121, 123, 125, 129, 144, 156, 157, 158, 159, 176
Greensboro Daily News 159
Gregg. Bvt. Brig. Gen. David 39
Grigg, Barbara Newsom 62
Groveton, Va. 23
Guilford County, N.C. 14, 28, 46, 76, 78, 80, 84, 88, 98, 110, 114, 115, 122, 124, 134, 137

Haas, W. F. 93
Hagerstown, Md. 24, 32, 53
Hahr, Maj. Franz J. 56
Haithcock, Jeff 171, 172, 173
Haithcock, Joshua 172, 173
Halfway Station 37, 56
Hampton, Gen. Wade 38
Hancock, John W. 147
Hancock, Gen. Winfield 34
Hannah 168
Hanner, J. C. 147
Hanover Junction 35
Hardin, Elizabeth C. "Lizzie" Harlin 94
Hardin, Lucy Routh 93
Hardin, William R. 93, 176
Hardin, Wincey 90
Hardin, Zimri 93
Hardin-Ellison Road 94
Hardin Family Cemetery 94, 176
Harlin, Elizabeth C. "Lizzie" 94
Harpers Ferry, Va. 24, 166; battle of 24, 69, 82, 107, 129
Harris, Maj. James G. 79, 156
Harris Farm 35
Harris' Landing, Va. 49
Harrisburg, Pa. 55
Hart, John 94
Hart's Island Prison, New York Harbor 81, 85, 90, 92, 95, 97, 104, 109, 126
Harvel, Elizabeth 79
Hatcher's Run, Va., battle of 38, 39, 83, 86, 90, 92, 95, 97, 109, 113, 114
Hayes (Hays), Anthony 94
Hayes (Hays), Elias W. 94, 95
Hayes (Hays), Elizabeth York 95
Hayes (Hays), James Madison 72, 94, 95, 147, 160, 176
Hayes (Hays), John 96

Hayes (Hays), Kernelia Blanchet 95
Hayes (Hays), Lovey Jane Allred 95
Hayes (Hays), Margaret Isabella Williams 96, 140
Hayes (Hays), Mary Jennings 95
Hayes (Hays), Nancy Johnson 96
Hayes (Hays), Oliver P. 95, 175
Hayes (Hays), Poline Leonard 95
Hayes (Hays), S. G. 96
Hayes (Hays), Samuel 95
Hayes (Hays), Sarah 96
Hayes (Hays), Susan A. Baldwin 96
Hayes (Hays), Tamer York 94
Hayes (Hays), Thomas B. 96
Hayes (Hays), William 96
Hayes (Hays), William A. 23, 96
Hayes (Hays), William Franklin 93, 96, 139, 140, 143, 178
Heilig, John 147
Hendricks County, Ind. 76
Henson, H. A. 140
Henson, J. G. 140
Henson, Joseph Alson 96, 140, 141, 143, 145, 160, 175
Henson, Matt 77
Henson, R. C. 140
Henson, Sarah Angeline Pugh 97, 140
Henson, Susan F. Burrow 97, 140
The Heritage of Randolph County, North Carolina, Volume 1 67, 114, 118, 125
Heth, Gen. Henry 29, 30, 33, 34, 36, 37, 40
Hicks, James Riley 97
Hicks, Jesse 97
Hicks, Mary Routh 97
Hicks, Ruth McDaniel 97
High Point, N.C. 13, 14, 46, 62, 107, 176
High Point and Asheboro Railroad 145
Hill, Gen. A. P. 21, 22, 23, 24, 26, 28, 29, 30, 32, 33, 34, 35, 36, 37, 38, 39, 40, 53, 73, 136
Hill, Gen. D. H. 21, 22
Hillsboro Military Academy 11
Hillsborough, N.C. 66
Hix, James R. 97
Hobson, Sarah Ellen 101
Hoke, Gen. J. F. 11
Hoke, Maj. Gen. Robert F. 36
Holder, Branson 97

Holder, J. W. 147
Holder, Lewis Franklin 97, 178
Holder, Lucinda (Lousinda) Turner 97
Holder, Rebecca Caviness 97
Holder, Sarah J. 97
Holly Spring Friends Meeting 76; cemetery 129, 176
Hollywood Cemetery 136
Holmes, Gen. Theophilus 16, 47
Home Guard 97, 98
Hood, Gen. John B. 22
Hooker, Maj. Gen. Joseph 26, 27, 62, 63, 65, 135
Hooker, W. C. 147
Horney, Alexander S. 9, 154, 155, 156
Horney, Capt. Elisha Clarkson 8, 9
Horney, Mattie 9, 10
Horney family 12
Hudson, N.C. 105
Hulin, Clarinda S. Crook 97, 98
Hulin, Emeline C. 98
Hulin, Frank J. 98
Hulin, Hiram 97
Hulin, Jesse 97
Hulin, John 97
Hulin, Linnie L. 98
Hulin, Nancy Sexton 97
Hulin, Nelson Kenny 97, 98, 178
Hulin, William 97
Hulin, Wilson K. 98
Hunton, Brig. Gen. Eppa 41
Hutson, Henry M. 98
Hutson, Susan Morris 98
Hutton, Martitia 79
Hwy. 49 112
Hyman, Col. Joseph 41

Illinois 102
Indiana 79, 111
Ingold, Johnnie 94
Ingram, H. C. 145, 147
Ingram, W. D. 147
Invalid Corps 83, 121
Iowa 107
Iredell County, N.C. 116, 117, 176
Irvine, Lt. W. T. 65
Ivey, Mary H. "Polly" York 98
Ivey, Stephen W. 98, 178

J. A. C. 17, 18
Jackson, John 32, 98
Jackson, Gen. Thomas J. 22, 23, 24, 26, 27, 49, 53, 54, 56, 57, 90, 91, 96, 132, 136, 137, 139, 140, 141, 143
James, M. R. 98, 99

James, Marshal 98
James River, Va. 37, 38, 47, 56
Jarratt's Station, Va., action at 38
Jarrell, Wallace E. 43, 172, 173
Jennings, David 99
Jennings, Mary 95
Jennings, Mary Allred 99
Jennings, Nancy 120
Jennings, Peter 99
Jericho Mills, Va., battle of 35, 78, 80, 83, 85, 89, 116, 124
Jerusalem Plank Road, action at 92
Joe? 165
Johnson, Maj. Gen. Bushrod 39
Johnson, Caroline A. 119
Johnson, F. L. 145
Johnson, Miss Irene 132
Johnson, James 99
Johnson, Mrs. M. E. 132
Johnson, Nancy 99
Johnson, Ransom 147
Johnson, Roger 171
Johnson, Willis 99
Johnson, Capt. Y. M. C. 132
Johnson County, N.C. 47
Johnson's Island Prison, Ohio 75
Johnston, Gen. Joseph E. 19, 20, 21, 47, 49, 50, 57, 58, 137
Johnston County, N.C. 173
Jolly, J. W. 147
Jones, A. H. 99
Jones, Bethania 99
Jones, Craven 99
Jones, Elizabeth 99
Jones, Emily 127
Jones, Mrs. G. H. 144
Jones, Lewis 99
Jones, Mary 100
Jones, Mary Ann E. 128
Jones, Mary C. Allred 99
Jones, Mountainville T. 98, 99, 175
Jones, William C. 99, 100
Jones' Farm, Va., action at 38, 109, 113
Jordansville, Va. 27
Julian, Hannah Sarah "Sally" 112
Julian, Sarah C. 150
Julian, N.C. 80, 81, 158
Junior Battalion 147

Kansas 126
Kelly, Sophia 125
Kentucky 119
Kephart, Mrs. E. E. 145
Kerr Bag Manufacturing Company 69, 107

Kershaw, Maj. Gen. Joseph B. 22, 41
Kildee Wesleyan Church cemetery 129, 176
Kilgo, Bishop John C. 156
Kilpatrick, Gen. Judson 32
Kime, Mrs. W. A. 159
Kime, W. C. 100
Kinney (Kinne) name 100
Kinney, Fannie Lane 121
Kinney, George 100
Kinney, Ruth McMasters 100
Kinney, Sibly Caroline 92
Kinney, Susanna 120
Kinney, Wesley 100
Kinston, N.C. 57, 129
Kirkman, Carrie Rebecca 68, 69,
Kirkman, J. H. 147
Kirkman, Martha Caroline 103
Kirkman, Mary Jane 102
Kivett, Alfred W. 100
Kivett, Alfred Washington 101
Kivett, Angeline 68
Kivett, Anna Scotton 100, 101, 102
Kivett, Daniel David 100, 102, 138
Kivett, Daniel M. 20, 100, 102, 137, 138
Kivett, Dolly Graves 100, 102
Kivett, Eli 100, 101, 102
Kivett, Elizabeth M. "Louisa" 104
Kivett, Elvira "Alva" 68
Kivett, Frances Reese 103
Kivett, Isabella 125
Kivett, Jacob 101, 176
Kivett, James Franklin "Sharpe" 101, 143, 178
Kivett, James Murdick 17, 42, 101, 176
Kivett, Joel A. 101, 143, 176
Kivett, John Aldridge 68, 103
Kivett, John Alfred 101
Kivett, John W., Jr. 32, 101, 178
Kivett, John Wesley, Sr. 102
Kivett, Kenneth M. 102, 176
Kivett, Leander A. 102
Kivett, Lucady Williams 102
Kivett, Lydia Belinda 101
Kivett, Margaret Williams 101
Kivett, Mariah 124
Kivett, Martha Caroline Kirkman 103
Kivett, Mary (May) 102
Kivett, Mary Jane Kirkman 102
Kivett, Mary Welborn 68, 103
Kivett, Mary Wrightman 103
Kivett, Nancy A. York 101

Kivett, Nathan P. 103
Kivett, Peter P. 102
Kivett, Rachel Isabel McDaniel 101
Kivett, Rick 103
Kivett, Sarah Ellen Hobson 101
Kivett, Sarah "Sally" Richardson 101
Kivett, Stanley "Sug" 19, 20, 100, 102, 137, 138, 176
Kivett, Talton 34, 103
Kivett, Tim 103
Kivett, Troy Thomas 68, 103, 178
Kivett, Capt. Warren B. 19, 20, 27, 49, 50, 68, 72, 103, 176
Kivett, William D. 2
Kivett, Zeno 68
Kivett family 2, 11, 149
Knob Noster, Mo. 126

Lamb, Alan 172, 173
Lamb, Capt. G. V. 145
Lamb, H. M. 145
Lane, Gen. James H. 30, 34, 37, 38, 39
Lane, John C. 24, 103
Lane, Rebecca 103
Lane, Sarah M. 84
Langley, Bartley Yancey 104
Langley, Delphina Marley 104
Langley, Edward Tyson "Tise" 104, 139, 178
Langley, Elizabeth 126
Langley, Elizabeth M. "Louisa" Kivett 104
Langley, Jenny Edwards 104
Langley, Mary 104
Langley, Nancy Warren 104
Langley, William 104
Langley, Zimri 104
Laughlin, Hugh 104
Laughlin, Mahala Hinshaw 104
Laughlin, N. G. 104
Laughlin, William T. 104, 176
Lawrence, A. E. Williams 75
Lawrence, Austin 74
Lawrence, Austin Willard 74
Lawrence, John Milton 49, 74, 166
Lawrence, Mary 74
Lawrence, Priscilla Trogdon 74
Ledman, Jane R. 121
Lednum, Mary Susan 75
Lee, Maj. Gen. Fitzhugh 39
Lee, Maj. Gen. G. W. Custis 41
Lee, Gen. Robert E. 21, 22, 24, 26, 27, 28, 29, 32, 33, 34, 35, 36, 37, 38, 40, 50, 53, 54, 55, 56, 57, 71, 90, 96, 114, 132, 136, 137, 139, 140, 141, 143, 159
Lee County, N.C. 106
Lee Springs, Va., skirmish at 82
Leesburg, Va. 24, 53
Lenoir, N.C. 106, 118
Lenoir County, N.C. 99, 129
Leonard, Anna Trogdon 78
Leonard, Mrs. J. D. 140
Leonard, L. 149
Leonard, Malinda 75
Leonard, Poline 95
Lewallen, Z. A. 147
Liberty, N.C. 10, 11, 68, 73, 80, 86, 91, 99, 101, 103, 127, 157, 158
Lincoln, Pres. Abraham 4, 5
Lineberry, Elizabeth 91
Lineberry, Matilda 91
Lineberry, Capt. Winfield Scott 145, 147, 159
Lingle, John 105
Lingle, Sarah Turnmire 105
Lingle, William Alfred 105
Loflin, the Rev. George 158
Long, Lt. Col. John O. 14, 20, 50
Longstreet, Gen. James 21, 22, 23, 26, 28, 29, 30, 32, 33, 34, 35
Lopp, Mary 87
Love (Lowe), W. E. 105
Lovejoy Methodist Cemetery 98
Lowder, Patrick 147
Lowe, Elizabeth Warren 105
Lowe, Grace 105
Lowe, James 105
Lowe, James P. 105
Lowe, William 105
Lowrance, Col. William Lee J. 29, 30, 31, 32
Lyndsay & Campbell's 150

MacRae, Brig. Gen. William 40
Mahone, Brig. Gen. William 36
Makepeace, George 12, 152, 153
Makepeace family 12
Mallet's Battalion of Camp Guards 114, 115
Malvern Hill, Va., battle of 22, 104, 122, 126, 141
Manassas, Va. 19, 52; first battle of 53; second battle of 23, 53, 74, 76, 79, 82, 83, 89, 90, 96, 109, 115, 116, 121, 124, 126, 138, 141, 143

Manassas Gap Railroad 23
Maness (Manis), A. 106
Marley, Delphina 104
Martin, Cheryl L. 67
Martin, Henry B. 145
Martinsburg, Va. 24, 25, 53, 54, 166
Marvin United Methodist Church cemetery, Iredell County, N.C. 117, 176
Marye's Heights, action at 26, 69
Maryland 53
Maryland Heights 24
Masten, Ursula A. 76, 158
May, J. M. 137
May, Okla. 107
McAlister, Col. A. C. 147, 156
McCanick's Mill 136, 137
McCaskill, J. A. 147
McClellan, Gen. George B. 19, 65
McColl, S.C. 106
McCollum, A. M. 147
McCrary, W. F. 147
McDaniel, Anderson Green 105
McDaniel, Mary Kivett 105
McDaniel, Rachel Isabel 101
McDaniel, Sophia 93
McDaniel, Zale 105
McDonald Mill 69
McDonough, Pvt. Michael 31, 32
McDowell, Brig. Gen. Irvin 53
McDowell County, N.C. 46
McGowan, Brig. Gen. Samuel 34, 40
McIntyre, Robert Tate 132
McLemore, Calvin D. 106
McLemore, John R. 106
McLemore, Margaret 106
McMasters, Cynthia L. Siler 75
McMasters, D. G. 147
McMasters, Huldah Welborn 75
McMasters, Lewis F. 19, 20, 46, 49, 50, 75, 165, 176
McMasters, Mary Susan Lednum 75
McMasters, Ruth 100
McMasters, William J. B. 75
McMasters Cemetery, Liberty, N.C. 68, 75, 91, 101, 102, 176
McMath, Mrs. Ella 144
McNeill, Mahala L. Sheppard 106
McNeill, William 106, 175
McPherson, W. H. 147
McPherson Ridge 29
Meade, Gen. George G. 33
Meadow Bridge 21, 50

Mechanicsville, Va., battle of 13, 21, 51, 69, 78, 85, 90, 93, 119, 120, 121, 122, 128, 136
Melvin, Rev. R. H. 159
Mexico 75
Middleton Academy 9, 12, 13, 46, 68, 107
Miles, Maj. Gen. Nelson A. 40
Millboro, N.C. 113, 156, 157
Miller, E. P., Jr. 106
Miller, Sue 106
Miller, W. M. 147
Mine Run, Va. 33, 108
Missouri 113
Mitchell, W. M. 145
Moffitt, Benjamin 45, 154
Moffitt, E. K. 147
Moffitt, M. H. 147
Moffitt's Mill, N.C. 86, 127, 145
Montgomery County, N.C. 73, 97, 98, 99
Moore, A. M. 145
Moore, the Rev. W. H., D. D. 72, 73
Moore County, N.C. 5, 27, 81, 84, 98, 106, 125, 156, 175
Morehead Township 114
Morgan, J. M. 147
Morgan, Nathan 147
Moring & Byrns 154
Morris, Mrs. 144
Morris, Private P. H. 145, 147
Morris, Susan 98
Morrison, Sam'l 147
Mt. Lebanon United Methodist Church cemetery 95, 105, 118, 176
Mt. Olivet School, Erect, N.C. 73
Mt. Pleasant Baptist Church cemetery 91, 101, 103, 176
Mt. Pleasant community 101, 128
Mt. Pleasant United Methodist cemetery, Davidson County, N.C. 87, 176
Murdock, A. G. 147

N. C. R. R. 149
N.C. State Militia 5, 7, 8, 147
Nashville, Tenn. 66
Negro 133
Nelson, H. H. 147
Nelson, Mrs. James 157
Nelson, Rebecca H. 112
Neosho County, Kan. 126
Neuse River, N.C., action at 58, 121
New Bern, N.C. 57, 72
New Bridge 22
New Jersey 66

New Market, Va. 27, 54
New Market Heights 38
New Orleans, La. 165
New Salem, N.C. 95
New York Troops 55
Newby, Nettie 110
Nine Mile Road 20
North Anna Campaign 35, 78, 88, 92, 108
North Anna River 35
North Carolina 4, 37, 47, 49, 52, 56, 57, 58, 66, 67, 72, 74, 102, 107, 113, 133, 140, 154
North Carolina Bulletin 7
North Carolina Confederate Pension Applications 67, 75, 78, 80, 82, 86, 90, 91, 93, 94, 96, 97, 103, 104, 105, 106, 108, 110, 113, 114, 117, 118, 119, 120, 121, 127, 129, 160
North Carolina Confederate Soldiers 1861-1865 (Broadfoot's Roster) 67, 84, 91, 93, 96, 100, 108, 122
North Carolina Museum of History 31
North Carolina State Archives 148
North Carolina Troops 1861–1865: A Roster 67, 97, 105, 108, 110

Oak Hill, N.C. 87
Oak Ridge Baptist Church cemetery, Vance County, N.C. 42, 109, 178
Oakwood Cemetery, Concord, N.C. 69, 176
Oakwood Cemetery, High Point, N.C. 124, 176
Oakwood Cemetery, Richmond, Va. 101, 102, 136, 176
Oakwood Confederate Cemetery, Raleigh, N.C. 74, 79, 127, 157, 178
Oath of Allegiance 75, 80, 81, 83, 85, 86, 87, 90, 92, 93, 95, 97, 100, 101, 102, 104, 109, 112, 113, 114, 115, 116, 118, 122, 126, 127
O'Brien, Alex 147
Oda, James 107
O'Dear, Nancy 108
O'Dear, William 108
Odell, Allie Addison White 69
Odell, Anna Trogdon 68, 69, 107
Odell, Elizabeth Forrester 107
Odell, J. M. Manufacturing Company 107
Odell, James 68, 69, 107

Index

Odell, James Alexander 9, 69, 107, 156
Odell, James L. 71
Odell, James M. 9, 46
Odell, James Madison 9, 107
Odell, John Laban 69, 70
Odell, Capt. John Milton 9, 11, 12, 13, 14, 19, 46, 68, 69, 70, 72, 107, 128, 139, 141, 143, 148, 149, 150, 152, 153, 154, 155, 156, 164, 165, 176
Odell, Maj. Laban D. 9, 12, 19, 25, 26, 27, 28, 46, 49, 68, 69, 70, 71, 107, 166, 176, 177
Odell, Mary Craven 69, 70
Odell, Mary J. Prescott 107
Odell, Rebecca Condra 107
Odell, W. R. 156
Odell, William Bedouin, Sr. 107
Odell Hardware Company 69, 107,
Odell Manufacturing Company 69 107, 156
Old Cold Harbor Crossroads 36
126th N.Y. Regiment 32
Orange County, N.C. 84, 88, 100, 108, 134
Orange Court House, Va. 26, 33, 55, 97, 140
Orange Plank Road 33
Orange Turnpike 27, 33
Ore Hill, N.C. 84
Oregonville, N.C. 83
Oseley, W. A. 108
Osgood, N.C. 70
Outliers 5, 110
Overman, E. M. 145
Overman, Senator 145
Owen, D. N. 145
Ox Hill (Chantilly), Va., battle of 24

Page, Hon. R. N. 73
Paris, Mary Emily 117
Parker's Store 33
Parrish, B. F. 147
Partisan Rangers 129
Patterson's Grove Christian Church cemetery 122, 178
Pearce?, W. M. 155
Pen, Alvens 108
Pender, Gen. William D. 21, 22, 23, 24, 25, 26, 27, 28, 29, 30, 52, 56
Peninsular Campaign 68
Pennsylvania 66, 79
Perry, D. 108
Perry, James 108
Perry, Seborn 150
Petersburg, Va. 13, 37, 38, 40, 51, 52, 56, 57, 92, 100, 133, 134, 136, 137, 140, 156; action at 39, 40, 72, 73, 81, 90, 92, 108, 109, 113, 126, 139, 143
Petersburg & Weldon Railroad 37, 38
Pettigrew, Gen. James Johnston 14, 16, 17, 18, 20, 21, 29, 30, 32, 47, 49, 50, 55, 163
Phelen, Mr. 58
Philadelphia, Pa. 62, 178
Philadelphia National Cemetery, Philadelphia, Pa. 79, 178
Pickett, Gen. George E. 30, 36, 39
Piedmont Historical Society of the 1860's 171
Plank Road 34
Pleasant Cross Christian Church 97, 140
Pleasant Grove Township 89, 129
Pleasant Ridge Christian Church cemetery 76, 158, 178
Poe, Harper 134
Point Lookout Prison, Md. 35, 42, 74, 75, 76, 78, 80, 81, 83, 85, 89, 90, 91, 92, 95, 100, 102, 103, 106, 109, 114, 116, 120, 124, 128; cemetery 81, 83, 102, 178
Pole Green Church 35
Pope, Gen. John 23
Potomac River 16, 19, 24, 26, 29, 32, 47, 48, 53, 54, 55, 62, 63, 64, 68, 164, 168
Pottery Festival, Seagrove, N.C. 174
Pounds, Archibald T. 75, 108
Pounds, J. L. 108, 158
Pounds, James M. 12, 19, 46, 75, 108, 158, 160, 175
Pounds, Malinda Leonard 75
Pounds, Minnie Belle 158
Pounds, Mourning Lowe 75, 108
Pounds, Randolph 158
Pounds, William A. 75, 108
Poupore, Fawnie 160
Prescott, Mary J. 107
Presnell, C. 145
Presnell, H. C. 147
Presnell, Nixon 145
Primitive Baptists 126, 140, 141
Providence Township 114
Providence United Methodist Church cemetery, Chatham County, N.C. 84, 178
Pugh, Alpheus "Alvin" 20, 21, 50, 108, 109, 165
Pugh, Barbary Lousina 128
Pugh, Caroline 120
Pugh, J. W. 145
Pugh, Lou Ann 45
Pugh, Martha E. 83
Pugh, Pithia Jane 111
Pugh, S. F. 147
Pugh, Sarah 109
Pugh, Sarah Angeline 97, 140
Pugh, Sarah Fields 109
Pugh, William 109
Pulley, Daniel P. 42, 109, 178
Pulley, John 109
Pulley, Lina Fitts 109
Pulley, Mary Ann Fuller 109
Pulley, Thomas Mark 109

Quakers 4, 129
Quantico Station, Va. 16
Quinney's Station, Va. 26, 54

Raccoon Ford, Va. 53
Raines, Marshall S. 109
Raleigh, N.C. 12, 14, 46, 52, 57, 58, 62, 72, 73, 79, 106, 137, 148, 149, 155, 160
Raleigh Guard 147
Ramseur, N.C. 82, 83, 110, 121, 129, 132, 134, 137, 139, 143, 144, 157, 158, 178
Ramseur M. E. Church South 144
Randleman, N.C. 118, 120, 157
Randolph Camp No. 1646, United Confederate Veterans 73, 75, 90, 95, 97, 114, 116, 144, 160
Randolph County Cemetery Records 110
Randolph County Court House 133, 147, 161, 173
Randolph County Finance Committee 148, 154
Randolph County Historical Society 66
Randolph Hornets 1, 12, 13, 62, 63, 64, 65, 66, 94, 148, 149, 150, 152, 153, 154
Randolph Living Historians 171
Randolph Room, Asheboro Public Library 6, 7, 14, 63, 64, 132, 147, 155, 161
Rankin, Elizabeth 92
Rapidan River 32, 33, 55
Rappahannock Bridge, Va., battle of 33
Rappahannock River 19, 23, 26, 27, 33, 54, 82
Reams' Station, Va., battle of 37, 76, 88, 109, 113, 115

Index

Red Cloud, Chief 126
"Red Strings" 5
Reece, Eleanor Armfield 110
Reece, Esther Caudle 110
Reece, Joseph L. 110
Reece, Joseph M. D. 110, 178
Reece, W. M. 44
Reece, William D. 110, 178
Reeder, Gary D. 67
Rehobeth United Methodist Church 82, 83
Richardson, Mike 171, 172, 173
Richardson, the Rev. N. R. 145
Richardson, Nancy 99
Richardson, Peter 99, 103
Richmond, Va. 11, 14, 15, 19, 22, 35, 37, 38, 40, 47, 49, 51, 52, 56, 62, 65, 72, 78, 79, 82, 86, 90, 91, 92, 94, 97, 99, 101, 102, 106, 111, 113, 115, 119, 123, 127, 129, 132, 134, 136, 137, 138, 139, 140, 141, 165, 166, 176
Richmond County, N.C. 98
Riddell's Shop, Va., action at 37
Riley's Battery 147
Ritter, Capt. John 5, 7
Robbins, Iredell 147
Robbins, James M. 75, 110, 175
Robbins, John 110
Robbins, John Madison 110
Robbins, Margaret Swaim 110
Robbins, Marmaduke Swaim 110
Robbins, Mary Frazier 75
Robbins, the Rev. Nathan 75
Robbins, Nettie Newby 110
Robbins, Rosanna Coltrane 76
Robbins, S. M. 110
Robbins, William Thomas 110, 176
Roberts, Dr. and Mrs. Marion B. 66
Rocketts 14, 47
Rockingham, N.C. 42, 83, 158
Rockingham County, N.C. 14, 92, 118
Rocky River United Methodist Church cemetery, Chatham County, N.C. 119, 178
Roll of Honor 91, 97, 103, 105, 106, 112, 122, 124, 125, 127
Rose, Caroline 77
Rosser, Maj. Gen. Thomas L. 39
Roster of North Carolina Troops in the War Between the States (Moore's Roster) 67, 74, 81, 90, 104, 105, 106, 110
Routh, Aaron 111
Routh, Agnes Spoon 111, 112

Routh, Dicy 111
Routh, Elizabeth Reitzel 111
Routh, Elizabeth Turner 111, 113
Routh, Emily Foust 113
Routh, George E. 111
Routh, Hannah Sarah "Sally" Julian 112
Routh, Isaac 111, 112
Routh, James 111
Routh, James M. 111, 112
Routh, Jesse 111, 113
Routh, John 111
Routh, Joseph Alson 111, 112, 176
Routh, Joshua 111, 113
Routh, Joshua Marion 111, 112, 176
Routh, Kyle 172, 173
Routh, Lillie Cude 111, 112
Routh, Mary 97
Routh, Moses 111
Routh, Nancy Hayes 111
Routh, Pithia Jane Pugh 111
Routh, Rebecca H. Nelson 112
Routh, Sally 112
Routh, Terry 172, 173
Routh, Wesley P. 112
Routh, William Clay 111, 112, 145, 176
Routh, William Riley 111, 113
Routh, Zachariah 111, 112
Routh family 112
Rowan County, N.C. 58
Rush, A. C. 147
Rush, A. J. 147
Rush, Lt. J. A. 145
Russell, T. L. 147
Rutherford College, N.C. 87, 159

Salem, N.C. 148, 149
Salem Manufacturing Cotton Mill 148
Salisbury, N.C. 58, 137, 145
San Diego, Calif. 110
Sandy Creek Baptist Association 4
Sandy Creek Baptist Church cemetery 86, 98, 103, 110, 122, 126, 141, 178
Sandy Creek community 44, 68, 107, 121, 122, 126
Sandy Ridge, N.C. 123
Sanford, N.C. 106, 175
Sayler's Creek, Va., battle of 40
Scales, Brig. Gen. Alfred M. 28, 29, 30, 31, 32, 33, 34, 35, 37, 38, 39, 40, 41, 56, 72, 73
Schoenberger, Fred 171, 172, 173
Scotland, Md. 178
Scott, Delilah 86

Scott, Enoch P. 113
Scott, W. B. 145
Scott, the Rev. W. L. 144
Scott, Gen. Winfield 53
Scotten, Jacob 113
Scotten, James Marshall 113
Scotten, Lucy 113
Scotten, Mary A. Staley 113
Scott's Old Field 5
Scronce family 115
Scronce, Jacob 115
Seccession 4, 5
2nd Battalion Arkansas Infantry 21, 23
Second N.C. Battalion: Company B 147; Company F 9, 145, 147; Company G 145; Company H 145
2nd New Hampshire Infantry 63
2nd Regiment Tennessee Infantry 16
Sedgwick, General John 27, 28
Seven Days Battles 50, 53, 56, 123, 127, 136, 138, 139, 141
Seven Pines, Va., battle of 20, 50, 68, 69, 74, 75, 78, 88, 89, 90, 97, 102, 106, 109, 110, 115, 118, 119, 127, 128, 136, 139, 141, 165
7th N.C. Infantry Regiment 156
70th Regiment N.C. Troops 11; Company E 147; Company F 9, 147
Shady Grove Baptist Church cemetery 96, 97, 101, 104, 121, 125, 139, 178
Sharpsburg, Md., battle of 24, 53, 78, 103, 138
Shaw, J. T. 147
Shenandoah River 53, 54
Shenandoah Valley 25, 28, 54
Shepherdstown, Md., battle of 24, 25, 69, 79, 126, 141
Shepherdstown Ford, Va., action at 82, 86, 104, 125, 129
Sheppard, Mahala L. 106
Sheridan, Maj. Gen. Philip 36, 39, 40
Sherman, Gen. William T. 57, 58
Shiloh United Methodist Church cemetery 80, 81, 93, 158, 178
Shipping Point Battery, Evansport, Va. 64
Shores, Andy 172, 173
Shouse, Catharina Geiger 113
Shouse, Edwin Thomas 113, 114
Shouse, Eli Augustus 113

Index

Shouse, Jacob 113
Shouse, James Leander 113
Shouse, Jeanette Brown 114
Shouse, Wiley 113
Sickles, Gen. Daniel B. 29, 55
Sikes, D. A. 147
Siler, Andrew J. 72, 114
Siler, Capt. Columbus Franklin 9, 19, 27, 28, 34, 38, 39, 40, 41, 49, 70, 72, 73, 75, 114, 157, 160, 178
Siler, Cynthia L. 75
Siler, Eliza 114
Siler, G. W. 159
Siler, H. Thompson 114, 147, 159, 160
Siler, Joseph A. 114
Siler, Mary E. Wood 114
Siler, P. T. 159
Siler, Ruth Barker 72, 114
Siler, W. D. 147
Siler, Wesley C. 32, 114
Siler City, N.C. 83
Silvey, Lydia Ann 88
Simms, Brig. Gen. James P. 41
Sioux Indian Tribe 126
16th N.C. Battalion 132; Company H 147
16th Regiment N.C. Troops 21, 22, 23, 26, 37, 52
6th Regiment N.C. Troops: Company G 145
61st Regiment N.C. Troops 147
69th Pennsylvania Infantry: Company A 102
63rd Regiment N.C. Troops: Company E 74; Company K 129
Skillicorn, Wm. 147
Slack, Eliza E. 117
Slavery 4
Smith, Ab 147
Smith, Edith Lineberry 114, 115
Smith, Henry C. 114
Smith, Herbert P. 114
Smith, Howard E. 114, 115
Smith, Madison 115
Smith, Reuben 114, 115
Smithfield, N.C., action at 58
Snipes, Nellie Mahalia 126
Snipes family 126
Soapstone Mt. 96, 128
Sommerville, Tenn. 72
South Carolina 4, 106, 123
South Side Railroad, action at 39, 40, 92
Southside Cotton Mills 158
Spencer, Lemuel 147
Spinks, Elizabeth Garner 115
Spinks, John D. 23, 115

Spinks, Sarah Martha 129
Spinks, William S. 115
Spoon, Sam'l 147
Spotsylvania Court House Va., battle of 34, 35, 56, 78, 92, 108, 125, 126, 141
Springs, Oak and Co. 5
Spronce, J. G. 115
Sprouse, J. G. 115
Sprouse family 115
Stafford Court House, Va. 15, 48
Staley, Hannah 121
Staley, John 109
Staley, Mrs. Lou 157
Staley, Margaret 109
Staley, Mary A. 113
Staley, Mary Elizabeth E. 89
Staley, Mollie Brown 158
Staley, Rebecca 124
Staley, Rebecca Melinda 90
Staley, Dr. Will 73
Staley, N.C. 86, 97, 101, 104
Stapleton, Jeff 172, 173
Star, N.C. 73
Star #437 Masonic Lodge 73
The State 65
Staunton, Va. 89, 166
Steamer *North Carolina* 132
Steed, J. H. & J. S. 154
Steel, Abner Branson 115, 145, 160, 175
Steel, Eunice Allridge 115
Steel, Jacob 115
Stephenson, W. M. 145
Stewart, Charles Wesley Abner 116
Stewart, Mary Emily Paris 116, 117
Stewart, Ralph 116
Stewart, Rebecca Johnson 116
Stewart, Thomas Jackson 116, 117, 176
Stokes County, N.C. 89, 92, 113, 118, 123
Stout, Eliza E. Slack 117, 118
Stout, Elizabeth 118
Stout, Lemuel 118
Stout, Lorenzo Dow, Jr. 41, 117, 175
Stout, Lorenzo Dow, Sr. 117
Stout, Martha Hendricks 117
Stout, Sarah E. Allred 118
Stout, William G. 99, 118, 176
Strickland, William O. 118
Stroud, Ok. 119
Strout, W. B. 118
Stuart, Gen. J. E. B. 28, 29, 54
Sudderth, William S. 118
Sugar Loaf (Carolina Beach), N.C. 57

Sugg, L. O. 147
Suggs, Dr. Joseph R. 65, 66
Sulphur Springs, Va., skirmish at 82
Sumner, Asa 118
Sumner, John R. 22, 118
Sumner, Mary 118
Sumner, Rachel Diffee 118
Sunset Knoll Cemetery, Ramseur, N.C. 121, 143, 178
Surry County, N.C. 92, 127
Surry County, Va. 109
Sutherland's Station, Va., battle of 40, 73
Swaim, Deritta Odell 156
Swaney, Ruben 147

Tabernacle Township 5
Tennessee 95, 119
10th N.C. Battalion Artillery: Company A 145, 147; Company E 147
10th Regiment N.C. Troops: Company C 147
Tenting on the Old Campground 145
Terrell, Fetney 85
3rd Regiment Maryland Cavalry: Company E 90
3rd Regiment N.C. Troops: Company B 147; Company F 147; Company H 147
3rd Regiment Pennsylvania Heavy Artillery 93
13th Mississippi Infantry 16, 47, 48
13th Regiment N.C. Troops 26, 27, 52
30th Regiment N.C. Troops: Company H 147
38th Regiment N.C. Troops 21, 23, 26, 52; Company H 9, 147
35th Georgia Infantry 16, 47
34th Regiment N.C. Troops 21, 23, 26, 29, 37, 52
32nd Regiment N.C. Troops: Company I 147
37th Regiment N.C. Troops 22
36th Regiment N.C. Troops: 2nd Company B 98; Company I 145
33rd Regiment N.C. Troops: Company I 147
Thomas, Dr. Brad 172, 173
Thomas, Brig. Gen. Edward L. 34, 35
Thomas, M. 147
Thomasville Township, Davidson County, N.C. 87
Thompson, A. F., MD 160
Thompson, Samuel 119

Index

Thompson, Sarah Womble 119
Thompson, Spencer D. 119, 178
The Times 17
Trimble, Gen. Isaac R. 16, 30, 33
Trinity, N.C. 5
Trinity Cemetery, Graves County, Ky. 178
Trogdon, Abigail 78
Trogdon, Anna 78, 162
Trogdon, Caroline A. Johnson 119
Trogdon, Caroline Pugh 120
Trogdon, Daniel 120
Trogdon, Emily Eliza Watson 120
Trogdon, Emsley 119
Trogdon, Fannie Lane Kinney 121
Trogdon, Hezekiah C. 119, 165
Trogdon, Jane Wagoner 119
Trogdon, Jeremiah F. 119
Trogdon, Lilly Allred 120
Trogdon, Linden Alred 119, 120, 175
Trogdon, Nancy Jennings 120
Trogdon, Priscilla 74
Trogdon, Samuel 22, 120
Trogdon, Sarah "Sallie" Stout 119
Trogdon, Solomon J. 120
Trogdon, Stephen Ward 5, 18, 19, 22, 25, 26, 120, 121, 160, 162, 163, 164, 165, 166, 167, 175
Trogdon, Susan 160
Trogdon, Susanna Kinney 120
Trogdon, Thomas L. 119
Trogdon, Vicey Allred 119
Troy, N.C. 73
Tucker, E. D. 145
Turner, Andrew Jackson 41, 121, 122, 178
Turner, Ernest 144
Turner, Hannah Holder Wright 122
Turner, Hannah Staley 121, 122
Turner, Jane R. Ledman 121
Turner, Sgt. John Tyler 1, 9, 10, 11, 12, 13, 14, 15, 16, 20, 21, 24, 26, 32, 33, 36, 43, 44, 50, 59, 90, 91, 96, 104, 105, 112, 121, 122, 126, 131, 132, 133, 134, 136, 137, 138, 139, 140, 141, 142, 143, 156, 178
Turner, Lucinda (Lousinda) 97
Turner, Maggie 144
Turner, Malinda York 121
Turner, Martin S. 121, 178
Turner, P. P. 144
Turner, Thomas 122

Turner, Walter 144
Turner's Romance 9, 121
12th N.C. Volunteers 14, 47
21st Regiment N.C. Troops: Company D 147; Company M 94, 134
29th Pennsylvania Infantry 63
22nd Battalion Va. Infantry 23
22nd Regiment N.C. Troops 16, 17, 19, 20, 21, 22, 23, 24, 25, 26, 27, 28, 29, 31, 32, 33, 34, 35, 37, 38, 40, 41, 43, 47, 49, 50, 52, 70, 71, 134, 136, 163; Company A 14, 85, 87, 94, 105, 106, 118; Company B 14; Company E 14, 88, 122, 134, 137; Company F 14; Company G 14; Company H 14, 92, 123; Company I 8, 14, 16, 17, 40, 145, 147; Company K 14, 118; Company L 8, 9, 10, 14, 18, 37, 40, 91, 118, 124, 132, 147, 167
27th Regiment N.C. Troops: Company E 132
26th (22nd) Regiment N.C. Troops 134
26th Regiment N.C. Troops: Company E 147; Company I 147
26th Regiment N.C. Troops (Reactivated) 171
Tyrell County, N.C. 14
Tysor, T. B. 145, 147

United Daughters of the Confederacy 111, 144
U.S. Army 76, 78, 90, 91, 93, 100, 109, 124, 128

Vance, Gov. Zebulon B. 52, 133
Vance County, N.C. 42, 109, 178
Vernon, Mo. 113, 176
Vestal, C. M. 147
Virginia 53, 55, 57, 64, 69, 74, 81, 88, 92, 96, 108, 109, 113, 126, 127, 137, 139, 140, 141, 162, 164, 165, 168

Wadeville, N.C. 73
Wagoner, Jane 119
Waisner, Mark 172, 173
Waisner, Matt 172, 173
Waisner, Terry 172, 173
Wake County, N.C. 57, 85
Walker, Gen. John G. 16
Wall, Alice 122
Wall, William 122
Wall, William B. 122
Walls, Elkanah 147

War for Southern Independence 131
Warren, Gen. G. K. 35
Warwick's Swamps 49
Washington, D.C. 16, 24, 48, 63, 80, 87, 93, 99, 102, 111, 112, 115, 116, 122, 162
Washington City, Ind. 105
Washington Navy Yard 65
Waterloo Bridge, Va., skirmish at 82
Watson, Emily Eliza 120
Webb, Rebecca D. 129
Webster, Eliza Ellison 122
Webster, James A. 122, 147, 178
Webster, Martha A. Foust 122
Webster, William B. 122
Weekly Times 62
Weldon, N.C. 57, 58, 137
Weldon Railroad 37, 56
Wesleyan Methodists 4
Whatley, Daniel J. 67
Whatley, L. McKay 8, 10, 12, 14, 69, 117
White, Addie Allison 69
Whiten, Major 58
White's Chapel United Methodist cemetery 128, 178
Whiting, Gen. W. H. 19
Wicker, Mrs. J. C. 158
Wilburn, B. E. 122
Wilburn, Peggy 71
Wilcox, Gen. Cadmus M. 30, 32, 33, 34, 35, 36, 38, 40, 41
Wilderness, Va. 54; battle of 33, 56, 73, 76, 80, 83, 86, 87, 91, 100, 103, 108, 115, 120
Wilkerson, Daniel C. 22, 123
Wilkerson, Delilah 123
Wilkerson, Ellen 123
Wilkerson, James 123
Wilkerson, James M. 123
Wilkes County, N.C. 92
Wilkins, Delyshee Joyce 123
Wilkins, John 123
Wilkins, Polly Ann Gann 123
Wilkins, Thomas 123
Wilkins, William J. 123, 178
Wilkins Cemetery, Stokes County, N.C. 123, 178
Willey, Anna 123
Willey, Rebecca Jane Cheek 123
Willey, William Parker 123, 176
Williams, A. E. 75
Williams, A. S. 145
Williams, Adam O. 124
Williams, America M. 125
Williams, Atha N. 124
Williams, Barbara 124
Williams, Benjamin 124
Williams, David Enos 124

Index

Williams, Diannah Breedlove 124
Williams, Etta 125
Williams, Henry S. 125
Williams, Isabella Kivett 125
Williams, Jacob 124, 125
Williams, Jacob, Sr. 124
Williams, James Madison 124
Williams, Joel 125
Williams, John L. 125
Williams, John Randolph 25, 125
Williams, Lillie J. 124
Williams, Lindsey 35, 125
Williams, Louisa Kivett 124, 125
Williams, Malvina Kivett 125
Williams, Margaret Isabella 96, 140
Williams, Margaret Lax 124
Williams, Mariah Kivett 124
Williams, Martha (Martitia) 124
Williams, Martine 125
Williams, Mary Jane Kirkman Kivett 102
Williams, Nancy Cox 124
Williams, Rebecca Staley 124
Williams, Riley 124, 125
Williams, Sophia Kelly 125
Williams, William Martin 125, 178
Williams, Zimeriah Nathanial 102, 147
Williamsburg, Va. 19, 20, 50, 65, 93
Williamsport, Md. 24, 32, 54, 55
Wilmington, N.C. 57, 137
Wilson, N.C. 52
Winchester, Va. 26, 27, 51, 54, 166, 167
Winder Hospital, Richmond, Va. 51
Winston, N.C. 134

Winston-Salem, N.C. 158
Wood, Mary E. 114
Wood, Mary Jane McMasters 80
Wood, Hon. W. P. 34, 72, 145, 147
Woodell, A. J. 145
Woosley, Joseph 125
Woosley, Lavina Krouse 125
Woosley, Nellie Mahalia Snipes 126
Woosley, William August 108, 125, 175
Wooten, Maj. Thomas J. 39
Worth, J. M. 154
Worth, Governor Jonathan 5, 6
Worth, Shubal G. 7, 8
Wrenn, Julia Ann 80
Wright, Abraham 126, 127, 141
Wright, Alfred Spinks 126
Wright, Anna Barbara Kivett 126, 127
Wright, Augusta A. 126
Wright, Barbara A. 126
Wright, David 41, 73, 126, 127, 141, 143, 178
Wright, Eli 126
Wright, Elizabeth Langley 126
Wright, Emily Jones 127
Wright, Hannah Holder 122
Wright, Isaac 126, 127
Wright, Jacob R. 126
Wright, John 126
Wright, John Darius "Doris" 126, 127
Wright, Judith Emily "Juda" Curtis 126
Wrightman, Mary 103

Yeargin, Daniel 127, 178
Yeargin, Isaac 127
Yeargin, Millicent Coble 127
York, Barbary Lousina Pugh 128

York, Braxton 22, 127, 129
York, Darius "Dorris" 46
York, Delphina Cox 18, 167, 169
York, Eliza Ward 129
York, Jabez 128
York, Jabez Lindsay 41, 128, 176
York, Jeremiah 127
York, Joseph 127
York, Larkin Culberson, Jr. 128, 143, 178
York, Larkin Culberson, Sr. 128
York, Leander 129, 154
York, Malinda 121
York, Martha "Patsy" Bray 128
York, Martitia 84
York, Martitia Curtis 129
York, Mary Ann E. Jones 128
York, Mary H. "Polly" 98
York, Mary Henson 127, 129
York, Matilda Elizabeth "Betsy" 82
York, Nancy A. 101
York, Pleasant 127, 129
York, Rebecca D. Webb 129
York, Samuel Clarkson 128, 129, 176
York, Sarah 127
York, Sarah J. Cross 128
York, Sarah Julian 128
York, Sarah Martha Spinks 129
York, Semore 128
York, Solomon 18, 147, 167, 169
York, Sophia "Tilly" Kivett 128
York, Spencer Donald 129
York, William J. 129
York, William Jasper 129
York, William Joseph 41, 129, 176
Yorktown, Va. 19, 49, 75, 88, 89, 105, 127, 128
Young, Captain 38

www.ingramcontent.com/pod-product-compliance
Lightning Source LLC
Chambersburg PA
CBHW081558300426
44116CB00015B/2925